Computer Performance Evaluation
Tools and Techniques For Effective Analysis

Computer Performance Evaluation
Tools and Techniques
For Effective Analysis

Michael F. Morris
Paul F. Roth

Van Nostrand Reinhold Data Processing Series

VAN NOSTRAND REINHOLD COMPANY
NEW YORK CINCINNATI TORONTO LONDON MELBOURNE

Van Nostrand Reinhold Company Regional Offices:
New York   Cincinnati

Van Nostrand Reinhold Company International Offices:
London   Toronto   Melbourne

Copyright © 1982 by Van Nostrand Reinhold Company

Library of Congress Catalog Card Number: 81-1613
ISBN: 0-442-80325-7

All rights reserved. No part of this work covered by the copyright hereon may be reproduced or used in any form or by any means—graphic, electronic, or mechanical, including photocopying, recording, taping, or information storage and retrieval systems—without permission of the publisher and authors.

Manufactured in the United States of America

Published by Van Nostrand Reinhold Company
135 West 50th Street, New York, N.Y. 10020

Published simultaneously in Canada by Van Nostrand Reinhold Ltd.

15 14 13 12 11 10 9 8 7 6 5 4 3 2 1

Library of Congress Cataloging in Publication Data

Morris, Michael F.
  Computer performance evaluation.

  (The Van Nostrand Reinhold data processing series)
  Includes index.
  1. Electronic digital computers—Evaluation.
I. Roth, Paul F. II. Title. III. Series: Van Nostrand Reinhold data processing series.
QA76.9.E94M67   001.64   81-1613
ISBN 0-442-80325-7   AACR2

This book is dedicated to Father Joseph Timothy O'Neill, his charming wife Lynn, and their six or so children. Without their warm hospitality and prolific inspiration, this work would never have been undertaken.

SERIES INTRODUCTION

The prudent management of computer resources has become more difficult in recent years. Now, the configuration is not just one CPU, a few disks, a printer, and a card reader. Instead, telecommunications, off-line entry, transaction reorders, cache memory, distributed processing, distributed data bases, multi-programming, real-time processing, "foreign" vendors, and multiple demands (such as production runs and testing), may be involved. Each adds complexity to the management task. Yet the high cost of money and of personnel mean that the demands to get the most from the computer have never been higher.

For these reasons, this book by Morris and Roth is welcome. It provides thorough and modern coverage of the techniques, tools, and practices of computer performance evaluation. The authors provide a well-balanced treatment, with emphasis on the software available. The authors wisely note that computer performance evaluation should be considered long before the operations stage in the life cycle. This book provides valuable and useful coverage of computer performance evaluation.

—Ned Chapin, Ph.D.
Series Editor

THE VAN NOSTRAND REINHOLD DATA PROCESSING SERIES
Edited by Ned Chapin, Ph.D.

IMS Programming Techniques: A Guide to Using DL/1
   Dan Kapp and Joseph L. Leben

Reducing COBOL Complexity Through Structured Programming
   Carma McClure

Composite/Structured Design
   Glenford J. Myers

Reliable Software Through Composite Design
   Glenford J. Myers

Top-Down Structured Programming Techniques
   Clement L. McGowen and John R. Kelly

Operating Systems Principles
   Stanley Kurzban, T.S. Heines and A.P. Sayers

Microcomputer Handbook
   Charles J. Sippl

Strategic Planning of Management Information Systems
   Paul Siegel

Flowcharts
   Ned Chapin

Introduction to Artificial Intelligence
   Philip C. Jackson, Jr.

Computers and Management for Business
   Douglas A. Colbert

Operating Systems Survey
   Anthony P. Sayers

Management of Information Technology: Case Studies
   Elizabeth B. Adams

Compiler Techniques
   Bary W. Pollack

Documentation Manual
   J. Van Duyn

Management of ADP Systems
   Marvin M. Wofsey

Hospitals: A System Approach
   Raymon D. Garrett

Hospital Computer Systems and Procedures, Vol I: Accounting Systems
Hospital Computer Systems and Procedures, Vol II: Medical Systems
   Raymon D. Garrett

Logic Design for Computer Control
   K.N. Dodd

Software Engineering Concepts and Techniques
   John Buxton, Peter Naur and Brian Randell

Information Management Systems: Data Base Primer
   Vivien Prothro

A Programmer's Guide to COBOL
   William J. Harrison

A Guide to Structured COBOL with Efficiency Techniques and Special Algorithms
   Pacifico A. Lim

Managing Software Development and Maintenance
   Carma L. McClure

Computer-Assisted Data Base Design
  George U. Hubbard

Evaluating Data Base Management Systems
  Judy King

Network Systems
  Roshan Lal Sharma, Ashok D. Inglé and Paulo T. Desousa

Logical Data Base Design
  Robert M. Curtice and Paul E. Jones, Jr.

Computer Performance Evaluation: Tools and Techniques for Effective Analysis
  Michael F. Morris and Paul F. Roth

Preface

Computer Performance Evaluation was written for data processing managers based entirely on practical experience. Unless specifically stated otherwise, all examples and figures included are based on actual projects. The purpose of this book is to provide insight and ideas from the many lessons that we have had to learn to help managers improve performance at their own computer installations. We think that any manager who is familiar with computer system operations and who has no more than a high school education should be able to understand and apply the information that is presented.

Two chapters were difficult to write at the same level of understandability as the rest. These are the chapters on *Analytic Models* and *Software Physics*. As presented, the Analytic Models chapter may look difficult to some managers when thumbing through the pages because there are still more equations included than we really wanted to use. They turned out to be necessary to impart the fundamentals of the subject. We have gone to extremes to explain any mathematical notations that are used at the risk of insulting the intelligence of readers with mathematical backgrounds. We apologize for this. The chapter on Software Physics may seem difficult because we have introduced some of the special vocabulary of the topic rather than staying with more familiar terms. We have done this because the terminology of software physics seems to be gaining increasing acceptance among data processing managers. We did not use the formal notation of software physics because it uses Greek letters and mathematical symbolism that is unappealing to many managers. Both of these chapters purposely take a different approach than other "tools and techniques" chapters. These two chapters are comprised almost entirely of practical examples. The Analytic Models chapter is one long example broken into several small and simple steps. The Software Physics chapter is a series of examples which deal with short, distinct phases of a general problem that is often addressed in computer installations.

Although computer installation managers are our intended audience, we have found that the material presented in this book is beneficial to senior corporate managers, to auditors, to quality control and quality assurance personnel, to computer technicians who aspire to management positions, and to technicians who are just being introduced to the discipline of computer performance evaluation. All of the material in this book has been presented and tested in public and private seminars throughout the United States, in Canada, Europe, and South America. Most of the information has been useful in university-level management courses. We believe that Dominico Ferrari's book (*System Performance Evaluation,* Prentice Hall, 1978) is, by itself, more adaptable to university-level computer science courses than is ours, but that the two books together would provide a very compatible basis for comprehensive courses in computer science curricula at the advanced undergraduate or graduate levels.

We believe that this book will be most useful as a topical reference on computer performance evaluation. It should be read through initially to become acquainted with its content. Later, Chapters 1, 2, 10, and 11 should serve as refreshers or introductions to the general issues of computer performance evaluation while Chapters 3 through 9 might be reread individually whenever their topics become important.

We appreciate receiving any criticisms or comments on this book that may be incorporated into subsequent editions to make the information more understandable or to expand the contents in ways thought to be important to the readers. Please write any such comments to us in care of the publisher.

Michael F. Morris and Paul F. Roth
Washington D.C.

Acknowledgments

The list of all individuals, companies, and government agencies who have contributed in one way or another to the material in this book or to the work needed to complete it is too long to include here. Nonetheless, we do thank all who furthered the completion of this work.

One person who must be singled out so that his role can be recognized is Orlando Petrocelli. Olly asked us to write this book in the first place, entered into a contract with us in 1970 to deliver a final manuscript by October 1973, and then waited patiently for several additional years while the computer performance evaluation field evolved too rapidly for a book to be feasible. Beyond this, his guidance and helpful suggestions were instrumental in arriving at the final format and content of this book. Thank you, Olly.

Other individuals who we feel we must name to acknowledge their part in completing this work by their suggestions, their assistance in conducting CPE projects, their reviews of all or parts of the manuscripts, or their help in other ways that they may not know of themselves, are: Joanne Ambrosio, Wally Anderson, Pete Anthony, Tom Bell, Joe Boyd, Jeff Buzen, Leo Cohen, Charley Davidson, Ruth Davis, Dick Dunlavey, Izzy Feldman, Jerry Findley, Gerry Galbo, Ted Gonter, Joe Harrison, Harold Highland, John Hoffman, Alice Howard, Phil Howard, Ed Joslin, Phil Kiviat, Ken Kolence, Rick Lejk, Art Lundquist, Halaine Maccabee, Al Meyerhoff, Ed Murray, Ron Novak, Ken Pollock, Don Scantlebury, Sue Solomon, Bob Ungvary, Virginia Walker, Dudley Warner, and Doug Wintermute.

Organizations which provided us either time or experience that was instrumental in preparing this book are: Boeing Computer Services, Burroughs Corporation, the Federal Computer Performance Evaluation and Simulation Center, the General Accounting Office, Management Advisory Services, the National Bureau of Standards, Peat, Marwick, Mitchell & Co., and the United States Air Force.

Contents

Preface		**xi**
1	**Introduction to Computer Performance Evaluation: An Overview of the Tools and Their Applications**	**1**
	A Survey of CPE Tools and Techniques	2
	The Life Cycle of CPE	9
	A Word of Caution	17
2	**Managing Computer Performance Evaluation Efforts**	**19**
	The Decision to Get Started in CPE	19
	Setting Preliminary Goals	21
	Selecting CPE Team Members	23
	Organizational Placement of the CPE Team	26
	CPE Project Administration	30
	The CPE Team Leader's Responsibilities	34
	Continuing CPE Activities	43
	Considerations for Smaller Systems	49
3	**Accounting Data**	**51**
	Categories of Accounting Data	52
	The Cost of Accounting Data	58
	The Importance of Environment	59
	Applications of Accounting Data	61
4	**Software Monitors and Program Optimizers**	**74**
	A Few Distinctions	74
	Definitions	75

xvi CONTENTS

Categories of Software Monitors	81
Strengths and Limitations	89
A Comment	92

5 Hardware Monitors 93

Physical Description	93
Using Hardware Monitors	102
Common-Sense Rules for Connection and Use of Hardware Monitors	108

6 Benchmarking 118

Background	118
Terminology	120
Why Benchmark?	121
Benchmark Characteristics	121
How to Benchmark	124
Benchmark Limitations	132
An Observation	133

7 Simulation 135

Essential Working Concepts	135
Definition	136
When to Use Simulation	138
The Process of Simulation	140
Discrete Event Simulation	152
Applications in the Computer System Life Cycle	159
Limitations and Strengths	162

8 Analytic Models 164

Definition	165
Queues	165
A Model of a Computer System	167
Applying the Model as a Predictive Tool	175
Strengths and Limitations	182

9	**Software Physics**	**184**
	Software Work and Software Power Definitions	185
	Software Power as a Measure of Throughput	190
	Software Power for Capacity	194
	Applications	201
10	**Reporting Performance to Management**	**209**
	Elements of a Performance Management Reporting System	209
	Reporting Formats	217
	Developing a Performance Management Reporting System	231
11	**A Structure for Continued Computer Performance Evaluation Projects**	**234**
	CPE for Existing Systems	235
	CPE for Proposed Systems	242
	General	246
	In Closing	247
Suggested Readings		**249**
Index		**253**

Computer Performance Evaluation
Tools and Techniques For Effective Analysis

1
INTRODUCTION TO COMPUTER PERFORMANCE EVALUATION:
An Overview of the Tools and Their Applications

Measuring, recording, analyzing, and predicting performance of human and mechanical events have been interesting and useful pastimes throughout recorded history. The first computer had no more than two operational programs before the idea occurred to insert check flags into the coding to obtain a measure of how far the program had gotten before it, or the machine, ceased operation. This measure was made useful by incorporating intermediate storage points just before each flag so that work completed before a failure would not need to be repeated.

The introduction of computer systems capable of simultaneous activity in the processor and in the peripheral devices, and the later introduction of multiprogramming, caused the number and complexity of questions about system performance to grow very rapidly. The profusion of such questions demanded special machinery and innovative programming in order to obtain answers. The creation and development of these special tools in the 1960s and early 1970s have thrust Computer Performance Evaluation into the position of a distinct discipline of the computer sciences.

2 COMPUTER PERFORMANCE EVALUATION

Computer Performance Evaluation (CPE) is the application of special tools, techniques, and analytical methods to improve the efficiency or productivity of existing or planned computer installations.

A SURVEY OF CPE TOOLS AND TECHNIQUES

The two most important and effective tools for evaluation of computer performance are available free in nearly every computer installation. They are *visual inspection* and *common sense*. Because these two tools are so widely known and used, they will not be treated separately here. But it should be understood that every CPE project starts with a thorough visual inspection of the suspected problem area and that the application of every CPE tool must be done by using common sense. Neglecting these as the two primary tools of CPE will cause severe misapplication of scarce resources to solving problems whose solutions should be obvious to even a casual observer who is moderately skilled in conducting performance improvement projects.

In addition to these two fundamental CPE tools, there are six others that are now in wide use. These are *accounting data reduction programs, program optimizers, software monitors, hardware monitors, benchmarks,* and *modeling*. These tools and their uses are the principal subjects of this book. They are briefly described below to prepare the reader for the CPE management topics covered in Chapter 2.

Accounting Data Reduction Programs

Accounting data throughout this book means information collected on the use of computer resources. A facility that generates information about the use of various resources within a computer system is now included in nearly every computer above the "mini" range. This information is typically available for each user program that causes system activity. The main reason for providing this resource accounting data has been for billing computer users for their use of the system on a program-by-program basis.

Numerous special purpose data reduction programs have been developed to take advantage of the availability of accounting data. Such programs are routinely furnished by most computer manufacturers as a part of their respective control programs. Because these data reduction capabilities usually have no identified extra charge passed on to the computer installation, these packages are generally regarded as "free" resources at the installation.

The easy availability of accounting data, coupled with limitations of manufacturer-supplied data reduction programs, has fostered the development of special programs that extract and report accounting information that is of much interest at many installations. Commercial development of such programs has spawned a wide variety of products that are collectively referred to here, along with manufacturer-supplied programs, as *accounting data reduction packages*. These commercial packages serve such diverse needs as configuration capacity management, job scheduling, library control, standards enforcement, job billing, and numerous other management-oriented functions. Some of these packages are even used as the primary CPE tool at many installations.

Accounting data reduction packages evolved from the check flags inserted in programs by users of the earliest computers. The evolution continued through manual logging and billing, to automated "trace routines," to the current comprehensive accounting data collection programs. Without exception, each step in the evolution of accounting data reduction packages was initiated by computer users. In general, the manufacturers simply adopted the more popular developments and furnished them to other users. Each step in the evolution was taken to solve or understand some real and practical problem in the operation or management of an installation. Because of the way that accounting data evolved, they are certainly the richest sources of information for most performance improvement projects. The use of accounting data reduction packages is integral to all continuing CPE efforts.

Software Monitors

Another descendent of the same lineage as accounting packages is the *software monitor*. Software monitors are specialized sets of code that are usually (but not always) made part of the computer's operating system and collect statistical information about the distribution of activity caused by the execution of particular programs or sets of programs. The major difference between software monitors and accounting packages is the level of detail that each is capable of examining. Software monitors can perform much closer examination of the step-by-step execution of instructions than can accounting packages.

Software monitors, like accounting packages, are sold commercially and are available primarily only for larger IBM systems. Like accounting packages, software monitors have been developed by individual computer installations and exist for nearly every brand of computer. Information on the availability of both commercial and user-developed monitors is generally obtainable through *users' groups* for the brand of interest.

Program Optimizers

A CPE tool that is almost a subset of both accounting packages and software monitors is the *program optimizer*. These are specialized sets of code, often written in the language of the program that is to be optimized, that are compiled with the application program of interest to collect information on the execution characteristics of that program when it is run with real or test data. Program optimizers are commercially available for the two major, high-level languages, FORTRAN and COBOL.

In spite of their name, most program optimizers do not, themselves, optimize programs. They produce reports that indicate the areas of a program where a programmer might decrease running time or computer resource usage by employing alternative techniques in the program. A major difference between these optimizers and most software monitors or accounting packages is that the optimizers can collect information like which parts of a program are *not* exercized by the data that are used. In a test environment, this capability is particularly important. Optimizers, since they are usually compiled into the application program itself, are compiler-dependent rather than system-dependent as are the related accounting packages and software monitors.

Hardware Monitors

A very different kind of CPE tool that descends from electronic devices like oscilloscopes is the *hardware monitor*. Hardware monitors are electronic equipment that may be attached to the internal circuitry of a computer system to sense changes of state at the various connection points. In their most basic and oldest form, these monitors sense and record or display information on the number and duration of events that occur at each connection point. This information may either be examined immediately or be saved for later reduction to reports by using a special computer program. Hardware monitors of this basic type are sometimes referred to as *basic monitors*. Basic monitors are totally system-independent and may be attached to any brand or model of computer so long as the attachment points, or probe points, are known and accessible for the signals that are of interest.

The second evolution of hardware monitors incorporated memories and special register adapters and even minicomputers to enlarge the monitors' capability for simultaneous measurement of large numbers of signals by allowing "Boolean" operations to be applied against events that are physically connected to the monitor. This produces reports that cover many combinations of the physically monitored signals that seem as though far larger numbers of basic signals, perhaps hundreds, were actually monitored. The *mapping monitors* are also system-independent, but a much more detailed knowledge of the subject computer system is needed to take full advantage of a mapping monitor's capabilities than for the basic monitor.

More recently, hardware monitors have been developed that "communicate" with programs within the subject computer to control the information that is collected by the monitor. These are referred to as *intelligent monitors* because they have attributes of both software and hardware monitors. Intelligent monitors are as system-dependent as software monitors. The architecture of the subject computer system must be effectively reproduced by the monitor so that operations can be recognized as they occur.

In contrast to accounting packages, software monitors, and source program optimizers, hardware monitors are not good tools for most beginners in the CPE field. Although there have been recent developments that greatly simplify the use of hardware monitors, useful information is not normally collected unless the monitor user has a thorough understanding of the computer's workload, formal training and practice in the use of the monitor, and a reasonably detailed knowledge of the architecture of the computer system to be monitored. Further, hardware monitors can generate data at such a detailed level and in such large amounts that inexperienced users often find themselves overwhelmed with data in a short time after the monitor is installed.

In the hands of experienced technicians, hardware monitors can be extremely valuable when some piece of otherwise unobtainable information must be measured. Except for the smallest of the basic monitors, hardware monitors are generally regarded as the measurement tool of last resort. This is not to imply that application of hardware monitors will not be rewarding. It is simply that, for the types of people who are usually asked to conduct CPE projects, hardware monitors are much more difficult to use than most other CPE tools.

Benchmarks

Benchmarks are programs or sets of programs that are used to represent a real workload that is in operation on an existing computer or that is planned to be in operation on an existing or proposed computer. Benchmarks are typically used to establish the relative capabilities of different computer systems or alternative configurations to process the workload represented by the benchmarks. Benchmarks are also useful to validate or verify the results produced by other CPE tools.

Benchmarks do not fit comfortably into either of the two broad categories of CPE tools: *measurement* or *predictive*. The four preceding tools (accounting data reduction packages, software monitors, source program optimizers, and hardware monitors) can only be used to measure existing computer workloads. The remaining CPE tool to be described below (modeling) is most useful for predicting the impact of alternative decisions. In the sense that benchmarks can only be used if the computer system of interest does exist, they may be regarded as measurement tools. However, one of the major uses of benchmarks is to estimate the future impact of a present decision. In this second sense, benchmarks are predictive tools.

A small set of benchmark programs that accurately represents the total workload of an installation is extremely valuable on a continuing basis to the CPE group. Periodic runs of such benchmarks allow the CPE group and the installation managers to assess changes made to the configuration and to the operating system. Such benchmarks also allow the CPE team to determine when their activities may actually have degraded system performance so that corrective action may be taken.

Modeling

There are often cases when the performance of a computer system or set of programs should be examined in detail before the system or programs exist. Such examinations are the most important role of *modeling*. Modeling is the creation and exercise of mathematical descriptions, or models, of those portions of the system that estimate the operational characteristics of the system as it should operate if implemented. Modeling may also be used to study existing systems when it is either too expensive, too time-consuming, or too dangerous to perform experiments directly on the real system. Modeling is done by means of analytic or simulation models.

A characteristic of modeling that sets it apart very distinctly from all other CPE tools is that the other tools are instruments by which problems may be solved. Modeling, on the other hand, can actually solve problems directly. That is, in applying the disciplines and techniques needed to use modeling, problems may be solved completely before the models are exercised. Beyond this, modeling is a discipline in its own right. It is widely used in most scientific and engineering fields. Each field develops its own specific modeling tools. In the CPE field, these tools are in the form of computer programs or sets of programs that are used as "packages" that can only model computer systems. In addition, there are special modeling languages that are tailored for creating detailed models of computer systems that are also widely used in CPE projects.

The differences between computer modeling languages and computer modeling packages are like the differences between software monitors and accounting packages. That is, the language tools are generally used when more detailed problems are to be studied while the package tools are most useful when overall systems are under examination. At the risk of extreme oversimplification: languages are generally used to develop models of activity that would last for, say, a minute or less on a computer system; packages are used to model activity that lasts for an hour or more.

8 COMPUTER PERFORMANCE EVALUATION

The major advantage of including modeling as a capability of a CPE group is that it provides an overall structure that guides the group from one problem area to the next in a logical manner, and that it provides in-depth understanding of the entire installation that is invaluable in recommending sound management decisions. The power of modeling is unique: it allows the performance of a total system or of any part of the system to be examined before making a major investment in the acquisition or construction of the system.

General

The tools of CPE are listed in Table 1-1 with regard to their availability, cost, and overhead. The starting point for nearly every installation is an accounting data reduction package. The second step is often the acquisition of a software monitor. Many CPE groups never go beyond these two tools and still produce timely and cost-effective projects on a continuing basis. The next CPE tool added is typically a program optimizer or a hardware monitor. The last addition to most CPE groups (although there are many that start

Table 1-1. Computer Performance Evaluation Tools.

TOOL	COMMERCIALLY AVAILABLE?	COST RANGE [a]	COMPUTER OVERHEAD
Accounting Data Reduction Packages	Yes	Low to Medium	Small
Software Monitors	Yes[b]	Low to Medium	Small to Moderate
Program Optimizers	Yes	Low	Moderate (by program)
Hardware Monitors:			
• Basic	Yes	Low to Medium	None
• Mapping	Yes	Medium to High	None
• Intelligent	Yes	High to Very High	Slight
Benchmarks	No	Internal Cost Only	Usually 100%
Modeling:			
• Languages	Yes	Low to Medium	Small
• Packages	Yes	Medium to High	Small

[a] Cost Ranges often change dramatically on these types of commercial products. They are shown here in relative terms for most products in each category solely for comparative purposes.
[b] These products are widely available for larger IBM systems but on a very limited basis for other systems.

with this) is a modeling capability. Benchmarks tend to evolve when they are needed to validate some particular point or when a major system acquisition is planned.

THE LIFE CYCLE OF CPE

Computer Performance Evaluation aims at improving the operational efficiency of the computer installation. *Efficiency* involves getting the greatest possible return from any investment in computing resources. Internal auditing, on the other hand, deals with the effectiveness of the installation. *Effectiveness* involves meeting those, and only those, requirements that serve the stated goal of the organization. CPE technicians and internal auditors may sometimes be mistaken for each other, but their respective roles are separate and distinct.

For example, a CPE technician might be asked to improve the running of some program that clearly should not be run at all. The CPE technician should, nevertheless, make the program run as efficiently as possible by producing the desired output with the smallest possible use of computing resources. An internal auditor asked to examine such a program should have a much different reaction that would, at the very least, aim at having that program removed from the workload.

The overriding interest of the CPE technician in the efficiency of the installation should not be forgotten. Of course, CPE technicians and internal auditors should be encouraged to work together as much as possible. Their similarities enable each to be quite helpful to the other. But the CPE group's principal concern should be the efficient use of all computing resources.

Efficiency of operation should be a consideration long before a computer system is delivered or even ordered. To ensure that the greatest return will be obtained from the data processing investment, CPE should be used during every phase of the life cycle of a computer system from the conceptual design of the workload through the reuse analysis of outdated equipment. Table 1-2 offers a condensed view of the life cycle of a computer system and of the CPE tools that are most useful during each activity of the phases.

10 COMPUTER PERFORMANCE EVALUATION

Table 1-2. The Life Cycle of a Computer System Related to the Tools of CPE.

PHASE	ACTIVITY	MODELING	BENCHMARKS	ACCOUNTING DATA	SOFTWARE MONITORS	HARDWARE MONITORS	PROGRAM OPTIMIZERS
Procurement	Conceptual Design of Workload	P					
	Detailed Workload Specification	P	S				
	Equipment Specification	P	S				
	Request for Proposals (RFP)	P	S				
	Review of RFP Responses	S	P				
	Select Equipment Supplier		P				
Installation	Tailor Workload to Equipment	S	P	S	S	S	S
	Configuring Equipment	S	P	S	S	S	
	Installation and Checkout		P			S	
	Acceptance Testing		P	S	S	S	
Operation	Workload Implementation		S	P	S	S	S
	Program Reviews	S		S	P	S	S
	Configuration Enhancement	S	S	P	S	S	
	Adding New Workload	S	S	P	S	S	S
	Projecting System Growth	P	S	S			
	Predicting System Saturation	P	S	S			
Transition	Review of New Systems	P	S				
	Review of Potential Data Processing Needs	P					
	Reuse Analysis of Owned Equipment	P	S				
	Conceptual Design of Foreseeable Workload	P					

P = Primary Tool
S = Supporting Tool

Procurement Phase

The life cycle of CPE should begin during the conceptual design of the workload that is to be automated or reautomated. It is at this point that the modeling capability is most powerful and most enlightening. As a clear idea of the magnitude of the workload is reached, the models become invaluable in the next step of the procurement phase: detailed workload specification. At this point, modeling allows many alternative specifications to be tested to determine such things as the type of peripheral device best suited to a particular file or the size of memory that will be needed to meet peak workload demands.

These modeling studies will overlap and lead into the equipment specifications which would determine reasonable ranges of relative speeds and capacities of the various components of the anticipated system. The understanding of the planned workload and equipment gained through early CPE application eases the creation or selection of representative benchmarks of the total system.

These benchmarks are of major importance in preparing the *requests for proposals,* or procurement documentation, for the pending equipment selection. By the time this step is reached, the future management of the computer installation should be able to forecast such necessary information as the approximate cost of the equipment that should be selected, the physical space and utilities needed, and the size of the operations staff. These forecasts could be based solely on the understanding of the organization's requirements as exposed by the application of modeling and the development of representive benchmarks.

Next in this phase, the benchmarks and models allow systematic reviews to be made of all proposals received from computer system suppliers. During this review, CPE should enable the prospective buyer to determine which proposals are most responsive to the requirements of the proposed workload. At this stage CPE will also help the buyer interact with all of the potential sellers of his new system. This encourages modifications to the proposals that will make each responsive bid both better tailored to the proposed workload and better priced through the competitive process. The proposal review is one of the most important steps in the system's life cycle and in the CPE effort because it is the one time when all potential suppliers are most intensely interested in the buyer's needs. Also, it is often the last time until the next procurement that the buyer has strong and immediate influence on the cost of the equipment that will be in his installation for several years.

The final step in the procurement phase, selection, is almost entirely outside the domain of CPE. Benchmarks are only used to determine which proposals are responsive. That is, the choice arrived at from benchmark runs is essentially binary; each proposed configuration can either perform or not perform the proposed workload. After this technical information is obtained from benchmark runs, the final selection decision must be made based on relative prices, delivery schedule, manufacturer support, conversion costs, and other factors that are beyond the scope of CPE.

Installation Phase

After the equipment supplier or suppliers have been chosen, additional CPE tools and activities come into use. When the new system is substantially different than the system being replaced or when the new system is coming into a previously noncomputerized environment, the workload may be tailored to fit the selected system on an existing, like system furnished by the winning bidder pending delivery of the selected system itself. During this activity the developing programs may be examined by using the output from the accounting package and, if it can be arranged, through application of software and hardware monitors. Information gained through these CPE efforts may show minor configuration modifications that should be requested before the new system is installed. Such modifications can have significant impact on the ultimate productivity and efficiency of the new system when it becomes operational.

For example, the impact of the operating system will be fully visible for the first time in an operational environment. Regardless of the care taken in the modeling and benchmarking activities, unanticipated effects of the control program will become apparent during the execution of developing programs. Also, the configuration of such things as input/output channels in either number or distribution may come into question during the workload tailoring step.

A non-CPE area that should not be ignored during the last of the preinstallation days is that of profitting by the experience of the operational managers and CPE technicians at the site of the furnished system. Even when these systems are at a service center of the winning bidder, the working relationship that can be developed with the on-site personnel often provides insight into peculiarities—both good and bad—of the system that would not otherwise be gained until long after the new system is up and running in a production environment.

Once the installation and checkout step begins, the weeks or months of CPE diligence will begin to pay off in the delivery of a system that very closely matches the demands of the workload. During this step, the CPE group should actively participate in the execution of diagnostic routines. If possible, the performance characteristics of each device should be noted and recorded by using a hardware monitor. Individual specifications of each component should be verified. For example, if the advertised transfer rate of a tape drive is, say, 100,000 characters per second, then the CPE group should be shown how to verify that this rate is attainable. Similar checks should also be made of such other things as printer speeds, disk access and transfer times, instruction execution times of the processor, and so forth. In short, each major performance characteristic of the new system should be checked to ensure that the components can perform at the rates that are to be paid for, and that the CPE group has some documented method to measure this performance when it is needed in the future.

If close attention has been paid during the installation and checkout step, the acceptance test will be both simple and meaningful. In accepting the installed equipment, the benchmarks that were used during the procurement phase should be rerun to verify that the total delivered system's performance equals that of the system upon which the benchmarks were demonstrated. This acceptance test is another extremely important part of the system's life cycle. It is the last chance that the buyer normally has to ensure that the system performance is as specified *before* payment must begin. It is also the last time that the highly skilled installation team from the supplier will be available at the buyer's site. Therefore, the buyer's management, operations staff, and CPE team should be convinced by the acceptance test that the system is indeed able to perform every test to their collective satisfaction. Once done, the computer system's manager must make the system deliver at the expected level without further certainty of such expert support from the supplier.

Operations Phase

The next activity in the system's life cycle, workload implementation, is usually the longest lasting by far. It may continue up to the last day before the system is replaced. CPE should play a major role throughout this activity. As each set of programs is installed, its impact on the existing workload should be examined to make recommendations on any modifications that might minimize this impact.

Continuing analysis of accounting data and, when available, software and hardware monitor data, will provide the insight to make performance improvement recommendations to the programmers who are responsible for implementing the changes.

As the workload grows and ages, activity begins that is aimed at programs that have been in production for some time. This is the domain of the software monitor. It is usually the need for program reviews that causes existing installations without a CPE group to realize that such a group would be worthwhile. The tasks of program review are reasonably simple and often remarkably productive. They involve methodical examination of the execution characteristics of existing programs to find those areas where substantial improvement might be possible. Program reviews tend to become the "time fillers" for established CPE groups. That is, they are performed whenever there is nothing more urgent that must be done.

As the system ages further, new products in the computer field will be announced. Those products that appear to offer significant performance improvements should be modeled as a part of the existing system and workload. This will allow the computer management to replace components in the system in a cost-effective manner and will aid in determining when it is time to begin to replace the entire system. The value of applying CPE during configuration enhancements is that the day when the entire system must be replaced is delayed. By delaying an enormous expenditure for a new computer system, the CPE group can provide enough cost-savings to justify their continuing existence.

As the system is enhanced, new jobs are usually proposed. Examination of accounting data can indicate where such jobs could be accommodated, and modeling during the design of the new programs will show how these jobs can best take advantage of existing capability. The knowledge that a workload's characteristics are being changed substantially by jobs that were not a part of the initial workload forecast should trigger the management and the CPE group to begin to analyze the potential extra workload. This may be done by using historical accounting data and standard statistical projection techniques to establish and predict trends in growth as a function of time. When growth has been projected for some reasonable time ahead—say six to twelve months—modeling may be used to test the capability of the existing system to handle the increasing workload and to predict necessary changes to ensure that the system will be able to do the work.

Sooner or later, a point will be reached in most systems where no amount of enhancement will enable the system to handle all of the foreseeable workload. This will usually be a by-product of the step referred to as "projecting system growth." In fact, it is the last growth projection that is limited by saturation of the system. Modeling is the principal tool for determining the system's point of saturation. Once saturation is determined, the operations phase is essentially completed except for that activity which must continue during transition to a replacement system.

Transition Phase

Once saturation has been predicted, the intensive examination of both new equipment announcements and potential data processing needs should be started. The existence of a CPE capability allows a degree of understanding that can be gained in no other way. Without the power of modeling and in-depth knowledge of the installation's performance history, there is likely to be some degree of panic at this point. There is really no room for panic in a heavily loaded computer installation that is known to be near its saturation level.

Continuing application of CPE enables the prediction of saturation to take place long enough ahead so that the transition phase will be orderly. Analysis of alternative uses of owned portions of the system may be made during the reentry of the procurement phase for the next system. Using the CPE group in reuse analyses is often overlooked even though it will give the equipment owner a substantial marketing advantage in selling the outdated system to someone with a compatible workload.

Finally, the life of the system ends as it began with application of modeling in the conceptual design of the next total workload. Computer Performance Evaluation is indeed useful throughout the life cycle of a computer system. The more heavily CPE is used, the more total system visibility the installation's management will have and the more efficient will be the distribution of computer resources to meet the demands for computing services.

WHEN TO STOP USING CPE

It should be apparent by now that the continuing use of CPE is not free. In fact, it is expensive. As the goal of CPE is efficiency, the practice of CPE should be examined relative to its own efficiency. This leads to the first reason to stop using CPE—when it is inefficient. That is, a CPE group should be disbanded and put to more productive work whenever the cost of operating the group is shown to be greater over a six- to twelve-month period than the value of the savings identified by the group.

A second reason for stopping an established CPE effort occurs when an owned system is operating to everyone's satisfaction (however "satisfaction" may be measured at the installation) with a stable workload and at costs that are considered reasonable. Such a system is the ultimate goal of all CPE projects. When it is attained, there is no reason to continue looking for improvements solely for the sake of finding improvements. Left alone, this situation will eventually lead to a prolonged period when the CPE investment exceeds cost savings, but there is no good reason to prolong the group when the desired efficiency level has been reached.

Third, CPE efforts sometimes result in decreased system size. There is a threshold of total installation costs beneath which there is no point in applying CPE. (This threshold is discussed in Chapter 2 under "Considerations for Smaller Systems.") Once the local minimum is attained, the CPE group should be moved on to some other system in larger organizations or disbanded in smaller organizations. Small computer systems profit more by expert programmers than through use of CPE. The out-of-work CPE technicians are usually extremely well prepared to return to programming at the expert level after helping to reduce installation size to a minimal configuration.

Finally, there are types of installations that cannot be concerned with computer operational efficiency. Examples of these are often found in true "real-time" environments like weapons control computers in military applications. Such systems may be vastly overpowered nearly all of the time so that during the few critical minutes or seconds when the massive computing power is needed, it is available. Similar situations may be noted in aviation control systems and occasionally in online reservation and banking systems. The goal of such systems is to provide immediate response in a "worst case" situation. The computer system in use must either meet this demand or be replaced by a more powerful machine, regardless of the excess capacity that may be available most of the time. The most extreme example of computers in this category might be the guidance computer on a purely defensive missile: such a computer is 100% *effective* only if it is never used—and while it is unused, it is 0% *efficient*. Systems that are judged solely on the basis of their effectiveness are not candidates for CPE projects.

A WORD OF CAUTION

In examining systems as complex as today's computers, it is not only important to know what to do, how to do it, and when to stop doing it, but it is also important to know when to be careful. There seems to be a widespread belief that someone will someday find an all-inclusive solution to the efficient use of computers. Pursuit of such a solution may well have as many valuable by-products, as did the pursuit for a way of turning lead into gold. But it seems almost as unlikely that such a pure solution will be found as that lead would one day become gold. Beware of any solution that promises to cure all of the computer installation's problems!

In working to increase the efficiency of a computer system, the experienced CPE technician views generalizations about computers and comparisons between computers with extreme skepticism. Every installation is somehow different than every other installation. Solutions that produce major benefits at one installation may well cause great harm when applied to another "similar" installation. Before accepting the results of a CPE project from some other installation, it is very important that the application and the intent of the project be thoroughly understood in the context of the installation where the project was done and in the context of the installation where the results might be applied. This caution should not be construed as criticism of interchange of CPE project results. Quite the contrary, such exchanges are so useful and productive that it is worthwhile to subscribe to professional and trade publications and to request CPE companies' reports to learn of the application methods of others in the field. But before applying the results of another's project in one's own installation, a complete understanding of the important facets of the project and of the goals of the project are necessary.

Conducting successful CPE projects demands that attention be given to the human factors that may affect the solutions. To be very candid, if a "politically" unacceptable solution is the only likely result of a project, then the CPE group should move on to some other problem where the solution has a chance of being productive. Further, when the people who will ultimately have to implement and live with the solution—operators, programmers, managers, etc.—are clearly incapable of doing so, then there is no point in working to find a solution. The people who must support or implement CPE solutions are as much a part of the computer system as is the central processor. These people cannot be ignored during the accomplishment of a CPE project or the project will surely fail.

2
Managing Computer Performance Evaluation Efforts

Establishing and operating a CPE group is very much like the initiation and management of any other high-technology activity. The purpose of this chapter is to highlight the special needs and obligations of using CPE and to tie these into more familiar, or "classical," management procedures wherever this is practical. The emphasis here is on providing a real and practical framework for application of CPE in a working environment. However, this chapter, more than any other, is directed specifically to installation managers and their staffs. The chapter has *no* intentional "academic" content.

THE DECISION TO GET STARTED IN CPE

When the cost of a computer installation reaches some threshold level, the management may make a decision to begin a CPE effort solely based on the expected return on their investment. In making such a decision, all costs in the computer installation that are subject to reduction by performance improvement projects should be included. That is, the equipment, operating supplies, operations personnel (including any systems programmers used solely to keep the computer in operation), and physical facilities such as rent and utilities are all factors in determining the investment that is subject to reduction through CPE application. Another way of looking at this cost is as the price of procuring all computer support from an outside service bureau. The cost of developing applications programs is intentionally omitted from this listing because it is a cost that is, in general, outside the domain of improvements found through CPE application.

When these total data processing costs have grown to a point where a modest increase in efficiency (say, 2 to 5%) of the overall productivity could represent a "saving" of at least the cost of two to three senior technicians, a business decision may be made to begin a CPE effort. During the first few years of CPE application, it is reasonable to expect savings, either in reduced expenditures or increased capacity at no increase in expenditures, in the range of 5% of the data processing costs each year. There are dramatic examples of CPE projects that have led to elimination of entire installations, but these are rare and should not enter into an investment-oriented decision to establish a CPE group. Expected savings of 5%, then, may be used as a practical limit of the amount that could be invested in a CPE capability with reasonable expectation of "earning" income from the investment.

A second and far more often used method of deciding to begin a CPE group might be termed a *problem-driven decision.* Typically, the installation management learns that some new workload will soon be added to the already heavily loaded computer or that routine examination of workload growth shows that the rate of growth is much higher than was expected or some influential member of the management staff may decide that it is time to replace the entire system with a later model, and so forth. Whatever the problem that causes or is about to cause a "crisis," someone must look deeply and carefully into the way that the existing resources are being used to meet demands. Then some method for redistributing the demands over the resources must be found to enable the installation to continue to handle its workload, or justification must be made for acquiring new equipment. A reasonable reaction to such situations is to start an intensive CPE effort.

A third "reason" has been noted recently for starting a CPE effort. This is, "Everyone else is doing it, why don't we?" This unacceptable reason for undertaking so substantial an investment as may be required for a CPE effort is no doubt due to the wide publicity that has been given to CPE in trade and professional publications and meetings. Computer Performance Evaluation should only be started for positive reasons, not for the lack of negative reasons. The best efforts are those that start conservatively to solve some specific problem.

Whatever the rationale for starting a CPE effort, the earliest efforts should stress the need to look first at the areas where there may be larger rewards. There is an "80-20" rule that is widely accepted in most management efforts that may be applied to CPE work. The "80-20" rule contends that 80% of all that must be known about any management task can be mastered in 20% of the time needed to master the entire task. The CPE corollary to this rule would be that 80% of the improvement possible in any computer system can be made in 20% of the time needed to completely improve the system. Both the rule and the corollary imply that there is an understood 100%, or perfection, level. This is not true in either case and it would be more correct to say that there is some larger benefit possible early in an endeavor than is likely later when the effort becomes a routine task. Relative to CPE, this is nearly always a true statement.

The rule of thumb to apply is to always look for the large numbers. In starting to examine a computer system, the jobs that use the largest amounts of resources are the ones to analyze first. Most production data processing systems have several hundred distinct programs which run each month. Almost without exception, fewer than 10% of these programs will account for more than 50% of the resource usage. If these 10% are not known at the installation, early CPE efforts may aim at the wrong targets from the outset.

SETTING PRELIMINARY GOALS

One conservative way of starting out in CPE that usually produces lasting and continuing efficiency gains depends upon setting an initial, easily attained goal. If an individual is given the assignment to "make the system run better," the reaction (which usually comes very slowly) is one of amazement at how complex the system really is. This kind of goal causes an attempt to collect all the information about everything so that every problem can be cured in a single pass. This does not work. A better method for bringing a novice into the CPE business is to set a simple, specific, and reachable goal for the first project. This will encourage the beginner to look at a problem that is of a reasonable size and it will usually lead to an early success.

It is also possible to try out CPE in this way without making any long-term training or capital investment commitment.

An initial goal might be to identify the two or three programs that use the largest amount of computer resources each week. Once these programs are found, the goal should be changed to one aimed at cutting the resources used by these programs by at least 5%.

Working towards a goal of this type allows the new CPE technician to discover what tools are available to identify large system users and encourages development of a healthy curiosity about the total system's workload. Further, the presence of someone in the installation who is actually assigned to find improvements will serve two purposes: first, others will become conscious of obvious inefficiencies at the installation and will try to make improvements themselves and, second, the new CPE technician will be used as a "suggestion box" for many insights into potential improvement areas that exist within every operations group. This work will also allow the CPE technician to discover what information is needed that is not available in the present system. And, when he knows that he must cut one of the major programs by 5%, he will have to devise some method of measuring the program's performance before and after the changes.

In general, it is extremely easy to reduce the resource usage of any large program by 5%. In fact, minor modifications in such programs often lead to 20 to 50% reductions. This is particularly true both in installations that have not been examined using CPE techniques previously and in installations where the computer system is strictly separated from the applications programmers. With any luck at all, the new CPE technician meets this first goal within six to eight weeks by cutting the identified programs' resource consumption by about 10 or 15%. In the process the technician will often develop strong justification to acquire some specific CPE tool to collect more detailed performance information that was not obtainable with his site's existing data collection capabilities. By meeting with success in the initial project and by knowing what tool to use for further projects of this type, a CPE effort would be underway that should produce continuing performance improvement at the installation.

A second example of an initial CPE goal that can be useful as a first project is to identify the one program that spends the longest average time in the installation. Here the time of interest is the period from deposit of the job at the input desk (or remote entry into the job stack) until output is delivered to the pickup point. Once identified, the goal would be to decrease this time by at least 5% but by no more than 10%. Obviously, the program identified would be one with very low priority. The reason for setting an upper limit on the acceptable improvement is to avoid "improvement" based solely on a request to handle that program faster. When it is clear that changing handling priority is not an acceptable solution, the usual result of this type of goal is that attention is given to the flow of all work through the installation. Typically, small changes are proposed to the arrangement of furniture or work stations and to the equipment layout and distribution of tasks among people who handle all input and output materials. The final impact of this type of effort will usually be that all programs spend a little less time in the installation. After an initial success in meeting a goal of this second type, it is best to redirect the new CPE technician with goals of the first type that require examination of the internals of the computer system. (Otherwise, the CPE technician may soon become regarded as a bothersome furniture mover.)

Many other equally simple preliminary goals that are of high importance at each individual installation may come to mind. These might involve usage levels of various parts of the equipment, unit costs of each item processed by a particular device, relative operating costs by shift, and so forth. The important thing is that the earliest goals are easily understood, easily met, and, above all, worthwhile. Simple and attainable goals at the beginning of a CPE effort are the key to continuing, long-term success. Use of such a goal-oriented approach tends to be quite conservative and it may be as long as six months before noticeable headway is made by the new technician. But once underway, the results of this kind of a start should be of much value to the installation.

SELECTING CPE TEAM MEMBERS

The assumption that a qualified technician is assigned the task of meeting initial goals is implicit in the above discussion. This is made explicit here. The single most important factor in CPE projects is the qualification of the individual or individuals who conduct the project. Further, the most successful CPE efforts are usually found to have three or more qualified individuals participating as a team. This does not mean that three or more people are needed on a full-time basis. It is usually sufficient to have a minimum personnel investment of about one man year per year, but it is best if this man year is divided among at least three people.

Necessary Background

It is difficult to find one individual with a background of enough depth to function across the spectrum of CPE applications. Although no substantial background is needed to identify problems in most computer installations, unusual qualifications are needed to find practical solutions to the problems. Nearly all significant improvements require either programming skills and knowledge of the system's architecture or a background as an electronics technician working with computer systems. Because of this, a skilled system programmer with applications programming experience is an ideal candidate for CPE work. A system programmer with a background in equipment maintenance is an even better choice.

Formal education is also a factor in selecting CPE team members; however, it is of much less importance than the working experience mentioned above. Education in a scientific discipline usually helps a person to examine situations systematically. A scientific education also exposes an individual to the fundamentals of mathematics and statistics. These traits—systematic thinking and a knowledge of mathematics and statistics—are helpful when the CPE effort develops and begins to address more difficult problems.

Another educational factor that can add immeasurably to a CPE team's effectiveness is academic diversification. The reason for this is subtle: in any developing field, the broader the participants' backgrounds, the more likely they are to discover parallels in other fields where similar problems may already have been solved.

Types of People

Original and innovative thought is a major part of any disciplined investigation. The CPE team needs at least one person who will function as the "thinker" or "innovator." This person will be the "spark plug" of the CPE team and he is seldom easy to find. A generally successful way to identify such an individual is to select a person who takes every assignment as a challenge to his thought process. This type of person is often found in the system programming branch of most computer organizations.

At the beginning and end of each CPE project a very different personality type is critical. This type is the "salesman." The idea of performing a CPE project may have to be "sold" to the people who will be affected before the project can be started and, when the project is completed, the management will have to be convinced of the need to implement the project recommendations. As used here, the "salesman" is the type of person who can grasp the important aspects of a project and present them in a clear and articulate manner so that others may be convinced of the need for beginning or implementing the CPE project.

To ensure that the ideas of the "thinker" are put into use and that the "salesman" has something to "sell," one other type of person is needed—a "worker." Conducting performance improvement projects is hard work. Pages and pages of documentation and analysis reports must be examined at a detailed level. Equipment may need to be physically moved or carried to accomplish some hardware monitoring tasks. Most of the time expended in a CPE project can only be described as detailed, tedious, and sometimes-physical labor. The "worker" type is by far of most importance to the lasting value of a CPE team. Although most important to the CPE effort, this individual is usually the least expensive and easiest to identify of the three types needed for the team. The "worker" need not be particularly well educated or brilliant, but he must be industrious. Fortunately, industrious people seem to be the rule rather than the exception among most groups of system programmers and computer engineers.

It should be clear that it is not easy to identify the proper people needed to form a successful CPE team. Because it is so difficult to select individuals to form a CPE group, it is becoming commonplace for organizations to simply hire proven CPE specialists away from other employers. From the viewpoint of personnel development and overall morale, it seems a better long-run practice to find potential CPE technicians among the existing staff. In the short-run, it is certainly cheaper to use people who are already in the organization.

Earlier, a suggestion was made that the minimum personnel investment in a CPE effort is one man year per year divided among three people. The distribution of this man year is more easily explained in terms of these three personality types than based upon education or experience considerations. Typically, time spent on a CPE project is about 10% "thinker-type", 20% "salesman-type", and 70% "worker-type." Lest this explanation be taken too simplistically, it is not intended that any of the people on a CPE team should be noncomputer-oriented. The personality types described here should be taken as traits found in computer specialists, not as individuals from the academic, marketing, or laboring vocations. Computer Performance Evaluation is a specialty for individuals who are already proven as computer specialists.

A Comment on Attitude

Computer Performance Evaluation requires not only imagination and innovation, it also requires a willingness to use the ideas and suggestions that may be available from outside the immediate environment of the CPE team. It is too often the case that an extremely capable system programmer is reluctant to try any changes that he did not think of himself. This is a poor attitude to bring into a CPE team. The best team members are open-minded and eager to examine potential improvement changes from any source. Extreme care should be taken to ensure that no individual whose outlook towards change is too conservative becomes one of the principal CPE team members. This attitude can defeat the purpose of the CPE effort. In short, beware of individuals with the "not invented here" syndrome.

ORGANIZATIONAL PLACEMENT OF THE CPE TEAM

A CPE team performs a classical *staff* function: it investigates existing methods, identifies and recommends alternative methods, and outlines ways of implementing these alternatives. Although the team must be able to implement the changes themselves, it is generally a misallocation of scarce talent to have them do so on a continuing basis. In larger data processing environments, the CPE team may be challenged periodically to do the recommended implementation of some project. It is reasonable to allow the team to do this about once each eight to twelve months. In the process of implementing its own recommendations, the team not only gains operational credibility, it also has an opportunity to update the team's programming or system design skills. This serves the important function of keeping the CPE team from becoming a group of *former* experts and enforces the idea that only useful and implementable recommendations from the CPE group are acceptable. The real work of the CPE team is to detail the specific work that should be performed by other members of the computer installation's staff to improve the overall performance of the total computer installation. The effectiveness of such a group is dependent on its being viewed as a *staff* function rather than as a *line* function (in classical management terms).

Reporting Authority

Another critical decision in establishing a CPE group is determining where the group should be placed within the organization. It appears that CPE teams which report to the individual who has financial control over computer equipment acquisitions have the greatest impact and success.* Such placement ensures that the recommendations of the CPE team will either be implemented or that very good reasons will be given as to why they cannot be used. Placing the CPE capability in the financial area will also encourage the team to view its own activities from a cost versus benefits viewpoint.

In very large organizations, it may be unrealistic to assign a working group like a CPE team at the high level of the individual responsible for financial management. In such cases, the reporting authority may be identified by asking, "To whom would a management consultant or external auditor report if he were to examine the computer installation?"

As a general rule, it is not a good idea to have the CPE team report to the computer installation manager unless the installation is very large. ("Very large" for this purpose is an installation that either has two or more brands of processors or that has a monthly lease cost—or equivalent—in excess of $100,000.) The reason for isolating the CPE team from managers of smaller installations is that most managers of such installations tend towards the view that ideas

---

* This opinion is not shared by all CPE practitioners. It is based on the authors' personal experiences and exposures in several alternative reporting structures.

for improvement that do not come from either the manufacturer or the users' group for "his" equipment are not likely to have merit. In addition, CPE efforts occasionally lead to elimination of entire systems, especially those that are relatively small at the outset. It is not realistic to expect that an installation manager would give fair consideration to a CPE recommendation regarding either elimination or drastic cutback of his own installation.

The CPE team will usually fit somewhere in the financial hierarchy of the organization. The exact location will depend on the size of the organization and of the data processing installation. In general, the higher the reporting authority of the CPE team, the more effective the CPE team will be.

Charter

The charter is the CPE team's license to operate. Whenever a group outside the immediate operational staff of a computer installation (as suggested above) is established for the purpose of improving the operation of the installation, it is mandatory that clear notice be given of the group's powers. This notice should be formal (written) and it should be given the widest possible distribution in the data processing environment. Such a notice serves as the group's charter to become involved in even the most routine aspects of computer support.

This charter need not be either lengthy or detailed. General direction will be best because it cannot be known ahead of time exactly which areas will produce the most plentiful savings. Such a charter should, as a minimum, include the following areas:

Equipment. Before ordering new equipment to replace, to add to, or to enhance the existing equipment's speed or capacity, the CPE team must be called upon to measure the levels of activity and the contentions of the system or portions of the system that would be affected by the proposed new equipment.

Programs. No new programs or systems of programs and no substantial changes to existing programs are to be implemented without first having the design or proposed changes reviewed by the CPE team. If the CPE team considers it necessary, the design or change must be modeled to predict its impact on the existing workload and to test any reasonable design alternatives before resources are committed to programming or implementing the system or change.

A charter that covers these areas will allow the CPE team to look at both existing systems and proposed changes *before* resources are dedicated to their accomplishment. To exercise this type of charter, the team will have to conduct a thorough examination of the entire system as it exists. Generally, this will be the first time that an impartial study of the existing system has been made by a group of knowledgeable individuals. This examination alone often produces enough material for immediate projects that will lead to initial savings exceeding the costs of establishing the CPE team.

Controls

A carefully selected CPE team that is properly placed in the organization and given a strong charter will be very influential at the working level. There may be a strong tendency to react too quickly to the team's suggestions. Therefore, it is important that rather strict controls be established to make sure that the team follows a detailed plan through to completion on each project before suggesting changes to those who may have to implement the changes. If such controls are not established, it is likely that changes will be made in anticipation before all aspects of the changes are evaluated.

This predicament may be avoided by including a statement in the charter that requires the written directive of some specified manager before any CPE team recommendation may be implemented. Whenever possible, the team should be required to provide at least two acceptable approaches to the solution of any problem along with reasons for and against each approach. Then the approach that will be implemented should be selected and directed by the specified manager. Without such control, the CPE team may quickly become the *de facto* manager of the data processing installation.

Job Descriptions

There are five distinct areas that should be covered in the formal descriptions of duties to be performed by the CPE team.

1. Working with documentation describing the logical and physical flow of signals and working through the computer system and its components
2. Performing measurement analysis and making changes in applications and control programs
3. Connecting, installing, or using such CPE tools or devices as may become available
4. Developing and using simulation and modeling techniques
5. Preparing and presenting reports describing CPE activities and recommendations for use by the organization's management

These areas may be elaborated as needed to meet major local requirements, but these five basic skill areas encompass the minimal needs to ensure that a CPE team can perform comprehensive and useful projects.

CPE PROJECT ADMINISTRATION

As with any employee group, CPE technicians should produce results that are worth more than their costs. Each member of the CPE team should know that the team will be judged on the value of its results and that the team will be dissolved if value does not exceed costs. To ensure that the team performs its day-to-day tasks in such a way that a reasonable review of the team's progress can be made, rather stringent policies are needed to administer each CPE project. These policies should address procedures, reporting, and project management.

Procedures

The specific areas that establish CPE group procedures are: problem definition, examination of present methods, postulating and testing potential changes, recommending suitable alternatives, and overseeing the implementation of recommended changes. It has already been stressed that the CPE team's recommendations should be made to management and that management should direct those changes that are chosen from among the CPE team's alternatives. The procedures should be stressed periodically to the team by the team's reporting authority. It is also useful to have written procedures manuals in cases where the CPE team grows to more than five members or in cases where the team performs projects at installations away from their home office.

Reporting

The only tangible product of most CPE teams is the project report that describes each significant activity. One format for these reports that has proven useful in several CPE environments is that of the standard "staff study." This format covers the following topics:

Summary. No more than one page stating the major findings and recommendations of the project. This should be the first page of the report
Purpose. An explanation of the reason for conducting the project
Scope. A description of the extent or limits on the project
Procedure. An explanation of what was done during the project and of the resources used during the project
Findings. Specific statements and supporting information about each significant thing that was learned during the project
Conclusions. An explanation of the process involved in using the Findings to arrive at the Recommendations
Recommendations. A listing of the actions that may be taken to improve performance in the area of the project and an estimate of the cost and benefit expected from each action

In this basic format, CPE project reports serve as the major communication device between the CPE team, management, and the individuals affected by the project. This type of report also serves as a lasting record of the team's major activities and as a source document for checking the accuracy of the team's predictions after changes have been made. As the number of completed projects grows, the project reports become a valuable source for planning new projects based upon those areas that have produced continuing, highly valuable results in the organization's own computer environment. Finally, reports of this type are useful as training documents when new people are brought into established CPE groups.

Project Management

Computer Performance Evaluation efforts are best regarded as "projects." That is, each effort tends to have a distinct purpose and a relatively short time is available to address this purpose. The CPE team itself may become a continuing body that requires standard management techniques, but the CPE tasks need to be managed on a project basis. The CPE team leader may be the regular project manager, but the growth of CPE in an organization often makes it impossible for any one individual to manage every active CPE project. Therefore, individual members of the team should be expected to take a turn at managing CPE projects. This section is directed to the functions of CPE team members serving as managers of individual performance improvement projects.

In classical management terms, every manager's tasks include the following five broad and general areas:

Planning. Determining requirements for people, facilities, and equipment, and estimating task durations and relationships between workload, expected results, and necessary deliverables

Organizing. Ensuring the availability of needed personnel, materials, facilities, and (most importantly) authority

Directing. Setting time and cost milestones and bounds on what must be done and making specific operational decisions

Controlling. Measuring performance against plans and taking any needed actions to correct malperformance

Coordinating. Ensuring that all concerned entities are aware of, and receptive to, the planned efforts, goals, and recommendations

These five general tasks are made specific in the context of a CPE project in Table 2-1 (CPE Project Manager's Responsibilities—Preparing for the CPE Project) and Table 2-2 (During the CPE Project). After the CPE project is completed, management responsibility for the project should be exercised by the CPE team leader rather than by the individual project managers. The post-project responsibility is to validate that the recommendations of the project, when implemented, are sound and accurate. This responsibility is dealt

Table 2-1. The CPE Project Manager's Responsibilities— Preparing for the CPE Project.

1. Understand and state the "customer's" problem as a solvable CPE problem.
2. Produce a clear, consistent, and appropriate project plan to:

   - determine what must be provided by all involved parties
   - ensure that all ideas will be explored and exploited
   - establish quality control
   - state project deliverables that address the problem
   - include all essential and no nonessential tasks
   - equate necessary resources to each task

3. Possess managerial and technical skills required for the project.
4. Obtain "customer's" agreement on the project plan.

---

with later in this chapter under "The CPE Team Leader's Responsibilities."

Each project manager should perform a large share of the work on his own project. Because of this individual's dual responsibility—both managerial and technical—care must be taken that no one team member is required to manage more that one major CPE project at a time. An ideal situation is reached when there are as many major projects underway as there are *trained* CPE technicians on the team and each is responsible for one project. Of course, the individual expertise of every CPE team member should be available to each active project as special talents are needed, even though it may mean that a project leader might occasionally work on another project than the one for which he is immediately responsible.

Table 2-2. The CPE Project Manager's Responsibilities— During the CPE Project.

1. Ensure that commitments to each task are met.
2. Prevent, detect, and correct any malperformance.
3. Exercise positive cost and quality controls.
4. Assess suitability of methods used for each task relative to known alternative methods.
5. Understand the technical details and products of each task and their relationships to the project's goals.
6. Review the adequacy of skills, facilities, equipment, and information used in the project.
7. Meet the scheduled completion date.

THE CPE TEAM LEADER'S RESPONSIBILITIES

Even under the strict requirement that each CPE team produce continuing savings in excess of the cost of the CPE effort, most CPE teams tend to thrive and grow into permanant sections of their organizations. It is not at all uncommon for a modest, part-time effort by two or three CPE technicians to grow to ten or more in less than two years. Because of this growth potential in most organizations, it is wise at the outset to make sure that someone on the team has the necessary managerial skills to oversee a group that might become larger than initially expected.

The team leader, whether the team numbers one or twenty, will necessarily be the "front man" for the organization's CPE effort. It is useful if this individual regards the people for whom CPE projects will be conducted as his "customers." This section is in the context of managing to ensure that both the customer's needs and the organization's needs are met by the CPE team's product: improved installation efficiency.

Table 2-3 lists the CPE team leader's management responsibilities. The narrative expansion of these responsibilities should be most useful after the CPE team has begun to function; however, it is reasonable for the prospective manager, technician, or customer to become acquainted with these responsibilities before becoming directly involved with CPE projects.

Table 2-3. The CPE Team Leader's Management Responsibilities.

1. Manage the objectives of each CPE project.
2. Schedule CPE projects and tasks.
3. Select and organize CPE team members.
4. Manage the scope of each CPE project.
5. Control the level of detail of each project.
6. Control CPE costs.
7. Manage project validation phase.
8. Manage CPE project report production.
9. Manage experimentation efforts.
10. Manage acquisition of CPE tools.
11. Maintain skill levels of CPE team members.
12. Conduct post-project reviews.

Manage the Objectives of Each CPE Project

Performing this function requires that the CPE team leader determine that answers exist to the following questions:

1. Does the customer know what he wants from the CPE project?
2. Does the customer have the authority and ability to implement the changes that are likely to result?
3. Are the kind of results that the customer expects both necessary and useful?
4. Is the customer motivated to support the CPE effort?

A negative answer to any one of these questions should signal the CPE team leader to use extreme caution before making a commitment to support the suggested project. Failure by the team leader to resolve any negative response will virtually guarantee that the objectives of the project will not be met.

Schedule CPE Projects and Tasks

Scheduling, a routine and relatively simple management responsibility, is too often overlooked. This results in an overcommitted CPE team that may have to rush projects too much to do a reasonable job on any of them.

Adequate scheduling will require that the CPE team leader use some quantitative or graphic method to assign CPE technicians, equipment, and facilities against all known tasks of CPE projects that are either underway or on the forecast of work to be done. Further, scheduling should ensure that the leader acts to acquire all necessary resources far enough ahead so that they will be available when they are needed. Finally, scheduling requires that the leader exercise positive controls to monitor progress and to make certain that each project is proceeding as planned.

Select and Organize CPE Team Members

Beyond the obvious tasks of recruiting or acquiring the right people for the CPE team, selecting and organizing CPE team members includes determining when the CPE team may need some kind of outside support. It also includes motivation of personnel to the specific goals of their assigned projects along with assignment of people to the individual projects. In most CPE teams the only organizing that is needed involves distributing the workload to make the best use of the individual team members' talents and to promote cross-training through on-the-job experience. In larger CPE groups, organizing personnel may include structuring the team into specialized subunits. For example, a large CPE group might be broken into three teams: one working with accounting data, one with monitors, and one with modeling. In other environments, large CPE groups might be structured into specialty groups according to computer manufacturers' products that are used by the overall organization.

Manage the Scope of Each CPE Project

To manage the scope of each project, the team leader must work with each of the CPE project managers to establish the smallest possible set of factors that contains all elements essential to the performance of the project. Boundaries must be set to limit the project and the possible effects of boundary conditions should be explored and stated explicitly when they may bear on the results of the CPE project. With a knowledge of all completed, current, or projected CPE projects, the team leader must determine whether each individual new project should be addressed at a specific or general level, or whether results of some other project may be adapted to the new effort.

Careful exercise of this responsibility will enable the team leader to recognize available project reports from outside his own organization that may have direct application in his environment. Managing the scope of each specific project also allows the leader to begin to categorize the team's past efforts so that new work with sufficient similarity to past projects may be handled more quickly than the earlier work.

Control the Level of Detail of Each Project

Controlling the level of detail of each project is one of the more difficult responsibilities to meet. The team leader must become involved enough in each project to assure that unnecessarily detailed work is not being done. The only practical way to meet this need is simply by continued insistence that the highest possible level of detail be used consistently and finer detail be allowed only when there is evidence that it is needed to complete a project.

Most major CPE savings result from projects that are conducted at very high, perhaps gross, levels of detail. The team leader should work continuously to demonstrate this to the team members based upon the results of their own past projects. It is also helpful to encourage team members to develop alternatives during a project that will allow them to go around areas that appear to demand very detailed work. With minimal encouragement, this approach tends to evolve as the team gains experience.

Control CPE Costs

Controlling CPE costs is a routine management function and is very important to the CPE team that is judged on its ability to produce more in savings than the team costs. Fulfilling this responsibility requires that the team leader establish control procedures to guard against poor usage of either people or equipment. Controlling CPE costs also demands that the leader use careful judgment to ensure that CPE resources applied to each project are consistent with the size and value of the project. Further, the team leader must be certain that no new tools are acquired unless substantial justification can be made for their acquisition.

Manage Project Validation Phase

Of major importance in validating the work of the CPE team is the thorough understanding and exposure of every assumption that must be made during the conduct of a project. The team leader must be very familiar with the accuracy of each CPE tool or technique that is used and he must assure that every tool is "debugged" and tested before it is used.

To ensure that both task and project validations are made, the team leader should develop a formal plan that outlines the validation procedure for each tool or technique that is as independent as possible of the specific use of the tool or technique. Such a plan would specify the confidence levels required to demonstrate the validity of each method and would assure that sensitivity tests were made whenever results are either unusually stable or unusually volatile.

The team leader should be familiar enough with the applications of every tool or technique to make "engineering estimates" of the nominal outcome of any CPE experiment *before* the experiment is conducted. It is often enlightening to examine a carefully conducted CPE project at the step-by-step level and ask the question, "Is this result possible?" The team leader must be able to spot those occasional cases where the answer is, "No."

Manage CPE Project Report Production

As has been pointed out earlier, the project reports are the only tangible product of the CPE team. The team leader must ensure that these reports are of sustained high quality. To do this, adequate documentation must be made of each major step in the project. The leader should be certain that a project notebook or other chronological log is kept for every project and that this record covers all such items as assumptions, decisions, specific actions, and so forth.

The CPE project managers will use these logs to prepare the final project report and the team leader will need access to the logs to be sure that every key assumption or fact in the report is supported by entries in the projects' logs. As soon as the project report is written, the team leader should review it in extreme detail for both content and context. A very important part of this review is a check to ensure that the purpose and impact of each recommendation is made clear in easily understood language.

Care must be taken in project report production that too much attention is not given to the individual project manager's literary style. Reports do need to be in an understandable narrative, but it is too much to insist that every report stand as a work that would be suitable for publication. Care must also be exercised in the other direction; even the best technical paper has no value if only the author can understand it. In general, the report should be as free of "jargon" as is reasonably possible and it should be written in short, simple words. The two sections incorporated in the format suggested earlier for CPE project reports that *must* be completely jargon-free are the Summary and the Recommendations. These are the two sections that management will use heavily, and management has neither the time nor the interest to learn the technical jargon of each specialty in an organization. When a term with a special meaning must be used, it should be defined in common terms when it is first mentioned. If a report contains several of such terms, it is useful to append a glossary or list of definitions to the report.

The project reports of successful CPE teams often become popular reading material in larger organizations. There are mixed blessings in this. It is encouraging to have the work recognized because this promotes high motivation among the team members, but it also requires that the team leader produce the reports in large quantities. When this increased circulation begins to occur, the leader should recognize that a significant new workload must be accounted for in his planning to make certain that this added work will fit into the team's and the individual projects' schedules. As long as the leader recognizes that the team is becoming involved in a "publishing business," there is seldom any real problem in managing the physical production of larger numbers of reports. But he must recognize this as soon as it begins to happen or project due dates may lose their meaning.

Manage Experimentation Efforts

CPE projects usually require that specific tests or experiments be conducted at several points during the project's life. Although the leader's responsibilities here are quite straightforward, they will demand that the team leader maintains a high level of technical expertise.

The leader should participate in the design of each new or unusual experiment to assure that the experiment's objectives are consistent with the project's objectives and to make certain that any necessary assumptions are clearly understood by those conducting the experiment. The leader must also establish the applicability and validity of any mathematical or statistical techniques that are to be used *before* the experiment is conducted. He will also need to be certain that analyses done during experiments are consistent and correct and that each experiment produces the desired results. Finally, the leader must check to see that clear and concise summaries of significant experiments are included in the project log and, when necessary, in the Procedure section of the project report.

Manage Acquisition of CPE Tools

Meeting this responsibility requires that the team leader stay abreast of a rapidly developing technology where new products seem to appear and old products to disappear quite frequently. There will always be pressure on the leader of an established CPE group to buy some new product. His task is to be sure that no CPE tool is acquired unless its use can be justified for an identified technical requirement that exists within the realm of the CPE team. The question that the leader should ask is, "Can the CPE team continue to function productively without this tool?" If this is too restrictive, he might ask instead, "Is the expected value of this tool, *as it would be applied here,* higher than the cost of acquiring and using the tool?"

The number of CPE tools used by a team has no correlation with the value of the projects conducted by the team. The leader should be as cautious and conservative in acquiring new tools as in any other activity connected with CPE projects.

The other side of meeting this responsibility is conducting periodic reviews of the use of CPE tools that the CPE group has previously acquired. Those tools that have either fallen into disuse or proven to be unacceptable should be removed from the team's "tool kit." There is nearly always a cost associated with just having a CPE tool even if it is not used. Periodic reviews of tools in use should also look back at tools that have been set aside in earlier reviews. Often a tool that was of little or no value to a developing CPE group will show much higher value after the team has gained breadth and experience in applying other tools.

One of the more enjoyable ways of keeping up with the CPE technology to meet the tool acquisition responsibility is through active participation in professional and commercial groups with special interests in CPE. Users' groups of most computer manufacturers often have a subset of individuals with such interests.

Maintain Skill Levels of CPE Team Members

The initial skills needed to apply CPE techniques are relatively easy to learn. New team members should require no more than one week of familiarization before they can be introduced to applications under the guidance of an experienced CPE technician. Short, two- or three-day seminars on CPE are useful for acquainting new team members with the spectrum of CPE tools and more popular applications, but these are seldom given at the level of detail needed to allow an attendee to apply CPE skills independently. Formal training is best obtained through the courses offered by CPE product vendors or by firms specializing in such training. Unless the CPE group is very large, say more than twenty members, there is no advantage to developing and conducting formal courses within the group.

It is not particularly difficult to bring new people in and get them trained to the level needed to perform projects. What is difficult is to develop the skills needed to recognize and work around the limitations of each special tool. The best way for the team leader to develop this skill is through periodic meetings of all team members. The CPE technician that is doing unusual or innovative work in his project should be asked to give a short status report on this work as the main topic of the meeting. The team leader should be prepared to ask enough questions about the project to start a discussion on the merits and potential pitfalls that the project manager may encounter. No more than one hour should be allowed for the status report and ensuing discussions. This should be followed by very short (no more than five minutes) presentations by each active CPE team member describing the project and tools that he has been involved with since the last group meeting. The atmosphere at these meetings should be as informal as possible to encourage a free flow of information between all team members. As a practical matter, a good time to schedule such gatherings is during the last hour or so of each pay day. This will encourage attendance in installations that still distribute paychecks personally. Alternatively, late in the day on every first and third, or second and fourth, Friday might be a reasonable schedule for these CPE team meetings.

A necessary skill that these meetings will help to develop is that of making oral presentations. Many CPE projects will require that the project manager make a formal presentation on the project results to high-level managers. The team leader who spends time helping his subordinates to develop effective briefing skills does a great service to their future audiences and earns the gratitude of his technicians. When it is known far enough in advance that a formal briefing will be a project requirement, the team leader may devote one or two meetings to "dry runs" of the presentation to provide constructive criticism to the prospective briefer.

Another use of periodic team meetings that should not be overlooked is that of giving recognition for jobs that have been unusually well done. On those rare occasions when a "customer" writes commending the CPE team or one of its members for good work, the team leader can use these meetings as a proper forum for communicating the commendation to the team or member and to add his own praise. Lacking such outside stimulus, it is still a simple thing for the team leader to tell the member that has done an outstanding job and that the work was appreciated by the team leader. Small efforts like these by the team leader often do more to promote continued high skill levels than all of the formal training that could be bought.

Conduct Post-Project Reviews

Once the project manager finishes a CPE project, the responsibility to follow up with the customer should shift to the team leader. As a matter of course, the team leader should contact the customer about thirty days after the project has been completed and the report delivered. The purpose of this contact is to allow and encourage the customer to ask any questions that may have come up since project completion. Too often such questions do not get directed back to the CPE group because the customer may feel that the questions would appear "stupid" or uninformed to the CPE specialists. The team leader must take the initiative to ensure that the customer can understand the project completely. A further purpose of this thirty-day follow-up is to learn how the implementation of project report recommendations is proceding. If the implementation is complete, arrangements should be made for the CPE team to check to assure that the recommendations actually produced the expected results.

A second follow-up should be made by the team leader much later after the recommended changes have all been completed and the changed portion of the total system has had time to stabilize. Typically this would be four to six months after project completion. The purpose of this follow-up is to see what new problems may have arisen in that customer's area so that discussions of further CPE projects may be started. This second follow-up is only of real importance as a formal management responsibility in very large organizations or when a centralized CPE group serves geographically decentralized computer centers. In smaller organizations or when the CPE group serves only one computer center, this second follow-up can be as informal as a casual meeting of the concerned parties in a hallway or cafeteria. This should not be taken to mean that the second follow-up is not important, only that it need not necessarily be a formal session.

CONTINUING CPE ACTIVITIES

Most of the continuing performance evaluation activities have been introduced in earlier sections about tools and techniques and under the specific responsibilities of the CPE team leader or of the project managers. This section brings these activities together in more general terms and describes a few continuing activities that are broader than those covered in earlier sections. The continuing activities may be grouped into six categories: determining installation measurement frequencies, capacity management, developing the CPE data base, integrating operations and measurement activities, examining and selecting new equipment, and establishing outside relationships.

Determining Installation Measurement Frequency

The determination of installation measurement frequency is almost exclusively within the domain of the principal CPE tool—common sense. One rule that nearly always applies in this area is that as a computer system's useful lifetime decreases, measurements are needed less frequently. Another general rule that usually applies is that detailed system profile measurements should be made at least once every six months for any computer that is in a multiprogramming environment.

The decision to measure a system's performance is generally based on such factors as the size of the investment in the computer center, the stability of the workload, and the capability of the personnel who operate the installation. Again using common sense, the measurement frequency would be either infrequent or never for an inexpensive center with a stable workload and a highly skilled operations staff. At the other extreme, continuous measurement may be needed for very expensive systems with dynamically changing workloads and an unskilled operations staff. The local mix of these three factors would suggest the interval that would apply at a specific installation.

Of course, even an established measurement frequency might need periodic exceptions to react to planned changes in the installation's workload. For example, it is useful to conduct system measurement projects before, during, and after the addition of large, new systems of programs, or of significant new users, or when the user mix is known to be changing.

It is an accepted practice at many large installations to conduct measurement activity at a gross level on a continuous basis using only accounting data (see Chapter 3). When these gross measures indicate that some part of the system's performance is unusual, more detailed measurements are made to determine the cause of the unusual performance. "Unusual" performance can only be identified if the "usual" performance is known and used as a standard of comparison on a regular basis. The establishment of normal or usual performance standards is discussed below as a part of "Developing the CPE Data Base," later, along with the use of accounting data (Chapter 3), and again in Chapters 10 and 11.

Although it may be difficult to set a specific measurement frequency for a particular system, it is quite simple to tell when the measurements are being made too often. The product of measurement is data. When no one is analyzing all of the detailed measurement data, the measurements are being made too frequently.

Capacity Management

Capacity management, a continuing activity, is the one that gets most of the publicity. It involves the "tuning" of the system to ensure that files are properly allocated, that programs are properly scheduled into a multiprogramming mix, and that the operating system and applications programs are optimized with respect to the equipment configuration.

Capacity management has been formally defined* in the CPE context as ". . . that set of functions concerned with maintaining the proper balance between workload and equipment configuration at the lowest costs and rates while taking into account such limiting factors as service, reliability, and total cost." As used in this book, capacity management places stress on the continuing assessment of relative costs of equipment components by their individual levels of usage. It is this activity that allows periodic changes to take advantage of possible trade-offs between cost and performance of the various parts of computer systems. This book is written from this capacity management viewpoint to the greatest possible extent for both existing and proposed computer systems.

Developing the CPE Data Base

The data base that grows naturally to support CPE projects has a high value and is of major importance to the continuing efforts of the CPE group. Information that is collected by one CPE tool is often used as input to, or in conjunction with, some other tool. It is necessary that continuing attention be given to common formats and structures that will allow such transferability of data.

Specifically, the CPE data base should be designed to provide interfaces between the various tools to standardize and simplify the routine application of the tools. Incorporation of additional features in these interfaces to allow editing of data should also be considered. Another consideration in developing the data base is its potential use in comparisons of installations in multiple installation environments and in comparisons of present projects with past projects. Recognition must be made of the fact that a CPE data base with more than just a few weeks of information will serve as the primary source for establishing continuing performance standards and for predicting future trends in the installation.

It is often effective when modeling is used by the CPE team to make the models the focal points for developing the CPE data base. That is, the outputs of other CPE tools may be used as the format

---

* Kolence, Kenneth W. *EDP Facility Accounting: Implementation,* Volume 1, Bank Administration Institute, Park Ridge, Illinois, 1975, p. 1.

outline for the models' inputs and outputs. Many installations develop this data management to the point that models may be driven directly by the information obtained from accounting packages or monitors. Such "automatic" input generation for models can cut many man weeks from modeling projects. When no modeling capability exists within the CPE group, accounting package reports can serve reasonably well as the CPE data base focal point.

One of the simple but productive uses of the CPE data base is as the information source for production of exception reports to indicate that something may be happening at the installation that deserves detailed examination. As the data base develops into a well-structured information source, special CPE programs may be developed or acquired commercially to perform periodic report extraction. Statistical methods incorporated into these programs can allow selection of activities that are outside some preselected statistical bound or control limit. This information serves as a pointer to the unusual activity area which may need detailed examination by the CPE team. These exception reporting mechanisms are often incorporated in accounting data reduction programs as described in later chapters.

The well-managed CPE data base serves as a record of long-term trends in the workload and the performance of the system. This historical information is very valuable for predicting growth of the total system. These predictions will be needed to support management decisions about installation expansions or replacements. The CPE data base development deserves nearly as much attention as does the development of the computer system's data base. The system's data base provides easy and efficient use of the system by its customers; the CPE data base helps the installation's staff to use the system efficiently.

Integrating Operations and Measurement Activity

The continuing existence and availability of a well organized CPE data base provides a strong focal point for integration of measurement activity into the routine operation of the installation. The data base may be greatly enhanced by encouraging the operations staff to suggest existing operations information that might be useful for improving the system's efficiency. Such things as console logs and system incident reports that are routinely kept by operators should be reviewed regularly by members of the CPE group. These reviews should be made openly, in the presence of the operators and with reliance on the operators for comments and clarifications.

The process of integrating the CPE and operations functions will be helped if the members of the CPE team explain the special tools that are available to assist the operations personnel in the selection of jobs for multiprogramming, in planning tape and disk pack usage, and in performing other operations-level scheduling tasks. Suggestions from operators should be solicited by the CPE team. Information flow between operators and CPE group members is necessary to the continued integration of operations and measurement activity.

This integration is important because many of the recommendations developed by the CPE group will depend on the operators for implementation. It must be understood that operator performance can be an overriding factor in the efficient use of contemporary computer systems.

An early and valuable by-product of efforts to integrate the CPE group into the operations team will be that the operators will also educate the CPE technicians. This education is usually in the form of tips on how the operators judge when any one program is running too long, or how they know when an unusual event is occuring within the equipment. Operators are also the most reliable source other than accounting data for immediate information at a relatively detailed level about which programs and systems are the major users of the various parts of the equipment. Finally, when hardware monitors are used, the operations personnel are usually a rich source of specific questions about the internal workings of "their" equipment. Paying attention to these questions allows the CPE technicians to develop insight into the system that could otherwise take a very long time.

Examining and Selecting New Equipment

This may not always be a continuing CPE team activity, but in the dynamic environment of most computer installations it is rare to find an installation that does not spend some part of each week considering equipment alternatives that may become available. The CPE group is the logical reviewer of suggestions about equipment changes or additions. If a charter as strong as has been suggested earlier is adopted, there will be no alternative but to seek the CPE team's review prior to each equipment change. The continuing activity in this area is, however, better treated as a logical duty of the CPE team than as a mandatory duty.

An ideal situation is reached when everyone with an interest in modifying the system automatically directs their comments and questions to the CPE team. The CPE team is the most logical group to respond to questions like, "What would happen if . . . ?"

Establishing Outside Relationships

It is truly amazing how completely isolated many computer installations are from the people who depend upon the installation for service. The routine activity of a CPE team requires that contacts be made with system programming staffs, application programming offices, manufacturers' representatives, and outside CPE groups in addition to almost daily contacts with the installation's operations staff. Because of this, the CPE group can act as a "bridge" between the installation and the "outside world."

It is often surprizing how quickly many computer "problems" are solved by developing communications between the operations staff and the other groups mentioned above. Many things that are considered problems by users are not known to the operators, but, once mentioned, very small procedural changes can completely eliminate the problem. Likewise, users sometimes make demands that are unreasonable for the operators simply because the users do not realize what must happen to satisfy their demands.

Outside relationships with the manufacturer's representatives are important to the CPE team. These relationships are most important because it seems almost an instinctive reaction of the manufacturer's maintenance personnel to want to restrict or resist any measurement activity. Beyond this, when using hardware monitors, the manufacturer's assistance may be needed to develop or check probe points, and, when monitoring leased equipment, the manufacturer's permission may be necessary before probes may be attached to the computer system. Finally, a good relationship with the manufacturer could lead to a healthy working-level contact between the CPE group and the research group of the manufacturer. Such a contact can greatly benefit the CPE group when it must address very difficult problems that concern details of the computer system's architecture. Further, this relationship is often helpful to the manufacturer because visibility of problems encountered in "real" installations is seldom available directly to their research groups.

CONSIDERATIONS FOR SMALLER SYSTEMS

There are computer centers that are simply too small to warrant the investment needed to use CPE on a continuing basis. Near the end of Chapter 1 ("When to Stop Using CPE"), a threshold level of installation cost was mentioned below which CPE would be impractical. At the beginning of this chapter ("The Decision to Get Started"), a claim was made that an affective CPE team should be expected to produce cost-savings with a value of no less than 5% of the total installation's cost during each of the first few years of CPE projects. Further, a minimum personnel investment to provide CPE support was given as at least one man year per year. In addition, the cost of providing suitable CPE tools may be estimated at about the same cost as a man year.

Putting all of these factors together leads to a simple calculation that can determine whether the installation is large enough to use CPE. For estimation purposes, the cost of a CPE technician may be taken as the same as the cost of a senior system programmer. The cost of the installation includes the annual lease cost of the equipment (or lease cost equivalent for owned systems), maintenance costs, operations personnel costs (including system programmers whose only tasks are to keep the computer in operation), installation operating supplies, rent and utility costs, and a share of the organizational overhead. In other words, all costs that would be borne by an outside supplier of computer services if the installation did not exist in-house. This total cost in smaller installations may be approximated as four times the annual lease cost of the equipment. This estimate should only be used to get an initial idea of the magnitude of the total cost, not for deciding whether or not the installation is actually large enough to support a CPE effort. The decision should be made based on precise cost data.

For example, suppose that a man year costs $20,000 in the organization. Then the annual cost of a minimal CPE effort should be expected to be near $40,000. This is 5% of $800,000. Therefore, if the total computer installation cost in this organization is more than $800,000 per year, a conservative decision could be made to begin using CPE. Savings of as much as 20% can result from the first year's CPE projects, but in smaller installations it is very risky to base a start-up decision on such an optimistic savings expectation. Use of the 20% factor would imply that a total installation cost of only $200,000 could justify a CPE effort in this example organization. This would be an unrealistic justification.

When actually using this simple calculation, borderline cases are best decided against CPE on a continuing basis. These cases are in the domain of special-purpose CPE projects conducted by outside groups or consultants.

If the installation of interest turns out to be too small, it need not be concluded that there is no room for improvement in the efficiency of the system. It is simply that the approach centers on individuals with very high levels of programming and operational expertise rather than on individuals skilled in CPE applications as discussed in this book.

3
Accounting Data

Accounting data as used throughout this book and in most computer installations means that information which is automatically collected by computer-manufacturer-supplied routines to describe the amount of computing resources consumed by or in support of each application program that is run on a computer system. This might more correctly be termed computer *resource* accounting data to avoid any confusion with the more widely known bookkeeping meaning of accounting data. Whenever the term "accounting data" is used here it should be taken in the specialized computer connotation to mean "resource accounting data."

It is becoming rare to find a computer installation that has no special programs or accounting packages to reduce accounting data into detailed records and reports of system events. Such packages were first developed to enable computer installation managers to bill computer users for data processing services. With the introduction of multiprogramming, users began to note that essentially identical runs were often charged very different prices. This caused computer managers to begin collecting additional data to find out why their prices were subject to these variations.

As knowledge was gained of their respective systems, many installation managers found their enhanced accounting data to be very valuable—so valuable that these managers were reluctant to accept new versions of manufacturers' control programs which would cause a reprogramming effort simply to continue to collect the necessary accounting data. Firm prodding forced computer manufacturers to follow the lead of their customers. Based on consolidations of customers' efforts, manufacturers began providing accounting packages with data collection capabilities far in excess of the

51

minimal needs for billing or cost allocation routines. The availability of this detailed information quickly made accounting data the logical starting point for CPE efforts.

This wide availability of detailed accounting data is a relatively recent occurrence. IBM's accounting package, SMF, or Systems Management Facility, was introduced in late 1970, about two years after Burroughs LOGGER accounting package came into use and just one year or so after most other manufacturers had enhanced their accounting data. Nearly all of these enhancements were direct reactions to users who were dissatisfied with billing based solely on simplistic metrics like "CPU seconds" per job. Most general-purpose computers above the "mini" category now collect reasonably detailed accounting data automatically.

CATEGORIES OF ACCOUNTING DATA

Operations Logs

The oldest form of accounting data is the manual operations log. As a minimum, these logs contain the job or program name and the time that the job was received at the computer facility and usually the time that it left the facility. Such manual logs are generally extensions of records that were begun to answer some specific historical question for the center manager. The detail, regularity, and accuracy of operations logs serve as a measure of the center or shift manager's level of interest in being able to answer queries regarding the handling of particular jobs.

One strength of manual operations logs is that they can provide information on such external events as key-punching or tape library activities. However, these logs seldom have sufficient detail to allow analysis of the internal efficiencies of a computer system. Nevertheless, these logs can serve as indicators for when to begin an analysis by using more powerful tools.

For example, it is not uncommon to note that most of the midnight shift's production is manually logged to the "out basket" during the last fifteen to thirty minutes of the shift. Once it is noted that products are not removed from the "out basket" until after the midnight shift goes home, the operators simplify their paperwork by doing all of the logging-out at the same time. There is nothing wrong with this practice, but when it exists it is a clear indication that turnaround times should be computed in days or shifts rather than in minutes or hours. This is an important observation for the performance evaluator. It may mean that the midnight shift can be assessed in very gross terms at the outset. The measure of performance in this case would be whether or not the shift completes all assigned jobs during its duty period. If work is nearly always completed, the performance questions to ask would be, "How long before the shift end is the work *really* finished?" When it can be determined that work finished very early during most midnight shifts or that the computer was operated far below its capacity, it would be reasonable to begin examining methods for cutting back or eliminating the shift.

Often the largest savings are found through the use of the simplest and least expensive tools. The issues that may be surfaced by examinations of operations logs can produce enough performance improvement to make such examinations worthwhile. Operations logs should not be ignored by CPE technicians.

Billing Information

Computer installations that charge real money for their services have a distinct advantage in beginning performance evaluation efforts. Most importantly, the true value of such installations can readily be established. When installation value exceeds installation cost, careful analyses can be made to determine the merit of beginning a CPE effort and CPE projects can be assessed in terms of value added to the installation. It is unfortunate that billing all computer usage to customers may cause the efficiency of individual programs to seem unimportant to some computer installation managers. Managers may assume that if the customer is willing to pay the price for running a program, then the only concern of the manager is to ensure that sufficient capacity is available to provide satisfactory service to the customer. In other words, the CPE efforts may only be directed at the efficiency of the hardware and its interconnections. This is a shortsighted viewpoint. In the increasingly competitive computer service market, customers have a way of migrating to those centers that provide both reasonable rates and help to improve the operation of individual applications programs.

Billing information is singularly good for placing values on each part of a computer configuration. Nearly all current billing packages assess costs according to use of specific system resources. Monthly summaries are generally available that show the installation manager the amount that each major component of his configuration earned during any month. Coupling this data with the time that each component was in use can yield the value per hour of the devices. Equating these values with the device costs per hour can rank performance improvement efforts in order of the revenue-generation importance of the configuration's components. This yields another logical starting methodology for applying CPE techniques where the larger benefits will be obtained. Many times the least expected component becomes the first to be examined when the billing information is used to establish CPE priorities.

For example, a card reader that is faster (more expensive) than necessary may become apparent when it is noted that its cost per hour of income-producing operation is higher than that of, say, the disk system. A slower card reader costing less per month and using more time to complete the same input workload may become more attractive when it is recognized that it would produce the same income as the faster device. Deeper analysis would be needed to determine whether the slower device might produce any unacceptable delays in customers' jobs. In the other direction, analysis of a cost- versus income-ordered listing can also suggest which devices may need to be upgraded to take advantage of the characteristics of the workload at the installation.

Even when the installation does not charge real money for its services, the billing information can still be obtained and used by the installation's management. The overhead associated with most billing information collection is generally such a small portion of the overhead for collecting system accounting data that managers find it to be worthwhile to use available cost allocation reports for their own enlightenment. Reviewing billing reports may have a significant impact on management's opinion of the value of the system's components. At the very least, methodical reviews of available billing information will tend to destroy relative value "myths" that are present at most computer centers.

The installation managers who feel that their responsibility to their users goes beyond simply providing enough hardware to meet the demands use billing information to direct attention to programs that may need a performance improvement effort. Usually, the center manager knows of programs run by different customers that provide substantially the same types of products to their respective users. It is a small task for the manager to track the relative cost for similar products with his total view of the installation's billing information. When great differences in cost are noted, the manager might suggest that a performance problem exists within one of the programs. This may be in the form of a suggestion that the user examine more detailed accounting data or employ a software monitor to check the execution of the problem program. When it is "politically" acceptable, the center manager might introduce the users with similar products but dissimilar costs so that one customer can help the other. Even the most naive customer would see such action as a genuine attempt to help the customer do his work better or at a lower cost. Installation managers and CPE technicians can derive great benefit from such a simple application of billing information.

System Accounting Packages

The next level of detail beyond billing information is generally represented by the packages that contain the billing routines. These are called the system accounting packages. These packages collect three types of information—identity, quantity, and time.

Identity data include such things as program name, charge code, and other information that is helpful for categorizing accounting data. This might include the name of the programmer, type of run (test or production), run priority, termination type, and so forth.

Quantity data cover things like the amount of memory requested or used, the storage space and count of records used by a program, the number of cards read or lines printed, and even the number of "pages" (or segments or overlays) used during the processing of a program. Some accounting packages also provide quantity data at the individual file level to account for such things as the actual number of logical records or both the block count and the number of records per block.

Time data associated with processor and other resource usage are also accumulated and presented by accounting packages. The time data may be accumulated to show actual usage from each start of use to each stop of use for devices, or it may simply show the time from the beginning of the first usage to the end of the last usage of a system resource. Packages that use the second and less accurate time data accumulation method seem to be slowly disappearing in favor of the much more precise accumulation method which measures each distinct resource event.

The initial strength of system accounting packages in CPE projects is more due to the standard reports that they make available than due to the specific data collection method that may be used. Standard reports of these accounting packages typically include processor time used, memory space requested and used, total elapsed time in the system, and the number of records input or output by device for each application program. The standard reports usually list information by individual program and allow some option for periodic summaries of totals by the various categories of data that are reported.

Standard reports may be coupled with utility programs that are available on most systems to consolidate several days or weeks of data into performance reports. Such consolidations are quite helpful in selecting those areas where CPE projects can have major impact. Scanning a consolidated listing of the total usage of system resources by program names can quickly indicate which specific programs have the potential of giving the largest performance improvement.

For example, examination of just such a listing of system accounting data for a large computer installation showed that one sorting program alone accounted for more than 400 hours of processing time per month when the total workload accounted for about 600 hours. The remaining 1000 programs regularly used at this installation accounted for a little less than 200 hours or one-third of the processing time. This is an extreme example, but it is all the more significant in that the installation managers did not know or even suspect that their workload was so overwhelmingly driven by this one program. Examination of this program uncovered a few very small changes in coding that would use available resources so much better that the program ran in about one-half of its previous time. The small changes were made and resulted in the elimination of one entire shift. The resources used to identify the problem had always been available but had never been used at the installation. The consolidation listing was extracted from a recent month of accounting data at the suggestion of a CPE consultant on a routine visit to arrange an in-depth project. The program used to extract, sort, and list the accounting data was, ironically, the very program that turned out to be the massive time user. Less than one man week of analyst and programmer time was needed to make the small changes that produced this monumental difference.

The payoff in this example may not be typical of immediate savings available through the use of such a simple approach as just listing and examining accounting data. However, the example should serve as a very real indicator of the value to installation managers of keeping track of the distribution of work performed by their computer systems.

The "standard" reports available from system accounting packages may be thought of as those that can be generated by existing utility and report generation programs without a programming effort as well as those reports that are actually produced directly from the accounting package. Most installations possess such a substantial capability in this report generation that programming is rarely necessary to satisfy a management information need for periodic accounting reports. This is not usually the case when system accounting packages are used for continuing management reporting or in detailed performance evaluation projects. In these two cases, either extensive programming or acquisition of an accounting data reduction package from some outside source may be necessary.

Comprehensive Accounting Packages

An extremely detailed level of program-related data is represented by the most recent accounting packages. These packages collect the same information as the billing and system accounting packages mentioned above and generate additional data to produce detailed reports on overall use of a system's total capacity. Comprehensive accounting packages are capable of providing much more information than any reasonable person would want on a continuing basis.

Hence, these packages are equipped with option "switches" to turn on selected information as the need may arise. Further, these packages are typically written to allow users to "exit" from the package to their own coding. These exit points are often used to embed statistical routines for testing the frequency of occurance of particular events so that data about such things as average program demands or peak resource usage may be collected. In addition, the exits may be used to create special performance evaluation report generators that would drive modeling packages for workload projection projects. Such modeling projects demand detailed workload models, and comprehensive accounting packages are ideal for supporting this type of project.

The additional information selectable through these packages includes such things as the time spent by each file on a specific device, the number of blocks (or physical records) and the number of individual records (or logical records) processed per file, the time spent accessing, transferring, and seeking records for any file that is processed, the time spent in the processor under control of the application program instructions and under operating system control, and the time that the processor spends waiting due to the activity of some other part of the configuration.

The major shortcoming of even the most comprehensive accounting packages is the lack of data collection capability on operating system activity. The second most significant limitation is the lack of data that can be collected on the execution of specific instructions within an applications program. In most other respects, comprehensive accounting packages can collect and report more than enough information to keep a CPE group both busy and productive. It is generally nonproductive to be concerned with these limitations until the strengths of accounting packages have been thoroughly exploited and the limitations begin to affect the thoroughness of the CPE projects.

THE COST OF ACCOUNTING DATA

Accounting data collection routines are programs. Like any other programs, these routines use computing resources in proportion to the amount of work that they perform. Measurements taken with hardware monitors on various types of systems indicate that the overhead for typical billing information is very slight—in the 1 to 3% range. System accounting packages have been observed with overhead rates of from 2 to 5% when collecting data for routine performance and management reporting needs. When all options of some comprehensive accounting packages are used at once, overhead can climb to 30% or even higher. It is more common for the overhead of a comprehensive accounting package in typical uses for CPE projects to operate at or below the 10% overhead level. In each case the overhead cost of accumulating and reducing accounting data is generally less than the value of the performance improvements made possible by use of the data.

THE IMPORTANCE OF ENVIRONMENT

The suitability of accounting data for performance improvement projects depends on the type of processing conducted at an installation. In serial environments, operations logs are necessarily the limit of suitable accounting systems. A serial-only computer is not capable of containing an accounting data collection routine along with an application program without resorting to programming techniques that are generally beyond the capability found at such installations. Multiprogrammable computers that are operated continuously in a serial mode usually are the objects of such gross mismanagement that information from accounting data would be meaningless as a starting point for system performance improvement. A serial environment is best treated by application of the well-proven methods of time study and production management disciplines. Computer performance evaluation techniques are outside the scope of most serially operated installations.

The multiprogramming computers that are the subjects of CPE projects fall into three major categories—batch, teleprocessing, and mixed batch-teleprocessing. In nearly every respect, and certainly for accounting data analysis, batch systems are the easiest to deal with and teleprocessing systems the most difficult. The mixed systems increase in difficulty as the portion of workload attributable to teleprocessing increases. This spectrum of difficulty is due to the increasing dependency on human performance and to decreasing visibility of activity in teleprocessing systems. There is an element of perversity that is manifested in teleprocessing systems in that an increasing load on the system slows the responsiveness, which causes the impatient human portion of the system to demand even more work from the system. Batch systems behave much more consistently.

Relative to accounting data, the spectrum of difficulty is compounded due to the lack of visibility of critical information in many teleprocessing systems. That is, in batch systems most work is under the direct control of software that is internal to the main computer system. Information about this work is accessible to the accounting data collection routines. In a teleprocessing system, large amounts of work in collecting, storing, forwarding, and in some cases even processing remote inquiries and in returning the responses to the proper terminal are under control of hardware and often of software that is physically outside of the main computer system. This data is not normally accessible by accounting data collection routines.

A further complication in analyzing teleprocessing systems with accounting packages is that typical teleprocessing programs stay in execution mode for very long periods—generally for an entire shift and sometimes for days or weeks. Most accounting data are simply accumulations of the identity, quantity, and time data that are collected throughout the execution of each program without regard for when the resource usage actually occurred during the running of the program. Although it is possible to time-stamp accounting data as they are collected, this usually requires addition of user code at the special exit points that are provided. Adding code increases overhead and heavily used teleprocessing systems can seldom afford increases in overhead that by their very nature must occur most often during those times when the activity is heaviest on the teleprocessing system. Beyond this, the structure of most accounting packages is still such that enhancing the existing (batch-oriented) data gives only a partial and very limited set of data for analyzing teleprocessing workloads.

There have been recent and encouraging developments of the use of accounting data in teleprocessing environments. Often the specialized accounting routines go by one of the oldest terms for accounting data collection programs—"trace" or "trace-driven" routines. These teleprocessing trace routines are the apparent next level of sophistication above comprehensive accounting systems. It is expected that the user community will eventually force the complete enhancement necessary to make accounting data as useful in teleprocessing system performance improvement projects as it has already proven to be in batch environments.

One productive application of accounting data as they are now generally available in teleprocessing environments is the examination of the use of various portions of the main computer configuration. For example, without impacting overhead too much, user exits may be employed to accumulate data in *reasonably* short intervals (say, five to ten minutes) to track such things as the type of inquiry or update or even interactive work that terminal users cause. Similarly, user exits may be used to identify the demands that teleprocessing users place on the various hardware components in reasonably short time periods. Listing such accounting data by time interval allows the performance evaluator to see what portions of the system are used by which general classes of teleprocessing activity. Such analyses can be useful in determining the need for more or faster hardware components and for establishing rudimentary schedules for terminal users with "compatible" workloads. In those few accounting packages which have sufficient system visibility to determine which terminal causes each demand, it is possible to create more useful schedules for use of specific terminals and to determine the relative utility values of each terminal. In general, analysis at this level would require a more specialized CPE tool such as a hardware or software monitor.

APPLICATIONS OF ACCOUNTING DATA

It should be understood by now that accounting data have a very broad use in performance improvement efforts. Installation managers have always been the major users of this accounting data. Although this is still the case, it is becoming more common to see accounting data reports circulate among programmers to provide them with routine visibility of their programs' performance. From the viewpoint of a CPE team, accounting reports for programmers represent a passive but worthwhile approach to performance improvement. The third contemporary user of accounting data is the CPE group in the conduct of its continuing efforts to improve total system performance. These three application areas are discussed below along with suggestions for easily implemented approaches in each area. Prior to these discussions, the need for conditioning data is pointed out to ensure that those who have never used accounting data will realize that the first application will be on the data itself.

Conditioning Data

Any information that is generated automatically should be examined for "reasonableness" before it is used. Accounting packages seem to be even more susceptible to spontaneous generation of "strange" data than most other programs. There is no general reason for this, but examination of "raw" data from accounting packages will usually show that bad records are not rare.

The most common errors, in order of frequency, are: duplicate records, incomplete records, and "garbage" records. Obviously, duplicate and garbage records must be found and removed from the accounting data base and incomplete records must be either eliminated or edited and "filled" before analysis can be started. This level of data conditioning is simple and quickly done, but it must not be skipped if the analyses are expected to be reliable. When billing has been based on the accounting data, conditioning at this level must certainly have already been incorporated into the accounting system.

As the accounting data becomes well understood, statistical methods may be employed to test the probable validity of each data point that will be used in a project. Once statistical validity tests have been incorporated into the conditioning routine, exception reporting techniques may be developed to highlight any variations in data that might make a data point questionable.

Management Reporting

Reports generated by manufacturer-supplied accounting packages present information that the manufacturer believes to be of interest and importance to installation managers. Some of these packages list everything collected in a single report while others provide extensive report selection and tailoring features. No matter how comprehensive the manufacturer's package may seem to be at first, it is unlikely that every data combination of interest to installation managers would be available through any accounting package from a computer manufacturer. Hence, managers should recognize at the outset that there will likely come a day when they must either allocate programming talent to the development of special accounting reports or resolve to purchase a management-oriented accounting data reduction package.

As an introductory exercise in the application of accounting data, each manager should select the dozen or so pieces of available accounting data that seem to be of high local importance and develop a report format that presents these data points in a manner that is helpful to the computer center manager. In preparing such a report, the format design should allow the complete report to be thoroughly understood in fifteen minutes or less. The report should cover at least one day's activity although shorter periods may be used in the initial development exercise. In selecting the parameters that are to be reported, a few test questions should be formulated. These questions might be stated as "hypotheses" about some part of the system or operation, and the report should be tailored to confirm or deny each hypothesis as simply as possible.

To illustrate this technique, suppose that an installation with a production environment of typical business programs were to be examined. Hypotheses that might be posed are, "The computer is I/O-bound." "The evening shift does the most work." Or even, "More core is needed." These hypotheses are typical of the assertions heard at many computer centers. Four of the many parameters that could be collected to address these hypotheses are *processor usage, channel usage, memory usage,* and *number of jobs completed.* A report to begin addressing these hypotheses should require a time interval of no less than one shift although it would be necessary to condition the accounting data on a much shorter interval.

One such preliminary accounting data report might consist of only three lines—one for each shift. The data could be presented as averages or absolute counts for each shift. Table 3-1 illustrates a report of this type. Additional columns are developed based on the collected accounting data and such other information as may be found to be needed *after* the first data selection has been made. (All

Table 3-1. Daily Performance Summary.
Monday

SHIFT	AVG % USE PROCESSOR	AVG % USE CHANNELS	AVG M BYTES MEMORY USED	NUMBER JOBS COMPLETED	BUSY FACTOR	I/O FACTOR	AVG MEM AVAIL	AVG PROGRAM SIZE
Midnights	31	62	1.560	41	12.3	2.0	0.440	0.520
Days	46	71	0.710	67	15.5	1.5	1.290	0.142
Evenings	62	83	1.200	109	67.3	1.4	0.800	0.267

necessary and no unnecessary data are rarely specified in advance the first time.) The main thing is to remember that the hypotheses must somehow either be confirmed or denied. It may be reasonable in this installation to calculate a "Busy Factor" by simply multiplying all of the four data points from the accounting data together. (This is not a suggested way of determining the busyness of a real installation. It is only a simplified approach used here as an example. More realistic methods will be outlined much later in this book for the profiling of activity levels at various installations. See Chapter 9.) A second metric to address the "I/O-bound" hypothesis might be termed an "I/O Factor" in this center. This could be derived by dividing channel usage by processor usage. The third hypothesis on the need for more memory really can't quite be addressed with the information specified so far. What is needed is the amount of available memory (which can be calculated directly by knowing only the selected data and the physical memory size of this configuration—this one is 2 M bytes) and the average program size (which cannot be determined from the specified data). At this point the likely "patch" to the report would be based on a manual gathering (still from accounting data) of enough information to determine average program size. For instance, only the average multiprogramming factor would be needed here. Average memory divided by average multiprogramming factor is equal to the average program size.

The idea of "forgetting" some of the necessary data is not given facetiously here. It is more the rule than the exception that the performance experiment will need to be reexamined as the experiment is underway. When this is done, it is entirely normal to have to go back and collect some other piece of information that was not foreseen as necessary to test some hypothesis.

From the data in Table 3-1 for this simplified approach, it does appear that this configuration may be I/O-bound and that, if this metric for "busy" is reliable, the evening shift certainly is the busiest. The need for more "core" is not so easily established. It seems that memory is not a limiting resource during day or evening shifts but that it may be during the midnight shift. (That is, on the average there is not enough memory available to insert one more average-sized program during the midnight shift.) In each case, management would be in a position to take further action. This elementary procedure has suggested the validity or invalidity of the three hypotheses and indicates which areas warrant more detailed examination.

Introductory management applications like this are only of real and lasting value when managers from the installation in question take the time to formulate their own hypotheses and define their own data needs. Then the follow-through, when the data are collected and perhaps augmented to test each hypothesis, will be interesting to the management and of value to the operation of the installation.

Finally, it is usually worthwhile to use this type of exercise to encourage feedback and communication among the installation's staff. In nearly every computer center there is someone who knows about a serious problem with the use of the computer *and how to solve the problem*. All too often these individuals simply cannot or will not communicate this information to the person who can do something about the problem's solution. Posting a simple report like Table 3-1 with space to write in comments can provide a focal point for surfacing performance improvement ideas that already exist in most installations.

As the managers become accustomed to regular accounting data reports, an effort is usually initiated to develop a series of regular reports for special areas of continuing management interest. When this begins to occur, it is time to give serious consideration to acquiring a commercially available accounting data reduction package. There are many of these products available. The cost of most such packages is typically much less than developing a series of management reporting programs at the installation. The spectrum of reports and options available through these packages goes far beyond those supplied by the manufacturers, and the packages are much more user-oriented. Given the wide applicability and moderate cost of commercial accounting data reduction packages, there is seldom a valid justification for developing management information reports from accounting data beyond the simplest one-time applications on an in-house basis.

Programmer Information

Computer programmers have become more and more distant from the machines that they cause to do work. As a rule, this is good because programmers that are close enough to the equipment's operation to become knowledgeable of the system's inner workings often use inordinate amounts of the computer's resources. On the other hand, this is bad because programmers who are completely innocent of the system's inner workings usually regard the computer as a "magic box" that does whatever is asked in almost no time at all. Reports from accounting data can provide programmers enough insight into the system's operation to eliminate the "magic box" attitude while still keeping the programmers a "safe" distance from the actual operation of the equipment.

The extra time needed to produce accounting reports for programmers in a production system is negligible relative to the performance improvement that these reports can cause. When accounting data have been collected regularly in support of management's needs, it is a small step to provide data that would be of interest to programmers. One type of information like this might be relationships of such things as the percentage of the total amount of time that each program uses versus the total number of executions of that program. These and other ratios may be prepared into reports that identify each program by the name of the responsible programmer. Such reports are of very much interest to any programmer whose name might show up on a bulletin board in the report covering some weekly or monthly period at the installation.

Table 3-2 is an example of a programmer information report based only on three easily available pieces of accounting data: pro-

ACCOUNTING DATA 67

Table 3-2. Programmer Information Report for Week of June 1-7.

PROGRAMMER	PROGRAM	(X) % OF TOTAL PROCESSOR	(Y) % OF TOTAL RUNS	(Z) % OF TOTAL REVENUE	X/Y	Z/X	Z/Y
Able, A	ABCDE01	9.96	1.79	6.44	5.56	0.65	3.60
Barker, B	BCDEF02	8.58	11.14	11.16	0.77	1.30	1.00
Cohen, C	CDEFG03	5.91	5.59	4.62	1.06	0.78	0.83
Dowd, D	DEFGH04	3.65	0.04	1.81	91.25	0.50	42.25
Eason, E	EFGHI05	3.58	0.02	1.92	179.00	0.53	96.00
Foxx, F	FGHIJ06	2.20	0.57	1.81	3.86	0.82	3.18
Getz, G	GHIJK07	2.00	0.80	2.12	2.50	1.06	2.65
Hill, H	HIJKL08	1.68	3.95	2.93	0.43	1.74	0.74
Ives, I	IJKLM09	1.54	0.03	1.70	51.33	1.10	56.67
Jones, J	JKLMN10	0.99	0.47	2.28	2.11	2.30	4.85
All Others		62.12	75.60	63.21	0.82	1.20	0.84

cessor usage, number of runs, and revenue. Each of these is on a program-by-program basis and is termed X, Y, and Z, respectively, for ease of reference and for developing the three relationships which are also shown in the table—X/Y or processor use per run, Z/X or revenue per processor use, and Z/Y or revenue per run. The basic X-Y-Z entries are shown as percentages of this center's totals for the period to protect the source of data. Implementations of this report would be more meaningful if processor usage were in minutes or hours, runs as an absolute count, and revenue in dollars. Changing to these more realistic units would, of course, cause changes in the numbers shown in the ratios; however, the relative values or ranking would remain as shown in this table.

Table 3-2 represents the "top ten" processor usage programs at this installation and the entries are arranged by descending order of processor usage. The "All Others" line includes the dozens of other programs that were run during this period and it is presented to allow a comparison point for each of the "top ten." The lack of correlation between X and Z or Y and Z simply means that the billing algorithm in use at this installation depends on many factors other than X and Y. It would be appropriate to select the most important factors at each installation for this type of report. Processor usage and run frequency are simply two of the several factors that could have been shown in this example. Another type of information that might be displayed in this type of report, along with X, Y, and Z and their ratios, is the percentage of change from the previous period's list. This data could be converted into two separate reports: a "good" list showing the ten programs with most improved ratios, and a "bad" list showing the ten whose ratios had decreased the most.

Given these types of cost and value comparisons, most programmers will take action on their own to bring resource consumption into line with revenue generation. This completely passive CPE approach can be extremely effective. Often a competition will commence among programmers to see who can cause the largest increase in ratios like Z/X. This is healthy and may easily be fostered. Some installations have gone to the extreme of posting a "ten most-wanted" programs list each month to encourage such competition.

Perhaps more important than the potential competitions that such postings may generate is that such lists can be expanded to include all programs so that every programmer has a basis for judging his own performance. These expanded listings might be broken into pages showing all programs that any one programmer controls. This enables each programmer to determine how his programs perform as revenue producers, relative to other programmers, to encourage self-development of those programming techniques that are most desired at that programmer's installation. Such reports might be considered programmer "motivation" reports. They are so easy to produce from the wealth of available accounting data that it is rather surprising that no commercial package has emerged to provide such motivation products.

Programmer information reports may be weighted according to the factors that are of greatest importance at the individual center. That is, if revenue is of much importance in an installation where the processor is a limiting resource, then any "good" listings should be biased to favor revenue per processor use (Z/X in Table 3-2) above any other performance statistic. Likewise, where an installation has some particular excess capacity, rankings may be slanted to favor programmers who take best advantage of the availability of this capacity.

The variations possible in programmer information reports are very wide but there are two factors to consider when this passive CPE approach is used. First, whenever weighting or biasing factors are employed, they must be made widely known to the programmers who may be judged by the combined impact of the weighting factors. And, second, once such reporting is started, it should be faithfully continued as long as programmers show an interest in the reports. It can be very frustrating when a lively competition is underway (perhaps unknown to the installation manager) and the reports suddenly stop being made available.

Performance Evaluation Projects

Established CPE groups with an assortment of tools generally rely most heavily on products of the accounting data. These products give a fast and automatic way to identify target programs or components for examination by monitors, to tailor simulation inputs, and to characterize total workloads for benchmarking use. Regardless of how CPE is begun at an installation, accounting data eventually becomes an integral part of the CPE group's activity. This is due to the *representativeness, acceptability,* and *availability* of accounting data.

No better representation of a system's workload can be obtained than the workload itself. This is what accounting data contains—a picture of the system's real workload. No matter what the shortcomings are, most managers come to regard accounting data as an acceptable indicator of the system's activity. These two reasons—representativeness and acceptability—are sufficient to make accounting data very attractive to a CPE technician. However, the overriding reason that virtually guarantees the use of accounting data in CPE projects is that the data is available at no added cost and in computer-readable form. This immediately usable information is so strongly appealing to the types of individuals who become involved in CPE that the representativeness and acceptability of accounting data are often of no importance at the outset. In general, it is only after some conclusion has been reached or recommendation made through the use of some other CPE tool that the accounting data's representativeness and acceptability may need validation.

As a startup tool, accounting data may be regarded as precise measures of the system's activity. As experience is gained in using a variety of CPE tools, the precision of accounting data will become rightfully suspect. No CPE technician should bypass an attempt to cross-validate accounting data with information from some other CPE tool. The anguish of resolving why there are differences in the data will be repaid by an understanding of the particular system's architecture that cannot be gained by any other means.

One of the first discrepancies found in accounting data relative to hardware or software monitor data is in measures of "overhead" processor time or operating system usage. The development of multiprogramming and "virtual" systems emphasizes this discrepancy. Accounting data typically reports much more application program time than does a hardware monitor. The specific reason for this varies by computer brand but usually comes down to assumptions made by the creators of the control program about the cause of particular activity in the control program. That is, "If it were not for that application program, this overhead would not have occurred; so allocate the overhead as application program time in the accounting data." Data from a hardware monitor (and in some cases from a software monitor) would measure actual application program activity directly and would not contain the allocated portion of the overhead. The intent here is not to criticize any method of allocating such information, but to point out that a careful observer of system performance should expect to discover seeming inconsistencies. Explaining these inconsistencies is a worthwhile exercise for a CPE technician.

Up to this point the performance information mentioned has been at a very general level. When discussing applications in CPE projects the performance information must be more specific. There may be a danger at the specific level that the terminology might not have meaning in some architectures or might be misunderstood at some installations. Recognizing this risk, Table 3-3 lists performance information that is generally available from accounting data. Terminology used in this table should be translatable into most architectures. The information is grouped under two major headings: *indicators* and *diagnostics*. Indicators are the types of information that CPE technicians monitor regularly to know when to respond to changes in system performance with more detailed examination of the system. These indicators are generally reflective of the installation's service to its users rather than of the usage levels of various

Table 3-3. Typical Performance Information from Accounting Data.

I. *Indicators*

- Number of Jobs Processed
- Turnaround Time
- Throughput Rate
- Abnormal Job Termination Rate
- Multiprogramming Level
- Processor Wait Time
- Device Wait Times
- Paging Rate
- Idle Time
- Revenue per Time and per Resource

II. *Diagnostics*

Operations

- System restarts
- Down Time
- File Mounting Times and Frequencies
- Equipment Errors
- Operator and Scheduling Errors

Systems

- Processor Activity
- Device Activities
- Memory Allocation and Use
- Tape and Disk Allocation and Use
- Interfile Contentions

Programs

- Elapsed Time
- Run Frequency
- Processor and I/O Time
- Job Termination Type
- Resources Allocated versus Used

Files

- Block Length
- I/O Activity
- Intrafile Contentions
- File Mount Frequency
- File Media

---

resources within the configuration. Diagnostics are the internal resource descriptors which CPE technicians generally only collect and examine on an as-needed basis for particular projects.

Table 3-3 is far from an exhaustive listing of data that are useful in CPE projects that comes from accounting data. The listing is offered to give an idea of the diversity of useful information that is widely available from accounting data and to suggest typical applications of the data in performance improvement efforts. Listing these items does not portray the depth of information that is available for any given brand of computer system.

For example, one of the entries in Table 3-3 under "Files," is "I/O Activity." On some systems this single entry could be expanded to the following for each program: file name, type/model device, number of records per block, input block count, output block count, and so forth. A few systems even include data about the time that a file could not be accessed due to some other activity in the system and the number of records or blocks that were passed to reach the record of interest. The point of this example is that the richness of the information depends on the comprehensiveness of the accounting data that are collected by the system under study. Systems with less comprehensive data collection capabilities might require software or hardware monitoring to collect what would be readily available as accounting data on some other systems. The manufacturer's manual describing the accounting data that are collected is normally adequate for determining the comprehensiveness of available accounting data.

The types of results that come from application of accounting data in CPE projects are quite diverse. Probably still most common is the correction or addition of blocking factors to increase the number of records read or written at one time to more closely match the installed equipment's characteristics. Trade journals frequently publish articles telling how a disk (or sometimes tape) file was found with 80-character unblocked records, which, when blocked to track size, decreased program run time by 50% or more. In spite of these frequent articles, it is still common to find card image records on disk at almost every computer installation. Another commonly reported change resulting from accounting data analyses is relocation of files of the same program to different devices of the same storage medium (usually disk) or to different media (usually from disk to tape or tape to disk). These simple changes can eliminate competition between the program's files for the same device or channel. Program run time reductions of 50% or more are also common in this type of project.

Scheduling problems may also be uncovered in early CPE application of accounting data. These problems may be seen in the relative activity and inactivity of various system resources as the characteristics of programs running together change. Detailed study of resource usage of major programs at an installation can result in a job catalog* showing which programs or categories of programs should be run together in the multiprogramming job stream. Cataloging programs according to resource usage is a worthwhile CPE application of accounting data in support of the installation's

---

* Cohen, Leo J. *Systems Performance Measurement & Analysis Course—Text,* Performance Development Corporation, Trenton, NJ, 1973.

scheduling task. Determining which types of programs run best together normally requires extensive experimentation at each installation.

Accounting data are by far the most used CPE tools throughout the longest part, the Operations Phase, of a computer system's life cycle (see Table 1-2). In many applications the accounting data are the pointers to the specific area where another CPE tool should be used. The usual way that these applications are implemented is through use of commercial accounting data reduction packages. Many of these packages provide reports which highlight areas in need of detailed examination. Continuing use of such packages enables the CPE group to develop standard procedures for use of all available CPE tools in general classes of performance problems that are pointed out by the accounting data.

The remarkably detailed and diversified applications of accounting data seem to grow almost daily. A wealth of up-to-date practical examples of these applications is available from companies which sell accounting data reduction packages and from users' groups of most brands of computer systems.

One of the most promising developments to the CPE field that has largely been made practical by the availability of accounting data and suitable reduction packages is Kolence's Theory of Software Physics.* This work provides a completely rigorous definition of "software work" and "power" in the context of modern computing equipment and extends these physics-like definitions to practical applications in billing and charging for system usage and in the broader field of computer system capacity management. Individuals with deep interest in the full potential of accounting data or in one possible theoretical basis for an all-encompassing description of computer system performance should become versed in Kolence's work in "software physics." An introduction to software physics is given in Chapter 9.

---

* Kolence, Kenneth W. *Introduction to Software Physics,* Institute for Software Engineering, Palo Alto, CA, 1976.

4
Software Monitors and Program Optimizers

Software monitors and program optimizers are programs that enable a computer to check its own performance. In a sense, these programs give the computer some of the characteristics of a hardware monitor. Although called by many other names (trace routine, check flags, etc.), software monitors were probably the first tool developed and used solely for examining the performance of computers. Program optimizers are derived from these same origins and may be viewed as special-purpose software monitors.

Other CPE tools may be of particular appeal to managers, mathematicians, or equipment specialists because of their own specialized backgrounds, but the one common experience in nearly every CPE technician's background is as a programmer. Since either a software monitor or a program optimizer is just another program, most performance evaluators find both of them appealing because of their understandability and ease of use.

A FEW DISTINCTIONS

Distinguishing between accounting packages and software monitors in a technical sense is difficult. In fact, they are nearly the same in every respect except their levels of detail and their principal intended users. Most information collected by software monitors is also collected by some existing accounting package. Software monitors are primarily concerned with individual programs or with specific equipment components while accounting packages are primarily concerned with all programs and all equipment. Software monitors are for CPE technicians and programmers to examine details of some part of a computer system's performance; accounting packages are for installation managers and CPE technicians to track overall use of the total system's capacity. Each may be useful in the role of the other.

Either a software monitor or an accounting package could be extended to perform all functions of both tools. This seems unlikely because of the different audiences to which each tool is directed and because the cost of such an encompassing product would probably be more than the total of the cost for two separate products. The reader is encouraged to draw parallels and contrasts between the uses of accounting packages and software monitors to develop an understanding of the subtle differences between these two tools.

Program optimizers are quite easy to distinguish from either accounting packages or software monitors, even though these optimizers may be considered as specialized software monitors. Program optimizers are generally transportable from one brand of computer to another while software monitors and accounting packages are not. This is so because program optimizers are usually written in the higher level language (like FORTRAN or COBOL) of the application program to be examined and are therefore compiler-dependent rather than system-dependent. Software monitors and accounting packages are typically written in a lower level language and made part of the operating system in use at the installation. Hence, software monitors and accounting packages are system-dependent rather than compiler-dependent. Program optimizers and software monitors both serve exactly the same audience—CPE technicians and programmers.

There is a semantic problem with the name of "program optimizers." These tools do not usually optimize programs. Rather, they produce reports on the functioning of programs which, when analyzed, facilitate program optimization. This tool might better be called a "program monitor" to more clearly imply its use and to highlight its strong relationship to software monitors. The generally accepted trade term, program optimizer, is used throughout this book.

DEFINITIONS

All commercially available and most locally developed software monitors are programs that displace or supplement a part of a system's control program to collect information about the execution of one or more programs or about the use of all or parts of the hardware configuration. Nearly all program optimizers are programs that are added to an application program to collect information about the execution of that particular application program. Program optimizers are nearly always *event-driven*. Software monitors may be either *event-driven, time-driven,* or a *combination* of both time- and event-driven. However a software monitor may be driven, *sampling* techniques are often used in controlling their operation. Program optimizers seldom use sampling techniques except when they employ a *self-adjusting* mechanism.

Sampling

A thorough discussion of the statistical technique called *sampling* is beyond the scope of this book.* A very brief and simplified explanation is offered here to ensure that the reader has at least a basic idea of the meaning of sampling.

In a very large population (such as the number of most types of events that take place in a computer system in a few minutes) the percentage makeup of the population can be estimated by checking only a portion of the members of the entire population as long as the members to be checked are chosen randomly. Here the terminology of statistics (population and members) will be dropped in favor of computer terminology (processing and events). Suppose processing was sampled ten times over a period of three or four minutes and that six of these samples showed the system to be executing a problem program; it could then be estimated that the system was in "problem program state" 60% of the time.

With only 10 samples over such a relatively long processing period, the accuracy of this 60% estimate would be very questionable. The degree of questionability (or "confidence interval" to a statistician) may be made quite small by taking larger numbers of samples. Figure 4-1 shows "confidence intervals" relative to sample size or events counted at varying levels of certainty ("confidence curves") that the estimate is correct. Suppose that the 60% problem program state had been based on 600 out of 1,000 event counts instead of only 6 out of 10. Then it would be a 90% certain bet that the

---

* See "Sampling" in any standard text covering probability and statistics.

SOFTWARE MONITORS AND PROGRAM OPTIMIZERS 77

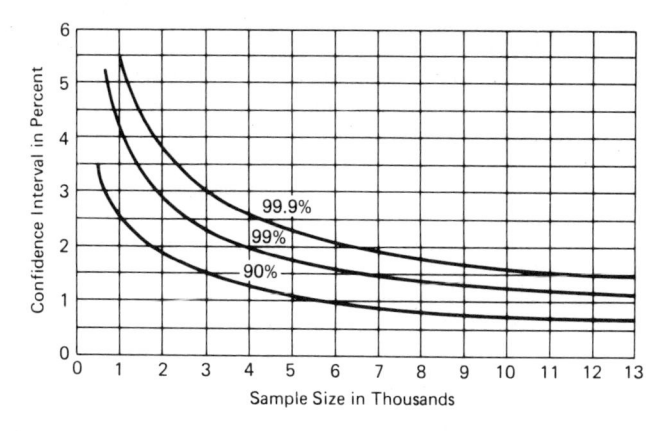

Figure 4-1. Confidence curves.

questionability of this estimate is about 2.5%, or that the system is in problem program state from 58.75 to 61.25% of the time when these 1000 samples were taken. In other words, if a person were to bet that this system was 58.75 to 61.25% problem program state in the interval in question, the person should expect to win the bet 90 times out of 100. (To follow this, just look across the horizontal axis of Figure 4-1 to the total number of samples taken—here 1000—go vertically up to the confidence curve desired—here the 90% curve—and then horizontally to the left to read the confidence interval—here about 2.5%. Then adjust the samples which are used to estimate the number of events—here 600 of 1000, or 60%—so that the interval occurs centered on the estimate. That is, for a 2.5% interval, subtract one-half—1.25%—from 60% for the lower estimate and add one-half to 60% for the higher estimate to determine the range implied by this sampling.)

Following the same methodology for 2000 samples, 60% of which were problem program state, would suggest an estimate of 59.1 to 60.9%. Six thousand samples would further narrow the 90% confidence interval to between 59.5 and 60.5%. If greater certainty is desired, say correct 99% or 99.9% of the time, the other curves would be used. That is, 600 of 1000 samples would imply an interval of from 58 to 62% at the 99% level, and from about 57.25 to 62.75% at the 99.9% certainty level.

If absolute certainty (100% confidence) is required, then sampling cannot be used. CPE projects rarely demand absolute accuracy, so sampling is widely used—particularly in software monitors. Users' manuals supplied with commercial software monitors tell how to use the particular monitor so that reliable data will be produced.

Event-Driven

Event-driven software monitors and program optimizers work either by means of *hooks* which are inserted into code that is to be studied or by collecting a fixed set of data each time some specific *change of state* occurs. The *hook* or the *change of state* would be the event that caused the monitor to operate.

A *hook* is simply a recognizable instruction that causes some selected set of data to be collected whenever the hook is encountered. In general, event-driven monitors using hooks can cause the most significant performance degradation when in use because activity initiated by the hook can exceed the activity that takes place between the hooks. *Sampling* techniques are therefore employed so that, say, every hundredth or thousandth occurrence of the hook is observed. This reduces the overhead of the hook method very substantially. When a large enough number of hook occurrences (sample size) are noted, this is a valid monitoring technique.

A *change of state* is the event which takes place when one type of computer activity stops and another type begins. For example, a *change of state* occurs when a processor stops executing instructions to await completion of an input or output sequence. (On an IBM system, this would be a change from "CPU Busy" to "CPU Wait.") Event-driven monitors that are triggered by a change of state usually collect information every time the change occurs rather than only for a sample of the occurrences. This is so because the changes of state used are typically events that happen relatively infrequently compared to the types of events that are associated with hooks.

Software monitors that are locally developed seem to be almost entirely event-driven and use both hooks and changes of state and sampling and nonsampling approaches. Program optimizers, whether commercial or locally developed, generally use a nonsampling, hook method because overhead is less important than precise data when examining only one of many programs. Rarely are commercial software monitors solely driven by events.

Time-Driven

A second data collection initiation method used in many software monitors but hardly ever for program optimizers involves examining activity periodically at some fixed interval throughout the monitor session. Any available internal clock may be used to cause the monitor to interrupt processing to collect a predefined set of information. This is the *time-driven* method of monitoring.

Overhead for a time-driven monitor may be determined very easily as long as the time for one data collection and processing cycle is known. For example, suppose that each cycle takes 3 milliseconds and the time interval used to start the cycle is 97 milliseconds from the end of the last cycle; then 3 out of each 100 milliseconds of processing time would be used as overhead for the software monitor giving a 3% processor overhead. Other components of overhead, such as the amount of memory required, may be observed directly.

The implication of this discussion of overhead is that the amount varies based on the length of the interval used to drive the monitor. When this is the case, the overhead may be reduced by simply increasing the timer interval. Time-driven monitors, by their very nature, only observe a sample of the events that may occur. Hence, the techniques needed to assure a valid sample as discussed above must *always* be used with time-driven software monitors. Too often, locally coded software monitors fail to consider the impact of sampling. This can cause the reported information from such software monitors to be potentially misleading.

Commercially available software monitors usually incorporate time-driven data collection for events that are of very short duration or that happen most frequently in the computer system. These would be events like execution of an "ADD" or "COMPARE" or other processor instruction. Software monitors with time-driven components are sold along with specific instructions on the minimum time period (which equates to minimum sample size) to use whenever the monitor is run. As long as these directions are followed, the monitor reports may be relied upon. In general, the time interval used is short enough so that runs of only two or three minutes are sufficiently accurate to be useful so there is seldom a problem with the precision of the measurements reported from these software monitors.

Combinations

Nearly all successful software monitors use a combination of all approaches defined above. This is because of the many orders of magnitude difference between the durations of events which occur in a computer system. Processor instructions occur in nanosecond or microsecond intervals while peripheral activities are measured in milliseconds or seconds, and job starts and stops can often be measured in minutes. The relationship of a nanosecond to a second is comparable to the relationship of a second to thirty years. No reasonable person would count events that took a second the same way as events that take thirty years.

Because of the magnitude of these differences it is common to combine time-driven and event-driven methods. The most frequent and shortest activities (like processor instructions) use time-driven techniques, less frequent or longer events (like changes from operating system state to problem program state) use event-driven methods with sampling, and the longest and least frequent activities (like a tape mount or a job start) record absolute counts using the event-driven method. There are exceptions to these generalizations, but the exceptions are quite rare.

Self-Adjusting

A final method which is occasionally used in software monitors and is frequently used in program optimizers may be referred to as *self-adjusting*. This involves internally altering the number of possible events that are examined in such a way that each set of events that is examined is a subset of the previous events and that each succeeding set of events is examined more closely than was the preceding set. The idea behind such an approach is to focus on the specific code in a program that consumes the largest amount of computer resources.

Implementations of this method serve as examples of the exceptions to the generalizations at the end of the preceding section. That is, a program optimizer might use a long time interval to examine a major program at first. Once the area of the program with the largest amount of activity is discovered, this part of the program might be examined using a sampling event-driven technique until the few lines of the program that accounted for most activity are discovered. These few lines of code might then be examined by collecting data on every event that they caused to determine exactly what changes would be needed to improve the program's overall performance. This is just the opposite of the general approach outlined above under "Combinations."

The reason for this reversal of what is a good general approach is simply to only spend overhead where it can return the most benefit. Locating a general area of high activity in a program does not deserve the detail of event-driven techniques while isolating specific instruction rates or sequences may repay the overhead of examining each event when the examination leads to program improvements.

CATEGORIES OF SOFTWARE MONITORS

There are three categories into which software monitors and program optimizers may be placed: those which are used for examining application programs, those for control programs, and those used to analyze the use of the equipment. These various categories are commonly called by many different names but here they will be referred to solely according to their major functions as *Application Program Analyzers, Control Program Analyzers,* and *Equipment Usage Analyzers,* respectively.

Application Program Analyzers

Application Program Analyzers, or APAs, include all program optimizers and those software monitors which collect and identify performance information on an individual application or "problem program" basis. Detailed examination and improvement, or "tuning," of such programs is almost the exclusive domain of APAs.

Application Program Analyzers are most useful in conjunction with a continuing program of accounting data analysis. Accounting data are used to identify and rank major resource-using programs for detailed study according to their individual ranking by using an APA. It is seldom productive to try to examine all application programs at once or to pick programs intuitively for APA projects. When accounting data are used to pick and rank APA target programs, the results are nearly always highly productive.

The types of CPE problems most often solved using APAs may be grouped under a general heading of "program efficiency." Program efficiency improvements are made by using APAs to sample the normal execution of an application program to collect statistics on the relative usage levels throughout the program so that heavily used and little-used portions of the program may be seen in a production environment. In general, only a small portion of a program's code will be found to account for a very large portion of resources used in processing the program. When this portion of the program has been identified via an APA, the individual instructions may be examined visually to determine what changes may be made to speed up this portion of the program. Typically, these changes involve such things as removal of unneeded instructions or use of faster algorithms in critical calculations. It is surprisingly common to find such things as instructions which reset counters in a program when the counters are never changed or that calculate and recalculate the same answers because the variables expected by the programmer turn out to be fixed values when the program is used.

One of the earliest dramatic examples used to illustrate CPE methods involved a program that ran for several hours each day on a large Control Data Corporation computer (CDC 6600). The program had been studied without locating major inefficiencies. No APA (either software monitor or program optimizer) was available for this type of computer or for FORTRAN, the language in which the program was written. To demonstrate the application of a then-newly available APA, the program was run on an IBM computer (IBM 360/65) and monitored with "PPE."* A single line of code was found to cause about 20% of the total processor usage. This line used the FORTRAN function which calculated the square root of any number. Examination of the program uncovered the fact that, although written to accept any positive value, a "two" was the only number that could be introduced into this function statement—so the computer had spent about 20% of its time calculating the square root of two. This line was removed and the well-known fixed value of the square root of two (1.4142...) was inserted where needed in the program. This extremely small change resulted in a saving of about one hour of CDC 6600 processor time each day.

Another frequent use of APAs is in the testing of new programs before they are put into production. One difficulty in testing new

---

* PPE, or Problem Program Evaluator, is an APA that is marketed by Boole and Babbage, Inc., of Palo Alto, California.

programs thoroughly is the creation of suitable sets of test data. Once created, it is not usually clear that the test data exercise all possible paths through the new program. APAs, particularly program optimizers, are available that produce reports covering not only the relative usage of each portion of the program but also which specific instructions have *not* been executed. Use of APAs in the development of new programs can ensure that all parts of each program have been tested before they become production programs. This is a valuable and too often overlooked CPE application. Although the value of not allowing mistakes to be made is difficult to quantify, this value must surely exceed the very modest cost of using APAs regularly in any test environment where a suitable APA is available.

The determination of an APA of either the software monitor or the program optimizer as "best" must be resolved at each installation. It is quite common in larger installations to have an APA of each type with the software monitor primarily used by the CPE group and the program optimizer mainly used by the test and development programmers or the application program quality control office.

It is interesting to note that some CPE groups have located major resource-using programs and examined them only to find that the reason the programs ran so long was that the coding of a program optimizer was inadvertently left in the production version of the application programs. As with any other tool, care must be taken when using these tools or their purpose may be defeated.

The methodology for applying APAs is simple and direct. Major programs are identified, usually by analysis of accounting data, and these programs are examined in order of importance using an APA. The most used instructions identified by the APA are visually examined to see what tasks these instructions perform, how these tasks are done, and to trace back through the logical flow of the program leading to these instructions. Once an understanding of these processes is reached, alternative methods or instructions are developed to accomplish the same functions more efficiently. This is usually one of the easier tasks of a CPE specialist but, without an APA to point out the areas where improvements would have the greatest effect, the task could well be impossible.

Control Program Analyzers

Control Program Analyzers, or CPAs, are like APAs except that the program to be examined is the operating system rather than one of the application programs. The composition and application methodology for a CPA are the same as those of an APA. Control Program Analyzers are discussed separately because it is so rare to find them in use at the types of installations that use APAs. The reason for this is that very few sites can afford to learn enough about the operating system to risk making any changes which might be suggested as the result of a performance evaluation project aimed at the operating system; therefore, there is little practical reason to undertake such projects.

Control Program Analyzers are not generally available on a commercial basis but they are quite widely available from users of most brands of computer systems. Users' groups are the best sources of information on the availability and usefulness of specific CPAs. Computer manufacturers normally use CPAs for development of their own control programs but these CPAs are rarely made available to users under normal circumstances.

There are conflicting factors that must be considered before undertaking CPA projects. First, the control program or operating system is easily the largest resource-consuming program of all programs run at a multiprogramming installation. Hence, the control program should be a high-priority candidate for performance improvement efforts. Second, operating systems must be so broadly general-purposed that they will operate properly regardless of the workload or equipment encountered at any user's installation. Such necessarily broad capability ensures that some inefficiencies will exist at every installation. Third, control program improvements could be shared among similar installations. This would multiply the benefits received from efforts invested in CPA projects. These three factors should provide strong encouragement for the conduction of regular CPA projects.

Unfortunately, the factors which discourage CPA projects are so significant that software monitors of the CPA category are seldom used with any degree of regularity outside the control program development staffs of computer system manufacturers. Principal among these factors is one which has already been suggested: very few installations are willing to make the substantial investment required to implement changes to the operating system that might be indicated by application of a CPA. Second, unless the user is an extremely important customer to the computer manufacturer who supplies the present control program, it is possible that the manufacturer may consider any "tampering" with the operating system as grounds for voiding existing guarantees or warranties on the operating system or the equipment under this program's control.

CPAs are most useful at installations which maintain their own control programs. Such installations usually occur at extremes of size. That is, the largest and smallest installations seem to be the only realistic candidates for continuing application of CPAs. Some of the largest installations are able to justify the cost of devoting a sizable group of system programmers to the development and maintenance of an operating system tailored directly to their workload and equipment mix. These installations are usually such important customers to their manufacturer that the "tampering" is more properly regarded as "tuning." Extremely small installations (generally users of minicomputers) with very stable or highly specialized workloads sometimes find the task of creating their own operating systems no more difficult than developing a major application program. Further, these small installations are much more independent of their equipment suppliers than is usually the case in medium- to large-sized installations.

Larger installations tend to start with the "standard" control program and, using a "borrowed" CPA, identify and remove those sections of code which are unnecessary and modify those which are most heavily used to arrive at an operating system that is tuned to the installation's own workload and equipment mix. Smaller installations often "start from scratch" to develop a control program with only those features demanded to service their own workload and equipment mix and then continue to modify or tune this skeletal control program for efficiency by using a CPA that they have developed along with the control program. At both extremes, users' groups are the primary media to communicate information about CPAs and their application to the various sectors of the user community. Typically, the large system users will disseminate information directly to other large system users at special interest sessions during meetings of the full users' group. At the other extreme, the "minicomputer" manufacturers may actually help the users to circulate information about special-purpose control programs and associated CPAs that have been developed by individual users and reported at users' group meetings. The overwhelming majority of computer installations between these two size extremes seldom either develops or applies CPAs for the reasons mentioned earlier. The only factor which seems likely to change this would be wide acceptance of "third party" control programs sold separately from suppliers other than the computer manufacturers. It would be reasonable to expect that such control programs might include a CPA capability to make the programs more attractive to prospective customers.

A typical application of a CPA is locating memory resident code in the "standard" operating system that is never used at a given installation. Such code is nearly impossible to find without a CPA. For example, Magnetic Ink Character Readers (MICRs) must be recognized by operating systems, regardless of whether or not a particular user has such equipment. If one MICR user demands very high priority servicing of these devices, the manufacturer, irrespective of whether or not all users have MICRs, might elect to make MICR servicing code resident in the "standard" operating system that is supplied to all users of the control program. This can cause every user to unknowingly devote valuable memory space and perhaps even processing time to poll this code even though only one other user has a real need for this feature. Any installation may estimate the potential for such extraneous code on their own system by looking through the catalog of available equipment and checking off the devices that are not present at their site. Beyond this, it must be remembered that the control program has to be able to serve the maximum possible configuration for every category of device; so the only installation which should not expect to find extraneous code would be one with the maximum number of all possible devices that could be configured with the operating system that is in use. It is doubtful that such a configuration exists—even at the manufacturer's control program development facility.

There is a practical side benefit that usually accrues to groups which employ CPAs to undertake control program-tuning projects.

By one means or another, such groups usually get into contact with similar groups within the technical staff of the manufacturer that supplies the "standard" operating system. In general, these computer manufacturer employees are totally isolated from end users of "their" control programs and information about "real-life" (as opposed to development and test) application of the operating system is as difficult for the developers to obtain as it is for the users to find out why the developers selected one default option over another. Development and application of a CPA at a user's installation opens a line of communication that is seldom opened by any other means. Both users and manufacturers gain by this direct contact between their technicians.

Equipment Usage Analyzers

Equipment Usage Analyzers, or EUAs, are the software monitors that are most like accounting packages. EUAs collect data on the amount and distribution of work for the various components of a computer system configuration both program by program and on a total system basis. This is essentially the same thing as is done by most accounting packages. The primary difference between an EUA and an accounting package is simply the level of detail at which the data are collected and presented.

An EUA allows a performance analyst to identify not only which specific disk or tape unit, for example, is in use (like an accounting package), but also to determine which other units are simultaneously in use or which cannot be used because of some other activity that is underway within the system. Further, the activity in process on a specific component is visible at a level that allows the analyst to propose alternative methods of arranging the processing so that the workload may be handled more efficiently. That is, the queues, or group of tasks waiting for particular devices may be examined to find specific equipment components that are "bottlenecks" to processing the workload as it is introduced into the system. Minimizing the effect of "bottlenecks," along with altering individual devices to those with speeds more nearly matching the installation's requirements, is referred to as *configuration tuning.* Configuration tuning is the major application area of EUAs.

It is worth noting that many of the very significant savings found through applications of software monitors are in the area of equipment usage analysis or configuration tuning. Not only are accounting packages widely used in this area of CPE, but hardware monitors also find major uses in configuration tuning; thus, there is no shortage of CPE tools for the major application area. The methodology for configuration tuning with EUAs (and other CPE tools) is now reasonably well understood and transferable among most data-processing installations.

The first step in configuration tuning involves collection of data on a total system basis. Examining this data at fifteen- or thirty-minute intervals for principal processing periods (say, one or two shifts per day for five to ten working days) allows the CPE analyst to determine the changing characteristics of the workload according to the time of day for the individual classes of equipment at the installation. Based on these characteristics, the analyst may recommend broad and general scheduling rules regarding the times when various types of movable work (work which can be shifted a few hours either way or from one shift to another) can best fit with the time critical work on the system.

When this level of scheduling has been adopted, the second step in configuration tuning may be taken. This calls for examination of the most heavily used files (typically, disk or drum files) to determine how they may be better distributed over available storage devices in order to balance the use of like devices and channels to these devices. This step often leads into use of APAs to accomplish such things as file blocking and rearrangement of sections of the program between main memory and disk or drum, or between "fast" and "slow" main memory. After this level of tuning or "workload balancing" has had effect, it is best to reexamine the characteristics of the equipment usage to ensure that the general scheduling rules developed in the first step in configuration tuning are still correct.

The third step aims at minimizing the time when any device or class of devices is running alone or "unoverlapped." That is, the level of simultaneous use of available devices is increased to the greatest possible extent without adversely impacting the service expected from the total system. This step often involves equipment changes like acquiring faster or slower devices or increasing or decreasing the number of devices in a particular class.

Once the scheduling rules have been established, the workload balanced, and the equipment matched to the workload, the configuration may be regarded as "tuned." The last step is to establish a schedule for periodic EUA examination of the configuration (typically, once per month) to ensure that the system remains "in tune" or that when the system begins to get "out of tune" it will be recognized and dealt with quickly.

Although this configuration tuning *methodology* is really quite simple, the actual application of an EUA in this manner is one of the more difficult tasks of the CPE specialist. In may take one year or longer before sufficient understanding is reached of the details of an installation's total workload and equipment configuration to employ this methodology. Because of this long learning period, it is usually best to start with APA projects, which are easy to do, and to progress into the more difficult EUA projects. Ultimately, these two categories of software monitors—APA and EUA—are most powerful when used in combination, just as all categories of software monitors are more powerful when combined with a regular accounting data analysis effort.

STRENGTHS AND LIMITATIONS

Software monitors and program optimizers are programs. As such, their major strengths and limitations are easily anticipated and understood in most computer centers. Because software monitors and program optimizers are so much like any other work at an installation, their strengths and limitations are seldom considered once these tools have come into use.

Strengths

The major advantage of these tools is simply that they are programs. In other words, programmers find that they are easy to install, easy to use, and their output is in familiar terminology. Second, commercially available software monitors and program optimizers are quite inexpensive. In some cases, users exchange their own software monitors without charge just as they do other programs. Last, software monitors are capable of collecting unusually detailed information on many different parts of the total system.

Beyond these generic strengths or advantages, each commercial supplier of software monitors or program optimizers can provide lists of the "advantages" of their particular product. These usually fall into the categories of special reports or other features incorporated for various users of their products. The real strengths of commercial monitors and optimizers, beyond those which are developed and exchanged between users, are the continuing maintenance efforts to keep the products up to date with current control program releases and the normally thorough and high-quality documentation that is provided with these products. Beyond these two advantages, the users of commercial monitors and optimizers will have someone to turn to when their supplier's product fails to perform properly. Because of these factors, commercial software monitors and program optimizers are much more prevalent than those that are developed and circulated by individual users.

Limitations

Like any other programs, software monitors and program optimizers use computer resources whenever they are put into operation. Specifically, these tools occupy space in memory and on some storage devices and use processing cycles while they are collecting the desired information. After collection, another part of the monitor or optimizer usually must be exercized to reduce the collected data into printed reports. Both of these runs represent the overhead of using these tools. Generally, only the collection phase is considered when overhead is discussed. During this phase, overhead is run time extension caused by the monitor or optimizer that receives most attention. That is, the memory and other storage used is regarded as of little or no importance, but slowing down any program's run time is viewed as overhead.

The amount of overhead that is seen as a time extension to the normal running time of application programs varies according to the mix of work during the monitored period and according to the speed of the equipment that is in use. In the first instance, if the monitor or optimizer uses resources that the normal workload does not use, then there will be little or no perceptible overhead; while if the monitor or optimizer must contend for the same resources as the workload, then the overhead may become substantial. In the case of equipment speed, monitors and optimizers are programs and faster processors and devices can complete programs in less time than slower equipment. Hence, collecting the same amount of information at the same level of detail on a small system as on a large system is often impractical. The variation in overheads caused by these CPE tools is also a function of the technique used—event- or time-driven, with or without sampling. In general, commercial monitors should be expected to extend run times of workload components from 2 to 10%. User-developed monitors and optimizers have a much wider variation, ranging from near the 2% level up to as much as 100%. (That is, when the monitor is introduced, the system stops.) There are cases where users have expended resources to develop a monitor or optimizer, only to discard the tool when its first run produced an unacceptable overhead. Often, this might have been cured quickly by incorporating sampling techniques rather than using the "count everything" approach taken in many user-developed monitors and optimizers.

This mention of sampling leads into another limitation in these CPE tools: the reported information may be invalid if the sample is not large enough. Here too, the commercial products come with instructions which, when followed, ensure that the information will be within acceptable bounds when sampling techniques have been used. User-developed monitors seldom contain instructions or "cautions" at this level.

The preceding limitations are minimal when software monitors and program optimizers are used carefully. The two remaining limitations are sometimes serious enough to cause a move to the use of hardware monitors. The first of these is that software monitors are system-dependent. They cannot be taken from a UNIVAC environment, for example, to a Burroughs environment, or even from one version of an operating system to another within the same brand of equipment in many cases. Program optimizers are either system-dependent or, typically, compiler-dependent. They cannot be taken from, say, an ALGOL to a PL1 environment. Second, only information that is accessible via software instructions can be collected by software monitors and only instructions within the target programs are available to program optimizers. Neither of these limitations are normally regarded as problems at installations with a homogeneous set of equipment and a workload written mainly in one or two of the major programming languages. But in installations with a variety of equipment and languages, or in geographically dispersed environments with a centralized CPE group, these limitations can be extremely important. When they do become important, the most common step is to begin looking at available hardware monitors.

A COMMENT

The topic of software monitors and program optimizers cannot be left with the negative connotation that is implied in the previous discussion of "Limitations." Users of the full range of CPE tools reported that they were more "satisfied" with software monitors than with any other CPE tool in a survey* of the membership of SIGMETRICS (the Association for Computing Machinery's Special Interest Group on Computer Performance Measurement and Evaluation).

During the Operation Phase of a computer system's life cycle, many (perhaps most) installations that have developed complete CPE capabilities seldom find a need to go beyond regular use of accounting data and periodic application of software monitors and program optimizers. Virtually every analysis of the value of using these tools versus the costs of using them shows software monitors and program optimizers to be overwhelmingly cost-effective.

---

*Morris, Michael F., "SIGMETRICS SURVEY—A Summary of the Responses," *Performance Evaluation Review,* **5,** Number 2, April 1976, pp. 19–62, ACM SIGMETRICS, New York, NY.

5
Hardware Monitors

Every technology has developed some device to record and examine physical phenomena which occur so that observers may understand and advance that technology. *Hardware monitors* were the first of the special devices for examining the internal workings of computer systems to become available for computer users. Hardware monitors are electromechanical devices which may be attached to the wiring inside a computer system to measure the activity which takes place within that portion of the system's circuitry.

Hardware monitors are like an oscilloscope, except that hardware monitors have special data displays and storage media and sometimes the capacity to process the data which they collect. Because hardware monitors are usually less familiar to computer specialists than other CPE tools, they are described here at a very basic level.

PHYSICAL DESCRIPTION

Hardware monitors range in complexity from that of a portable alarm-clock television to that of a stand-alone minicomputer system. These monitors weigh from fifteen to over five hundred pounds and cost from about $5,000 to over $200,000. The smallest hardware monitors fit easily on a typewriter table while the largest occupy as much space as two or three tape drives. A hardware monitor may be placed in any convenient location within about one hundred feet of the most distant device that is to be monitored. If desired, line amplifiers may be used to increase this distance.

Connection

Cables must be attached within the computer system where signals are available and run on or under the flooring to the monitor's location. Connections to the computer are made at the engineering test points or "probe points" within the protective cabinets housing the processors, controllers, peripherals, communications devices, and so forth. Special hardware monitor probes are attached to the probe points to sense changes of state which are transmitted to the monitor to be displayed directly or collected to prepare reports on the observed activity.

The hardware monitor probes have low resistance (or high impedance) so that they are not normally "noticed" by the circuitry and may therefore be left attached while the system is in operation. The probe's circuitry is housed in a plastic cover ranging in size from a little larger than a cigarette package down to less than one-half the size of a single cigarette. Short leads, usually less than twelve inches long, with female fittings or "universal" probe point adapters, run from one end of the probe housing for connection to the computer test points. A second lead from the housing is used for connection to any convenient ground pin. Some probes have a third lead for sensing the voltage level of the signal which is to be monitored. Those with only two leads have some adjusting mechanism on the probe housing to set the probe to the correct voltage-sensing level.

Hardware monitor probes that are used to monitor test points that are quite close together, say within twelve to sixteen inches of each other, are often supplied in "ganged" probe housings. Generally, these ganged housings have four separate probes each. In this case there are usually only five leads: one for each of the four signals to be monitored, and one to serve as a common ground for all four signals. These multiple probe housings save time in running the necessary cables and use less space inside the system's cabinets than would four single probes.

Signals Monitored

The voltage levels monitored on most computers is generally in the range of minus five to plus five volts. The probe voltage settings keep signals that are too small from being counted as activity. For example, if the signals to be monitored were known to vary between zero (no signal) and plus three volts (signal), setting the probe voltage as plus 1.5 volts would establish a threshold, or "bias," below which electrical activity, or "noise," would be ignored and above which would be recognized as presence of a signal. Figure 5-1

HARDWARE MONITORS 95

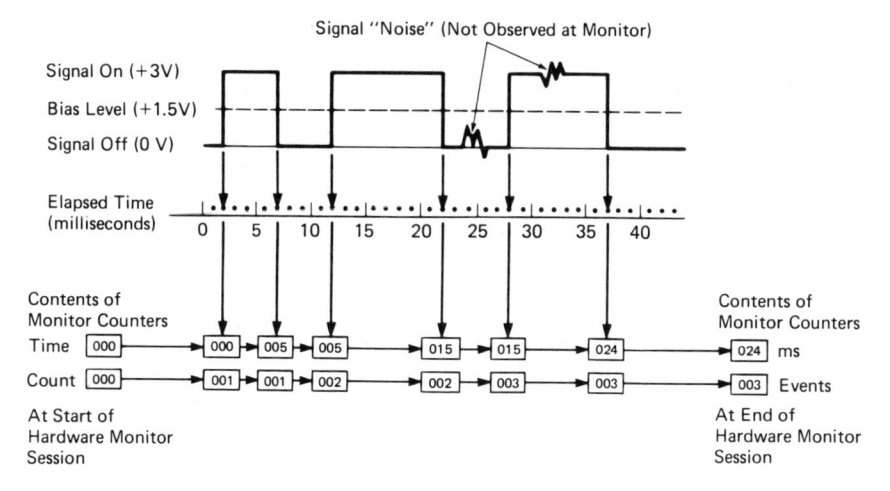

```
Signal On (+3V)          Signal "Noise" (Not Observed at Monitor)
Bias Level (+1.5V)
Signal Off (0 V)

Elapsed Time
(milliseconds)    0    5   10   15   20   25   30   35   40
```

Contents of   Contents of
Monitor Counters   Monitor Counters
Time [000] → [000] → [005] → [005] → [015] → [015] → [024] → [024] ms
Count [000] → [001] → [001] → [002] → [002] → [003] → [003] → [003] Events
At Start of   At End of
Hardware Monitor   Hardware Monitor
Session   Session

Figure 5-1. Counting and timing a signal.

is a schematic of a signal and its associated bias illustrating two basic types of information that can be collected by a hardware monitor from such a signal.

The two types of information shown being collected in Figure 5-1 are the count of the occurrence of the signal and the accumulated time during which that signal was active. These two pieces of information could be collected using one probe by feeding these data into two counters in the monitor. One of these two counters would be set in "event mode" to count the number of occurrences of the signal and the other in "time mode" to accumulate the total duration of the signal.

The "event" under examination in Figure 5-1 could be any signal that is available through a logic pin anywhere in the entire computer system. The use of the collected data would naturally depend on the nature of the event and the purpose of the CPE project. The event that occurs with the signal in this figure could be the accessing of records on one of the system's disk units. If this were the case, the analyst could determine that the average time to access a record on this unit would be 8 milliseconds per access (24 milliseconds ÷ 3 accesses) from the contents of the two counters at the end of the hardware monitor session. The monitor could be left to collect this information for any length of time, say one day or one week, and the average record access time for this unit with the real workload would be known.

Logic Boards

Hardware monitors can combine several signals and perform operations of "Boolean Algebra" on them by means of *logic boards* before the results are displayed or recorded. For example, the fact that a processor is waiting while some peripheral is busy may be of interest. Signals showing CPU WAIT time and CHANNEL BUSY time could be individually wired into the input side of an *AND GATE* so that an output would only come from this gate if the processor was waiting while the channel was busy. This resulting output could then be timed or counted (or both) and collected for further analysis.

Logic boards usually contain the two elementary Boolean operators (AND and OR) along with various other wiring conveniences such as "fan outs" (to provide multiple copies of a signal), inverters (to change a signal from positive to negative or from "true" to "false"), decoders (to convert from hexadecimal numbers to decimal numbers or vice versa), and other features depending on the particular brand of monitor under discussion. These hardware monitor logic boards will be quite familiar to individuals whose experience dates back to the earlier days of data processing when "plug boards" were in wide use. Others will find them quite easy to use after a brief familiarization with the meanings of the various functions of the logic panel and after practice with wiring a few different experiments.

Figure 5-2 is an example of a logic board on a very reduced scale. Most of these panels have hundreds of *hubs* or wiring connection points. Figure 5-2 shows only forty hubs. The four hubs on the left-hand side of the figure would be for connection of up to four probes from various parts of the computer system. These hubs are labeled A, B, C, and D, in the figure and only the first three of these hubs are shown with probes attached to them. Each probe signal could be split into three copies via the "fan-out" hubs shown next to each signal input hub. These hubs are referred to as A1, A2, A3, B, and so forth. In the center portion of the figure, four *GATE*s are shown. The top two are AND GATEs and the bottom two are OR GATEs.

HARDWARE MONITORS 97

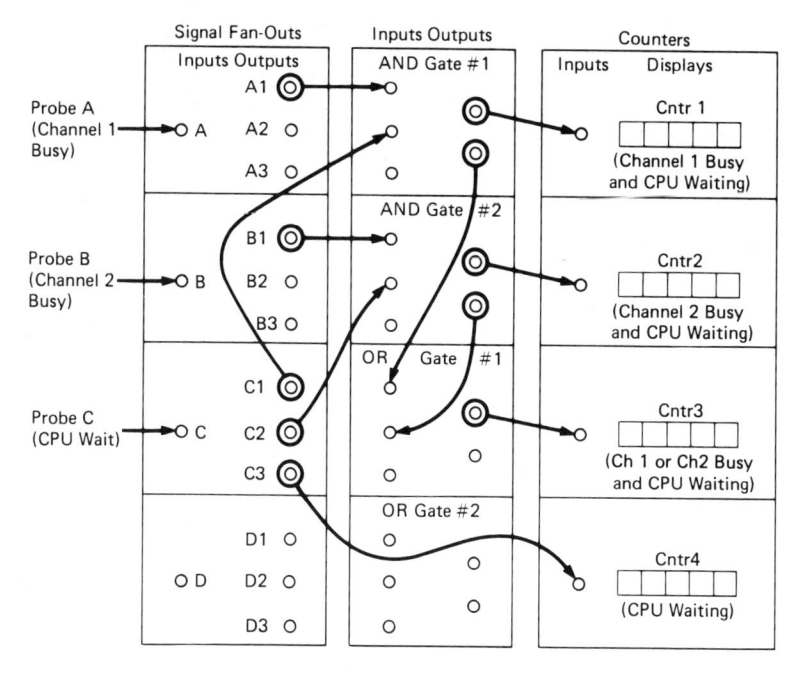

Figure 5-2. Example of a logic board.

Up to three signals may be input to any of these four gates and up to two identical signals may be taken out of each gate. On the right side of the figure there are four hubs, which drive the associated counters, labeled Cntr1, Cntr2, Cntr3, and Cntr4.

Note that there is no physical connection implied between Probe A and AND GATE #1 and Cntr1 simply because they are adjacent on the logic board. This is also the case in "real" logic boards. The only connections are those which are completed by connecting wires from the output hub of one function to the input hub of another. These connecting wires are shown as heavy arrows in Figure 5-2. Unused hubs may be considered to have no effect at all. (This is not always true on real logic boards. Sometimes, unused AND GATE input hubs may need to have constant signals introduced to ensure that the Boolean AND condition will be satisfied when the other signals occur.)

The connections between the hubs shown in Figure 5-2 are most easily explained by example. Suppose that the three probes entering from the left were *A:* Channel 1 BUSY, *B:* Channel 2 BUSY, and *C:* CPU WAIT. Further suppose that the problem is to determine the time during which each of four events occurs. Event 1: Channel 1 is busy while the CPU is waiting, event 2: Channel 2 is busy while the CPU is waiting, event 3: either of these two channels is busy while the CPU is waiting, and event 4: the total time that the CPU is waiting regardless of channel activity.

Using standard notation with a dot (•) representing the Boolean AND operation, and a plus (+) representing OR, these problems may be written as follows with each event assigned (⟶) to the respective counter.

Event 1:	CH1•WAIT	= A•C	⟶	Cntr1
Event 2:	CH2•WAIT	= B•C	⟶	Cntr2
Event 3:	(CH1+CH2)•WAIT	= (A+B)•C	⟶	Cntr3
Event 4:	WAIT	= C	⟶	Cntr4

Following Probe A (Channel 1 BUSY) through the wiring of the logic board in Figure 2: fan out output A1 is input to AND GATE #1 (along with the CPU WAIT signal from C1); one of this AND GATE's output signals is displayed on Cntr1 and the other output signal is wired as an input to OR GATE #1 (along with one result from AND GATE #2); the output of OR GATE #1 is used to drive Cntr3. Probe B (Channel 2 BUSY) is treated identically starting with AND GATE #2 driving Cntr2. Probe C (CPU WAIT) is used with each of the preceding probes as described above and is also, without Boolean operation, wired directly from fan out C3 to drive Cntr4.

There are alternative ways of wiring even this very simple set of problems. For instance, neither Probe A nor Probe B is required to go through the first portion on the left hand side of the figure since only one "copy" of each signal is used. Probe A could be connected directly into AND GATE #1 and Probe B into AND GATE #2 input hubs. Also note that Event 3 (Channel 1 OR Channel 2 BUSY AND CPU WAIT) is written as (A+B)•C, but is shown wired in the figure as (A•C)+(B•C), which is logically identical but easier to wire when signals for (A•C) and (B•C) are already available (as outputs from AND GATEs #1 and #2, respectively).

Although it is not particularly difficult to perform the wiring chores for these logic boards, it will take a little thought and practice at the outset and careful planning before each experiment is set up to be certain that the information which is collected is really the information that was intended. Hardware monitor suppliers provide formatted work sheets to help in laying out experiments on their logic panels. These work sheets should *always* be used—even for the simplest experiments. They not only help to ensure that the intended data are collected, but they also document the experiment for any report which may result and they may be useful as a guidebook for repeating experiments at another time or place.

Other Factors

The counters shown in Figure 5-2 are normally only provided on the smallest hardware monitors. Most monitors collect "counters" as magnetic tape records which are processed into specific reports after the hardware monitoring session. The counters shown in the figure may be regarded as parts of a tape record that is written periodically throughout the hardware monitor session. It is possible to visually observe any monitored signal or "counter" on nearly every monitor by routing the signal to an available display device. All signals are normally observed in this way when a hardware monitor is first connected to verify that the correct data are being collected. But, except for the smallest monitors, it is not common to watch counters or displays as data are collected for a project.

Hardware monitors have internal clocks. The clock places a time stamp on each record (or set of "counters") that is written during a monitor session. These time stamps allow the analyst to correlate the hardware monitor reports—which are produced after the session—with other information that is available about the system's activity. Usually, the hardware monitor information is analyzed along with accounting data reports or, occasionally, with reports produced by software monitors or program optimizers. Hence, the monitor's clock is normally synchronized with the computer system's internal time at the beginning of each monitor session.

Cables need to be run between the probe locations and the monitor location so that layout planning must be done before a hardware monitor may be used. Depending on relative equipment locations, these cables may be as long as one hundred feet. Cable *concentrators* can be used to enable several probes to be joined and run to the monitor location over one large cable.

Because the need for cables is directly dependent on each installation's physical layout, a scale drawing should be prepared to show where the monitor and all necessary cables will be placed. This schematic will indicate the proper number and sizes of cable to order and, if it is kept up to date, it will help the monitor user to arrange experiment changes with minimal relaying of the cables.

Laying cables is usually disruptive in the computer room and is always the dirtiest and most difficult physical work involved in using a hardware monitor. This undesirable work is reduced substantially by planning aimed at minimizing the initial cabling task and the relaying of cables to support added experiments. If the hardware monitor is to be moved from one computer system to another, the planning should provide for collection and transportation of the cables. These cables can take as much space when prepared for shipment as does the entire hardware monitor. Because of the bulkiness of the cables and the work involved to install them, it may be reasonable to acquire a set of cables for each site where the monitor will be used and to leave these cables in place so that only the monitor and probes would need to be moved from site to site.

Comparators

Comparators are often acquired with hardware monitors. A comparator is a device that checks observed signals against a preset value or values to determine whether the signal is of interest to the experiment. For example, the highest and lowest addresses of some software routine in memory may be set in a comparator so that any time there is activity within the preset bounds the event will be relayed to the monitor for collection. Such information may be helpful in operating system-optimization projects. Another common comparator application, which is quite easy for most computer system architectures to measure, is the exact amount of time that a processor spends doing specific instructions. This information is useful when trying to decide whether to add computer hardware to perform an operation currently done by software or to remove hardware features that are infrequently used.

Comparators normally have the capability of checking at least two distinct sets of 24- or 32-bit "addresses." These addresses can also be used in sets of eight bits, or one byte, which allows four bytes of data to be checked on each of the two settings of a 32-bit comparator. The box which contains the comparator also usually has a logic board to allow Boolean operations and signal manipulations like those described earlier in connection with the hardware monitor itself (see "Logic Boards").

Comparators enhance the capability of smaller hardware monitors rather dramatically because they allow collection of data from the computer at the bit level. This means that the exact contents of registers may be read and collected as the system operates, and the status of the register under examination can be reproduced after the session for extremely detailed analysis projects. Such projects may require use of several comparators and development of programs to interpret the data that are collected. In general, users move to larger hardware monitors which can perform such operations directly before such complex tasks are undertaken using a small monitor and a large number of comparators.

After the hardware monitor and all associated devices and cabling have been installed, the only extra work required to support the monitor's operation is the occasional changing of tape reels on the monitor's tape drive and execution of the data reduction program. As these are familiar tasks at computer installations, they are only mentioned here as jobs that must be done while the monitor is in use.

Figure 5-3 depicts an installed hardware monitor and a few of the computer components that are typically connected to a monitor to suggest what the physical presense of a hardware monitor involves at a computer center. This illustration is greatly simplified and should not be viewed as a comprehensive example. The cables shown between the components and the monitor would normally be out of sight under the false floor and there might be several cables running from any one component to the monitor.

Once installed and in operation, the hardware monitor cannot normally be moved more than a few feet without disconnecting and, perhaps, rerunning some of the cables from the probes to the monitor. Neither the original connection nor rerunning of probes and cables necessarily demands that normal processing be sus-

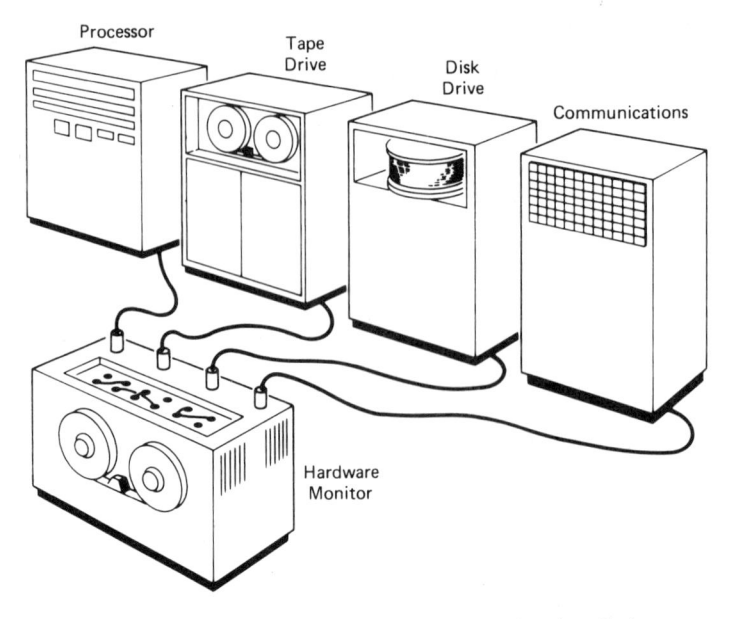

Figure 5-3. Conceptual view of a hardware monitor installation.

pended, but it is best to schedule these activities at a time when the computer system can be stopped just in case all does not go smoothly. (This topic is discussed further in the next section.)

USING HARDWARE MONITORS

Categories of Hardware Monitors

There are three distinct types of hardware monitors: *basic monitors, mapping monitors,* and *intelligent monitors*. Each type is a subset of the next larger type of monitor. That is, a mapping monitor can do everything a basic monitor can do plus something more, and an intelligent monitor can do more than a mapping monitor. All three types of hardware monitors are in wide use.

Basic. Basic hardware monitors can count and time signals. Most basic monitors have some provision for recording the count and time information on magnetic tape although a few only display the data as they are sensed and have no provisions for recording data for later reduction. In addition, most basic monitors have logic panels to allow extensive Boolean operations to be done. In general, basic monitors are completely system-independent and can be connected to any system; however, basic monitors are becoming available which are designed to perform only one type of data collection on a specific brand of computer system. Typical applications of such special-purpose basic monitors include keeping a continuing record of the response times at terminals or of processor and peripheral busy times. Costs of special-purpose basic monitors range around $5,000 while the more widely usable basic monitors are from $5,000 to about $20,000.

Mapping. The second generation of hardware monitors incorporated memories and facilities to connect large numbers of probes. With a mapping monitor it became feasible to not only count and time signals, but also to determine the values or contents of certain locations in the computer's memory or registers. Mapping monitors made it possible to create logical "maps" or distributions of activity as it took place throughout the computer system. It also became possible to insert a special code in the target computer which could "communicate" with the hardware monitor to allow the monitor to "know" when a particular program or activity was taking place. A common application of mapping monitors would be to collect data on the frequency of use of each instruction in the processor. The contents of a mapping monitor's memory may periodically be copied in its entirety onto a magnetic tape. This allows such monitors to appear to have large numbers of "counters"—say, more than one hundred. This "pseudocounter" capability is probably more used in actual applications than is the capability to map memory or instruction usage. Mapping monitors range from about $15,000 to $50,000.

Intelligent. The third generation of hardware monitors contains its own processor. This allows the monitor to be programmed for any number of different experiments without rewiring logic panels or, in many cases, without disconnecting and reconnecting probes. This approach reduces the on-site technical expertise needed to a minimum as the intelligent monitor may use "canned" programs supplied by the manufacturer to avoid costly experiment development and debugging at the user's installation. The cost of this ease of use is paid for in the lack of system independence of intelligent monitors, although it is possible to develop monitor programs for any type of computer system. A major advantage of some intelligent monitors is that the collected data may be reduced on the monitor's computer rather than on the target computer system. When this is done there is *no* overhead associated with using a hardware monitor. It should be recognized that intelligent hardware monitors are not only *like* computers, they *are* computers. They may have their own tape drives, disks, printers, and communications, and they may be connected in networks to communicate with each other as they collect and analyze data for several computers simultaneously. In fact, intelligent monitors may be used as small, stand-alone computer systems for such routine applications as inventory control, time accounting, payroll, and so forth. Intelligent monitors cost from about $30,000 to over $200,000.

General. Most basic and mapping monitors are either portable, or at least, transportable. Intelligent monitors are usually much too large and bulky to be considered transportable. Hence, if traveling applications are intended, it is usually easiest to use a basic or mapping monitor. Intelligent monitors are well suited to permanent installation at large computer centers.

When to Use versus Other CPE Tools

The principal factor in determining which CPE tool to use is *availability*. Nearly every large computer installation now has some set of programs to reduce computer resource accounting data into management reports. Many installations also have some form of software monitor. Most applications may be fulfilled by using accounting data or software monitors.

When information must be obtained that is "invisible" to the system's software, then hardware monitors are the only available tool. As computer systems become more and more dispersed and interconnected via communications devices, the amount of important activity which is invisible to software increases. Hence, it is reasonable to expect that performance evaluation specialists may be required to use hardware monitors more often for routine applications in the future.

Another area where hardware monitors may be necessary is when extremely precise measurements are required at a very detailed level. Such measures are often necessary when applying software physics to configurations that have never been measured with great precision.

Another reason for deciding to use a hardware monitor comes up when the evaluator must be certain that the collected data are totally independent and has not been altered by anyone at the target site. This may be a singular advantage in audit applications over tools like accounting data reduction programs and software monitors which may be subject to modification by the site which furnishes the tool to the auditor.

Finally, there are instances where it may simply be *opportune* for a performance evaluator to try using a hardware monitor. Although only a relatively small number of installations have hardware monitors, the number is increasing, particularly in very large computer centers. When a performance evaluation specialist finds that a hardware monitor is already attached to a computer which is to be examined, it may be worthwhile for the specialist to incorporate some of the monitor's data into the normal review of the installation.

As has been mentioned earlier, hardware monitors should be regarded as the measurement tool of last resort. When measures must be made at a very detailed level, when no software tools exist, or when the measures must be totally system-independent, this "last resort" may be the only option.

Probe Points

Once the decision is made to use a hardware monitor, the most technically demanding task must be undertaken. This task is determining which signals need to be monitored and locating the logic pins to obtain the necessary signals. It is a problem that requires the participation of engineers from the manufacturer of the computer system which is to be monitored.

One of the easiest ways to determine which signals to monitor is to follow the approaches outlined in software physics (See Chapter 9). Then all that must be decided is the level at which the configuration should be examined. For most projects, it is not necessary to go to any greater detail than channels for major classes of equipment (like tape channels and disk channels) and processor and communications activity. At this level all that needs to be requested are the locations of the logic pins which indicate the number of bits (or bytes or words) transferred into or out of the equipment class and the execution time for that equipment class to accomplish the transfer. This is sufficient information to establish an activity profile for a configuration that would enable an evaluation specialist to determine how much capacity is available and how much is in use at the installation.

The probe points that are ultimately identified should be located on a scaled schematic of the configuration. This allows groups of signals to be identified which may be collected by using probes with multiple leads rather than single—thus reducing the chore of laying cable. Generally, the on-site engineer can estimate how far apart the probe points are in any cabinet. The continued cooperation of the engineer should be actively sought while planning the layout of probes and cables. This not only makes the performance evaluation specialist's task easier, but it also helps the engineer to prepare for the monitoring of his equipment.

As soon as the signals which are to be monitored have been identified, the manufacturer or manufacturers of the components which will be probed should be contacted formally and informed of the intent to connect devices to their equipment. The purpose of this notification is twofold: first, many contracts require such written notice be given thirty days in advance by the user to the manufacturer and, second, the letter serves as a formal request that the manufacturer supply probe point locations for the signals which are to be monitored. In general, the manufacturer will not respond directly to the request for probe point locations. Instead, they will designate a contact (usually the field engineer for the site to be monitored) to assist in identifying the probe points locally. Once a contact has been specified, probe point identification progresses quite rapidly. It is mandatory that ample notes be taken to document each probe location used. This task cannot be delayed as it is generally impossible afterwards to reconstruct all of the reasons why one specific pin was selected from a list of dozens.

On-Site Assistance

The engineer is usually the only one that knows the nonstandard modifications that are present within the equipment. These modifications exist in nearly every computer that has had a field-installed change or significant amounts of maintenance. Often, the engineer will make such modifications according to his own specifications instead of the manufacturer's. Unless the aim is to discover such things, the engineer must be a cooperative participant in all stages of a hardware monitor project. A side benefit of this early inclusion is that the engineer will be able to get the "odds and ends" cleaned up before "his" circuitry is exposed to the probing eyes of the hardware monitor specialist.

The engineer's normal curiosity for electronic devices, coupled with his proprietary feeling toward the computer system, usually make it quite easy to get the site engineer involved in the hardware-monitoring projects. The engineer will quickly realize that connecting the monitor is just like connecting his oscilloscope and he will generally enjoy his role as "teacher" to the specialists. In exploratory monitor projects where no specific goal has been set before connecting the monitor, the site engineer is usually the best source for suggestions on what parts of the configuration to look at once he has become involved in the project.

A final reason for involving the site engineer in the monitoring project is that he is the one that would have to repair the computer system if any damage were done. In spite of claims to the contrary, systems have been damaged during the connection, use, and disconnection of hardware monitors. The damages can nearly always be traced to carelessness on the part of the hardware monitor specialist but there have been incidents of damage which were alleged to have been caused by faulty electronic components in the hardware monitor. The possibility of causing damages may be greatly reduced by following a set of common-sense rules during the connection and use of hardware monitors.

COMMON-SENSE RULES FOR CONNECTION AND USE OF HARDWARE MONITORS

1. Notify the manufacturer(s) of the site's equipment that hardware monitors will be connected to their equipment. Ask for help.
2. Determine what signals are to be monitored and where the probe points are physically located that test these signals.
3. Determine where the monitor will be least bothersome to normal operations and place it there before starting any work towards connection.
4. Identify the power source(s) for the monitor and components, plug in and *test the monitor* (and each component), calibrate all probes, then turn the monitor and components off.
5. Ensure that all power sources are continuous and separate from the computer system's power sources so that shutting down the computer does not shut down the monitor.
6. Label all cables according to scheme recommended in hardware monitor manufacturer's documentation, then make all cable connections—start at the cabinets where the probes will later be connected and work toward the hardware monitor.
7. Lay all cables out of the way of normal computer room activity (under the floor or in cable troughs). Connect probe cables to hardware monitor as each is laid.
8. Electrical safety check: Remove all rings, watches, bracelets, etc., tie back long hair, remove neckties, and roll up long sleeves.
9. Suspend each probe near the point where it will be attached making sure that the probe hangs free of the computer logic panels. Use nonconductive material for this suspension. (Nylon filament tape works very well for this.)
10. Hold the probe tip close to the probe point to ensure that very little weight will have to be supported by the probe point and that the probe tip will easily reach the probe point location. Check every probe tip in a multiple housing. Make any needed adjustments in the height of the suspensions made in step 9 above.
11. After all cables are in place and connected and all probes are suspended, check all connections again, replace all floor panels

or cable troughs, and clean up any mess made during the cable laying and equipment placement. Replace *all* covers on computer cabinets. Put away unused cables or other monitor equipment. This is a good point to take a break and recheck to make sure that all is in order and to wait until the computer can be put in an "idle" or "stop" condition for probe connection.
12. Turn on the power for the monitor and all components. This is very important as most probes are powered and should not be connected to a logic pin unless the probe has power applied to it.
13. When the computer is ready ("idle" or "stopped"), remove the cover of a cabinet where probes are to be connected. Make the area comfortable for probe connection so that it is not necessary to strain to reach the probe points.
14. If the site engineer has not been involved up to this point, get him and repeat step 8 above.
15. The engineer should be asked to make the probe connection with the monitor specialist by identifying each probe tip and reading aloud the probe point location. In every case, the ground lead should be connected first to any convenient ground pin within a few inches of the probe point. This allows the individual who will make the connection to find the probe point once without connecting to it (ground pins are easy to identify and are usually available in abundance).
16. If it is possible with the ground lead attached, manually variable probes should be checked again to make sure that they are set at the proper voltage level. Three-lead probes should have the reference voltage lead connected at this time.
17. The probe point should again be called out and independently found by both participants (small wooden dowels or "chopsticks" sharpened in a pencil sharpener are handy for pointers in this step). When both agree that they have found the same, correct probe point, the probe tip should be connected.
18. When all probes are connected at this cabinet, the cover should be replaced and the next location sought repeating steps 15 through 17 until all probes are connected.
19. Validate that the signal obtained on each probe is the signal that should be on that probe. Test programs may have to be created ahead of time to do this validation.

20. After all probes are connected and validated, the monitor's clock should be set to coincide with the computer system's clock and the planned project undertaken.
21. During the course of the project it may become necessary to move the probes to different points. These moves should be undertaken with the same care used during the initial installation of the probes.
22. Disconnecting the monitor should also be done with great care, particularly as the project's data collection phase is completed and there may be a tendency to rush at this point.

There is nothing in this list that would not be deduced after going through a few hardware monitor projects in a safety-conscious environment. The physical attributes of monitors and computers require that caution and good judgment be exercised to avoid causing unnecessary problems. Apart from precautions taken to assure that no damage is done to equipment, it is also a good idea to have a first aid kit handy in case any injuries occur. The most common injuries are small cuts from handling wires and pinched or bruised fingers from removing and replacing floor panels. On rare occasions people get electrical shocks when working with the hardware monitor. Essentially all instances of injury are the result of carelessness.

Output

It is very important to recognize that the product of a hardware-monitoring session is usually a magnetic tape with many records, each containing information about a short interval of system activity. These tapes amount to the source data which must be processed into reports for anlysis by the CPE specialist. When the tapes have begun to be created, it is necessary to find time on an appropriate computer for running each tape against the monitor's data reduction program. In general, "an appropriate computer" means a medium-to large-scale IBM system.

Because of this constraint on data reduction, it is wise to identify the data reduction facility when the monitor is being obtained. This should ensure that data reduction runs may be attempted as soon as the first data tape is created. An early run of the monitor's first tape is necessary to ensure that the data have reached the tape without error and that the data is as expected. It is best if each tape can be

HARDWARE MONITORS 111

reduced shortly after it is created. This will enable the monitor specialist to take corrective action right away should such be indicated by the contents of a tape.

Figure 5-4 is an example of hardware monitor data. This figure should suggest the futility of trying to use "raw" data for analysis. Figure 5-5 shows part of this data after a pass through the data reduction program (DYNAPAR) of the monitor supplier (COMTEN). Figure 5-6 is a further reduction and consolidation of the raw data into reports for a particular analysis. These reports were generated by special programs developed for a particular monitor project. It is quite common to have to write special programs to create information in the format needed for each monitor project.

The output of a hardware monitor can be the most discouraging feature of using a monitor, particularly when the project has not been planned with care. This is because so much output can be generated with so little effort after the monitor is installed, that the amount of data can overwhelm the analyst. Great care should be taken with such simple items as specifying the interval for reporting data. The fact that data are available on a second-by-second basis should not sway the analyst to ask for reports on a second or even minute basis. It generally takes at least one page (usually two) to report each monitor interval. As there are 1440 minutes or 86,400 seconds in a day, a one-minute reporting interval will cause a very large report to be generated. A one-second interval report would be absurd for monitor periods of a day or longer.

If extremely detailed analysis is required, it is best to start with fifteen-minute or one-hour intervals to identify the exact period which requires analysis. Typically, no more than two hours need be subjected to detailed analysis to understand some behavior phenomenon—as long as the right two hours are selected. Then this selected period could be reduced using fifteen-second or one-minute reporting intervals.

```
OG  @LH--BDR/CK7"T"  |  |  |  |  |LH7&B<BALKTK  A  F  AID<DAF  A<DHDAF
OGA@LH80R%B/LK<UDF  J<D<U  F&A<UHDDF  A<DDU  F  J<U<U  F&J<UD
OGB@LHO  B*B/LK&J(4<D  F  A(4ID  F-A<UDD  W  J(D(U-F  J<UID  F  A(UFU  A(
OGP@LL/  B%7/LK     F  J  D  DDF  J  DOMAF  /  4  U  F  /HU  U  F  A  UAD  F-JDD
OGQ@LL6-B*BJLK/JA4  M  F&J  M  D  F&JH4HU-F&J  4AD-F&JHU  M  F&J  U  M-F
OG  @LLMOB<BALKDF  J  D  M  W  J  D  D  FAJHD  D  F  J  D  UAF  AIU  M  F  /  DM
```

Figure 5-4. "Raw" hardware monitor data.

CYBER 74 D-8028 DATA
DYNAPROBE/DYNAPAR INTERMEDIATE COUNTER SUMMARIES   JOB 10 17
                                                          FROM 15.15.02.4 ON 10/30/80 TO 15.45.00.1 ON 10/30/80

COUNTER	DESCRIPTION	(BASE = T01)	TOTALS FOR LAST 1797.7 SECONDS	ACCUM. TOTALS FOR 10190.4 SECONDS
C01	7428 FAST HEAD IDLE		1570.5 SEC 87.36 PCT	9188.6 SEC 90.17 PCT
C02	CONTROL		71.7 SEC 3.99 PCT	284.2 SEC 2.79 PCT
C03	USER		155.5 SEC 8.65 PCT	717.5 SEC 7.04 PCT
C04	SLOW IDLE		12.4 SEC 0.69 PCT	63.3 SEC 0.62 PCT
C05	CONTROL		0.0 SEC 0.0 PCT	0.0 SEC 0.0 PCT
C06	USER		1785.2 SEC 99.31 PCT	10127.0 SEC 99.38 PCT
C07	PPU A READ BUSY		216.3 SEC 12.03 PCT	1130.8 SEC 11.10 PCT
C08	7428 PPU A WRITE BUSY		13.3 SEC 0.74 PCT	48.8 SEC 0.48 PCT
C09	B READ		152.2 SEC 8.47 PCT	888.7 SEC 8.72 PCT
C10	B WRITE		7.7 SEC 0.43 PCT	21.9 SEC 0.22 PCT
C11	7416 IDLE		1648.6 SEC 91.71 PCT	9772.7 SEC 95.90 PCT
C12	CONTROL		33.7 SEC 1.68 PCT	123.1 SEC 1.21 PCT
C13	USER		115.2 SEC 6.41 PCT	284.9 SEC 2.84 PCT
C14	PPU A READ BUSY		162.2 SEC 9.02 PCT	909.2 SEC 8.92 PCT
C15	7416 PPU A WRITE BUSY		7.2 SEC 0.40 PCT	32.0 SEC 0.31 PCT

I	C16	7416 B READ	75.8 SEC	4.22 PCT	390.5 SEC	3.83 PCT I
I	C17	B WRITE	1.5 SEC	0.08 PCT	4.0 SEC	0.04 PCT I
I	C18	CH 24 BUSY	50.8 SEC	2.83 PCT	145.2 SEC	1.43 PCT I
I	C19	25	52.3 SEC	2.91 PCT	144.7 SEC	1.42 PCT I
I	C20	26	13.5 SEC	0.75 PCT	120.5 SEC	1.18 PCT I
I	C21	27	16.1 SEC	0.90 PCT	121.7 SEC	1.19 PCT I
I	C22	30	63.8 SEC	3.55 PCT	155.6 SEC	1.53 PCT I
I	C23	31	0.0 SEC	0.00 PCT	50.1 SEC	0.49 PCT I
I	C24	32	30.3 SEC	1.69 PCT	151.5 SEC	1.49 PCT I
I	C25	33	8.8 SEC	0.49 PCT	112.7 SEC	1.11 PCT I
I	C26	7428 CH 03	341.6 SEC	19.01 PCT	1906.7 SEC	18.71 PCT I
I	T01	TOTAL RECORDED TIME	1797.7 SEC	100.00 PCT	10190.4 SEC	100.00 PCT I
I	T02	MONITOR PAUSE STATE TIME	0.0 SEC	0.0 PCT	0.0 SEC	0.0 PCT I
I	T03	MONITOR STOP STATE TIME	0.0 SEC	0.0 PCT	0.0 SEC	0.0 PCT I
I	D01	7428 CP0 BUSY TIME	227.2 SEC	12.64 PCT	1001.7 SEC	9.83 PCT I
I	D02	7428 CP1 BUSY TIME	1785.2 SEC	99.31 PCT	10127.0 SEC	99.38 PCT I
I	D03	7416 CP0 BUSY TIME	149.0 SEC	8.29 PCT	412.1 SEC	4.04 PCT I

Figure 5-5. DYNAPAR reduction of hardware monitor data.

DATE	SH	MEASURED TIME	SEC	CPU BUSY	PCT BSY	MEM REF/SECOND	PWR RATE	POWER AVAILABLE	WORK DONE
901	1	0056	3,550.0	43.8	1.2	1,897,723	17.0	60,632.2	477.0
901	1	0156	3,595.0	21.8	0.6	1,880,376	16.9	60,839.5	250.5
901	1	0257	3,663.0	14.7	0.4	1,886,912	16.9	62,205.8	174.0
901	1	0356	3,582.0	14.3	0.4	1,887,660	16.9	60,854.4	170.3
901	1	0456	3,550.0	18.3	0.5	1,895,273	17.0	60,553.9	211.7
901	1	0556	3,610.0	23.7	0.6	1,899,300	17.0	61,708.2	268.0
901	1	0655	3,577.3	219.5	6.1	1,955,240	17.5	62,950.3	2,268.0
901	1	0756	3,609.0	1,053.6	29.1	2,031,841	18.2	65,996.2	19,358.1

Figure 5-6. Special program reduction of hardware monitor data.

The key to successful handling of hardware monitor output is to ensure that only necessary data are collected and that reports on this data are carefully planned before they are generated.

Limitations

The biggest problem with basic and mapping hardware monitors is that there is no easy way to correlate the data they collect with the specific programs that are executed. Several schemes have been used to synchronize accounting packages, software monitors, or manual program logs with hardware monitors so that the system activity could be equated with the system workload. These methods usually cause more manual analysis work than they repay. There have also been special programs incorporated into systems that "communicate" with hardware monitors. These have not enjoyed success, either. Attempts to automatically tie monitor data to specific programs tend to eliminate the "no overhead" and "system independence" advantages of hardware monitors.

A second limitation is that some computer functions that are imbedded in the control program of certain computers cannot be tracked by hardware monitors without expensive or elaborate additions to either the monitor or the computer. One example of this is the function known as WAIT in IBM 360s and 370s. This function is readily available for these IBM computers and can be monitored with the simplest of hardware monitors. But on many other types of computers, the processor never "waits." When there is nothing to do, the control program fully occupies the processor to look for something to do. Generally, this is done by a loop of instructions in the operating system. Finding the WAIT time in these types of computers requires at least a two-address comparator connected to the memory address register (if there is one) and a rather detailed knowledge of the control program. Even with the necessary equipment and knowledge, it is usually only possible to find a level of activity that includes all of the WAIT time plus whatever other time is also used up in the same loop. In practice, WAIT time can be well enough isolated on most computers to perform useful analyses of "I/O-bound" conditions, but it is not always easy to do.

Another factor that limits the use of hardware monitors is that the cooperation and sometimes the permission of the computer manufacturer is needed to connect the monitor. The requirement that a site engineer be immediately available or working with the monitor analyst as mentioned earlier could be a significant stumbling block to the performance of hardware monitor projects. This is not usually a problem when the system to be monitored is owned, but when it is leased the owner could impose restraints that would preclude connection of a hardware monitor.

The next limitation is one of training and experience. Before any hardware monitor can be used, training is necessary to learn how to connect probes and how to operate the monitor, and experience is needed to decide what parts of the system should be monitored. The type of individual who is competent to work with the circuitry inside a computer does not emerge spontaneously. This is particularly true of system programmers and analysts who are typically called upon to become hardware-monitoring specialists. A reasonable investment in training should be expected before a hardware monitor will produce useful results.

Installation of a hardware monitor is an unusual event in most computer facilities. It is also a rather large physical job to place all needed cables to get ready to monitor. Operations personnel will be very curious about the new "black box" that is as unfathomable to them as their "black box" has been to most of their customers for years. Installing a hardware monitor should therefore be expected to cause significant disruption to the normal activity at a computer center.

A further problem with the use of these monitors is that they can cause computer malfunctions. The most common cause of such problems is associated with careless practices while connecting or disconnecting probes. There have been reports of computer problems caused by the monitors themselves, but these are singularly difficult to document. One which has been documented appears typical of this type of problem.* An early monitor, called a CPA7700, with a comparator connected to a Burroughs B3500, was in checkout testing to see every conceivable nonmalicious change that the monitor and its components would cause. Switching the signal inverter on the comparator from "normal" to "invert" mode and back repeatedly with the B3500 processing normally caused memory faults that affected the output of programs in progress. The fault was not corrected on this particular monitor but subsequent versions of the equipment were reported to be fixed. It is wise to proceed with extreme caution when any change in a monitor's setting is made while the monitor is connected to an operating computer.

Finally, a limitation that is noted every time a computer fails when a hardware monitor is connected is that the failure will always be blamed on the monitor. The experienced monitor user will learn to keep the site engineer close at hand whenever any change is made and to stop and trace the real cause of any failure that happens during these changes. Failures that occur while the monitor is connected, but when no changes are being made, are usually impossible to trace to the monitor.

Cost

It should be recognized that, even though hardware monitors have specific known prices, the true cost of using them is much higher than their prices imply. For example, a configuration of three basic and mapping hardware monitors was leased for three months to use in the review of five computer centers. The lease price for these monitors was just over $20,000. The total cost to use the monitors was nearly $200,000 when hardware monitor specialist costs, data reduction, and other support costs were added to the monitor cost. The analyses of hardware monitor data and report preparation brought total project time to about nine months.

This was an unusually large hardware monitoring project. A more

---

* Air Force Data Systems Design Center, "Operations Research Report S10-70," October, 1970.

typical review involving only one medium-sized computer center would probably cost in the $20,000 to $30,000 range and take two to four months.

The items which must be accounted for in determining the cost of a monitor include: monitor and supporting equipment lease cost, consultant time to identify and verify probe points and to assist or perform installation, operation, and removal of equipment, computer time to generate reports from hardware monitor data, equipment shipping costs, and travel and per diem costs. In general, the monitoring equipment should represent between 10% and 20% of the total hardware monitor project costs for one-time projects using leased equipment and outside consultants.

6
Benchmarking

Benchmarking is a very old measurement tool which originated in the land surveying field. In surveying, a benchmark is a horizontal incision on a rock or other permanent geographic feature whose location and elevation has been precisely surveyed. An angle iron is driven into this incision to serve as a "bench" on which a surveyor's leveling staff may be set. This benchmark serves as a point of reference for surveying the relative locations or elevations of other surrounding geographic points. The term *benchmark* has evolved to mean a standard for comparison or a point of reference for other products or activities which are similar to the one which has been chosen to serve as the benchmark.

In the computer field, a benchmark is a set of executable instructions which may be used to compare the relative performance of two or more computer systems. A benchmark is usually composed of computer programs, but it may also include scripts of narrative instructions that direct a person or a machine to perform certain specific tasks during the course of the comparison test. The process of benchmarking is conducting controlled experiments to collect measures of system performance which may be compared from one system to another.

BACKGROUND

The first computers were compared more to some number of human beings doing the same task than to other computers. For such purposes it was only necessary to know the number of digits entered and the types of mathematical operations performed to make statements like, "This computer solved a problem in twenty minutes which would have taken one hundred people with calculators one thousand years to complete." It was quite easy to justify solving certain problems on computers in those days because there was no practical alternative if these problems were to be solved at all. As the number and variety of computers increased and came into commercial use, methods for comparing one computer's performance to another's for the same workload were needed. Initially, the approach used for comparing computers to humans were used. That is, the number and size of calculations were timed and totaled for each machine under examination and the machine with the fastest time was usually quite obvious. It was a simple case of which machine had the fastest "adder" and which could carry the most digits before overflowing.

The event which caused the first real difficulty in comparing one computer to another was the increasing use of early computers for business purposes rather than for strictly scientific or mathematical applications. This event caused interest to be directed towards more than just the computer; the whole computer system became important. That is, the input, output, and storage devices began to have as much or more impact on total performance as did the processor or computer. The approach used to make comparisons of these types of workloads was to establish typical sets or "mixes" of computer programs. One of the most widely used of these was the "Gibson Mix."* This approach tested several sets of applications in both the business and scientific fields and published the execution time of available computer systems executing each of these mixes. Selecting the computer system for a particular installation then became a problem of reducing the planned workload into multiples of each program in "Gibson's Mix." For example, a workload might be characterized as "six of type A, four of type B, eleven of type C," and so forth. Then the prospective user would simply multiply the published execution times by the numbers which characterized his workload to find the expected total workload's comparative speed on each available computer system.

The development of computer systems which could execute multiple programs simultaneously fostered the development of benchmarks as we know them today. The introduction of ranges of periph-

---

* J. C. Gibson, "The Gibson Mix," *IBM Report,* TR-00.2043, Poughkeepsie, N.Y., IBM, 1970.

eral devices of varying speeds and capacities further complicated the comparison of systems and the introduction of terminals and online applications has made benchmarking current systems extremely difficult. The value derived from performing benchmarks has increased proportionally with the difficulty of this activity when the purpose of benchmarking is to select a computer system which will become part of the organization's daily operation for an extended period.

TERMINOLOGY

The basic unit of any benchmark is called the *benchmark kernal*. A benchmark kernal may be at the level of a machine instruction like an "add" or a "divide" and so forth, or it may be at a higher level like "edit" or "sort." The next higher level element of a benchmark is called a *benchmark instruction*. A benchmark instruction is like a line of code or a subroutine in a computer program. It is made up of benchmark kernals. A *benchmark instruction mix* is completely analogous to a computer program. The benchmark instruction mixes are composed of individual benchmark instructions. The collection of all benchmark instruction mixes is the "benchmark."

The technology of emulation has been incorporated into benchmarking in recent years. This has been done by using a separate computer from the one which is being benchmarked to serve as a terminal activity generator, or "remote terminal emulator" (RTE). The RTE may be a small computer brought in to serve this one purpose or it may be an available, full-sized machine that is adapted temporarily for emulation purposes. The RTE generates activity that looks to the system being tested as if it was the activity of some number of terminals. Usually the programs in the RTE are parameter-driven so that the benchmark group may alter the modeled system's characteristics over a large range of emulated activity. The incorporation of RTEs has made the use of benchmarks for typical workloads containing both batch and teleprocessing demands both simpler and more representative of reality. Remote terminal emulators are considered here as a technique of benchmarking rather than as a separate and distinct tool for CPE. Essentially all major computer manufacturers have RTE equipment for demonstrating or benchmarking a prospective customer's terminal workload.

Benchmarks are both *measurement* tools, like monitors and accounting packages, and *predictive* tools, like simulation and analytic models. In recognition that a system must exist to be benchmarked, some regard benchmarks as purely measurement tools. But the wide use of benchmarks to estimate how some new system would perform one's own workload, *if* it were to be acquired and installed, makes it difficult not to view benchmarks as predictive tools.

A *script* is a listing of step-by-step instructions and procedures which must be followed during all or part of a benchmark test. Scripts may also include the data which are to be used by the instructions. Usually scripts are employed to specify terminal activity which is to be done during the running of a benchmark. Scripts may be followed by individual terminal operators or they may be entered into the computer and serve as terminal emulators. When scripts are used to drive emulators, they are generally loaded into the RTE prior to the benchmark run and initiated at some predefined time during the run. RTE scripts may define very large terminal networks with extensive activity of differing types. Scripts that are entered by individuals are usually very short and contain repetitions of the same set of actions for as many times as are needed to generate the desired workload.

WHY BENCHMARK?

There is a very powerful appeal in the use of benchmarks for examining and selecting new computer systems or components. This appeal extends to both the prospective buyer and the prospective seller. It is simply the widely accepted "try it before you buy it" rule applied to computer systems. Ideally, the best test would be that of trying one's own real workload on each possible computer system. The practical limitations make such testing impossible in all but the most limited types of applications. Hence, the idea of a small, representative sample or a benchmark becomes necessary if only to avoid the practical problem of testing against the real workload.

Other reasons, beyond the practical ones, exist for benchmarking. Many governmental agencies and some large commercial concerns have procurement rules which require that computer systems be demonstrated competitively by using representative samples of the workload that the new system will have to support. The decision about whether one specific system or configuration of a system is faster than another can be answered quite convincingly with a benchmark and a stopwatch. Most computer system manufacturers are set up to handle customer-supplied benchmarks or will provide sets of their own demonstration programs to show how their equipment will perform under different workloads or conditions. Benchmarking is a marketing approach for these manufacturers, just as a test drive is a marketing approach for an automobile dealer. The buyer of a computer system who furnishes benchmarks to all interested bidders enjoys the advantage of having a controlled demonstration of a known workload on a full range of competitive manufacturers' equipment, and can then focus the procurement on getting the best price for equipment that suits the buyer's workload. This changes the likely outcome of the procurement from favoring the vendor with the best marketing staff to favoring the vendor with the best price/performance ratio for the buyer's applications.

Benchmarks are not used only as procurement aids. They are often used to validate the projected impact of some operational or procedural change that has been proposed. For example, if a new version of an operating system is projected to yield a performance improvement on some class of applications, it is quite common to test a small representative sample (or benchmark) of those applications running under the new operating system while collecting careful measurements of the execution characteristics for comparison with measures of the applications running under the original version of the operating system. This kind of benchmarking is quite easy to perform, and the value of knowing what the real impact of such changes would be is normally well worth the effort.

One of the most frequent applications of benchmarks is in testing the validity of predictions about proposed changes that are the results of CPE projects. The proposed changes are made in the representative benchmark and their effect is measured as in the example mentioned above of a new operating system version. It may also be the case that CPE project recommendations are implemented without testing with benchmarks. In these cases, the actual workload will serve as the "after-the-fact" benchmark. That is, the performance changes in each workload component would be regarded as the measure of the value of the change. This is particularly the case for online users and the response times that they witness. No matter what area the CPE recommendations refer to, any impact on response times will be widely seen and attributed to the group that made the recommendations. Because of this, a well-informed CPE team will always test their recommendations to see what their impact would be on such public measurements as response times. The value of benchmarking of this type may well determine the continuing existence of a CPE effort.

The reasons for benchmarking as either a procurement tool or as a test of performance predictions are entirely pragmatic. They are quite similar to a cost/benefit study where the value of an alternative is compared directly to the price of that alternative. Benchmarking is done to prevent spending more than the merits of an alternative deserve.

BENCHMARK CHARACTERISTICS

A good benchmark will be run more than once. Benchmarks are for making comparisons. When several comparisons must be made, benchmarks that need only a *short run* for each set of comparisons are highly desirable.

Benchmarks always represent either a real or potentially real workload. Usually, large sets of real or proposed programs are represented by a few benchmark programs. These few benchmark programs must be prepared very carefully to make certain that they are truly *representative* of the real workload.

Since the entire purpose of benchmarks is to obtain measurements of performance under varying conditions, benchmarks should contain internal collectors of as much information as is practical. That is, benchmarks should be *self-auditing*.

There are several ways of selecting or creating benchmarks. The least acceptable is by relying on the intuition of managers or technicians to decide what would be the best representation of the system's workload. The best approach is to perform a careful analysis of the structure and makeup of the current workload and to use the results of this analysis to create or select programs which will serve as the benchmark. Whatever the purpose of the benchmarking project is, the content of the benchmark must be *justifiable* in every sense of the word.

Table 6-1 presents these four characteristics to both summarize and emphasize their importance.

Inherrent in these characteristics is the fact that benchmarks must be cost-effective. The objective of the specific benchmarking project should be carefully considered to be sure that a fully justified, self-auditing, representative, and short-running benchmark is produced at a minimal cost. Beyond the cost of creating the benchmark, paying careful attention to these characteristics will also minimize the cost of using the benchmarks and will enhance the value of the results obtained from the benchmarking project.

HOW TO BENCHMARK

Benchmarks may be created for systems which already exist, systems which are proposed, or combinations of existing and proposed systems. The typical benchmark comprises both existing and proposed workloads. The approach used for creating benchmarks of these types of workloads is the same, but the basis upon which a benchmark of an existing workload is created is at a different level than is that of a proposed workload's benchmark. Existing workloads are usually analyzed at the *instruction level* while proposed workloads are analyzed at the *task level*. The source of detailed information for creating the benchmarks is also necessarily different. Data for existing systems may be obtained from accounting packages, software or hardware monitors while data for proposed workloads would require simulation or analytic models.

The next consideration in creating a benchmark is the management objective that the benchmark is intended to satisfy. The most common objectives of benchmarking have been categorized as shown in Table 6-2.*

A benchmark that is intended for testing competitive systems in a procurement evaluation would be a representation of the total load that the new system would have to support. Emphasis would ordinarily be on testing the processors, channels, and immediate access devices while there might be no test of, say, printers or communications lines. On the other hand, a benchmark for component certification would only need to contain a load that would drive the

---

* Wyrick, Thomas F., "Benchmarking Distributed Systems: Objectives and Techniques," International Conference on the Performance of Computer Installations, June 22-23, 1978, Gardone Riviera, Italy.

Table 6-1. Characteristics of a Benchmark.

1. Short-Running (relative to real workload)
2. Representative
3. Self-Auditing
4. Justifiable

Table 6-2. Benchmarking Objectives.

1. Procurement Evaluation
2. Design Analysis
3. System Integration
4. Component Certification
5. Service Quality Determination
6. Stress Load Analysis
7. Regression Testing
8. Performance Improvement
9. Migration Planning

component in question at its specified limits. For example, an 1100-line-per-minute printer might be certified by a simple demonstration of printing 11,000 lines in ten minutes (considering speed losses for such things as page line feeds). A benchmark for analyzing peak or stress loads would typically only focus on those one or two resources that are bottlenecks in the system when it is under heavy loads. The benchmark need not be all-encompassing of everything in the system. If such an approach were taken, the cost of most benchmark projects would be prohibitive. The objective of the project should set the limits on the benchmark's comprehensiveness.

With the similarities and differences between existing and proposed workload benchmarking and the limitations caused by the specific objective of a benchmark project in view, the development of benchmarks for either existing or proposed workloads is discussed below. The major class of benchmarks which represent combinations of both existing and proposed workloads is not discussed specifically. The approach in these cases is simply partly that for existing systems and partly that for proposed systems.

Benchmarking Existing Systems

A benchmark of a system that is already running on existing equipment is reasonably easy to create. It is important to recognize whether the benchmark will be used only on the existing equipment or whether it may be used to compare other equipment—such as in a procurement evaluation. When the benchmark may be used to evaluate other equipment, the initial analysis must be based on the coding of the existing programs rather than on the execution characteristics of these programs on the existing equipment. The reason for this is that each configuration imparts its own execution characteristics on any program or workload which it processes. If the hardware and operating system that are in place are measured to create a benchmark for procurement purposes, the true workload of existing programs will almost certainly be very badly stated. The execution characteristics of any given program may be substantially different on one manufacturer's configuration than on any other's. It is best to recognize that no matter what the immediate purpose of a benchmark is, if the benchmark is carefully constructed and widely accepted, it may become a comparison benchmark later. In other words, the starting point for developing a benchmark of an existing workload is the coding of the current programs.

The specific programs that should be examined may be selected based upon the current system resource consumption of all programs. It is best if resource consumption is measured in the money cost for processing the full workload for at least one month. Then the individual runs may be rank ordered according to the cost of each with the highest cost run at the top of the list. If the benchmark is to represent the entire workload, the programs or runs that account for about 80% of the total cost for the month from the top of the ordered listing should be selected as those used as the benchmark's basis. This may seem like a large number of programs but if only the top cost programs are selected, the number is usually surprisingly small relative to the total number of programs that are executed in a month. In general, much less than 20% of the jobs (usually more like 5%) constitute 80% or more of a system's workload. A caution that should be mentioned here is that *all* work must be considered, not just production jobs or those that are charged against outside users of the computer system. This is necessary as nearly all larger installations use more computer resources within the computer division itself than for any functional user. Whether this is good or bad is not important here; what is important here is that the entire load must be examined regardless of the reason for any component of the work.

Having selected these *driver* programs—the jobs that drive the total computer resource consumption—individual program coding analysis may begin. This analysis is greatly assisted by using an APA-type software monitor. Such a monitor shows which code is executed in what relative proportions. This code may be examined at the instruction level to determine the benchmark kernals of the workload. The kernals which account for up to 80% of the processing may be listed in rank order just as the jobs were earlier. These kernals are developed for each driver program and they will be used to create "synthetic" programs that represent, on a one-for-one basis, each driver program. As the development of individual synthetic programs progresses, it may become necessary to remove the least-used instructions from the benchmark kernal in order to adjust the running time of the synthetic program.

The importance of the least-used instruction in a kernal to the running time may be seen by studying the numbers shown in Table 6-3. If a kernal were to be selected that represents 84% of the example driver program which executes 273,600 instructions, only 84 instructions would be needed in the kernal. If this kernal required more execution time than desired, an 83% kernal of 28 instructions, or an 80% kernal of 14 instructions, or a 74% kernal of only 8 instructions could be used. Note that the fractional values of the instructions used in kernals are carried in this table. This should be done in the

Table 6-3. Benchmark Kernal Development.

INSTRUCTION	REAL DRIVER PROGRAM			SYNTHETIC PROGRAM			
	NUMBER OF USES	PERCENT OF USE	CUMULATIVE % OF TOTAL	NUMBER OF USES IF:			
				84%	83%	80%	74%
AA	57456	21	21	21	7	$4(3\frac{1}{2})$	$2(2\frac{1}{3})$
BB	49248	18	39	18	6	3	2
CC	38304	14	53	14	$5(4\frac{2}{3})$	$2(2\frac{1}{3})$	$2(1\frac{5}{9})$
DD	32832	12	65	12	4	2	$1(1\frac{1}{3})$
EE	24624	9	74	9	3	$2(1\frac{1}{2})$	1
FF	16416	6	80	6	2	1	—
GG	8208	3	83	3	1	—	—
HH	2736	1	84	1	—	—	—
All Others	43776	16	100	—	—	—	—
Totals	273600	100	—	84	28	14	8

work papers created during benchmark development so that it will be easy to decide which instruction counts to change if the benchmark needs to be adjusted later. For example, if a slightly smaller running time is necessary for the 74% kernal, instruction CC might be changed from 2 occurances to 1.

As the kernals are collected into benchmark instruction mixes and the mixes are built into synthetic programs, the individual synthetic programs should be scaled to each other. This is done in a manner that is entirely analogous to the kernal development shown in Table 6-3. And, again, the least used synthetic program will control the total running time of the synthetic jobstream or total workload benchmark.

When each synthetic program is completed in an executable form, it must be validated against the program or job that it represents. Table 6-4 shows the parameters that are useful for this validation in most architectures. Judgment must be used to adapt this list of parameters to some types of architectures.

The parameters shown as P1 through P8 are measures of CPU and channel active times, whether alone, overlapped, or total. P9 through P11 quantify the use of main memory. P12, P13, and P14 (which would normally become much more than three parameters based on the configuration which currently exists at the installation under

Table 6-4. Parameters of a Benchmark.

P1	CPU Active Time
P2	CPU Only Active Time
P3	CPU and Channel Active Simultaneously
P4	Channels Only Active Time
P5	Channels Active Time
P6	CPU Waiting While Channel Active Time
P7	Problem or Normal State Time
P8	Supervisor or Control State Time
P9	Memory Allocated
P10	Memory in Use
P11	Number of Programs Active Simultaneously
P12	Number of Directly Accessed Records[a]
P13	Number of Tape Accessed Records
P14	Number of Unit Accessed Records[b]

[a] P12 includes DISK, drum, low-speed memory, and data cell records. Each category device should be specified separately in systems which have more than one of these types of devices.

[b] P14 covers lines printed, cards read or punched, terminal messages in or out, and any other I/Os that are not susceptible to blocking. Each unit record device would also be specified separately.

study) account for external peripheral activity. All of these parameters are normally obtainable from computer resource accounting data from medium- and large-scale computer systems. If available, a hardware monitor may be useful in making precise measures of the real driver program and of its corresponding synthetic benchmark program for cross-validation.

The fact that the resource usage parameters of the current system are used in the validation of the benchmark programs should not be confused with the point made earlier that the actual program code be used as the basis for the benchmark development. Here, the code has already given the constructs of the synthetic programs and the synthetic programs have been run on the existing equipment. The comparison would therefore include the effects of the operating system and the current configuration on the independently created synthetic programs. These synthetic programs should be prepared in the language that is in use for the real program except that the "standard" version of the language should be used. That is, no special features of one manufacturer's compiler should be used when coding the synthetic program so that the benchmark will be easily transportable from one vendor's equipment to another's. As long as standard versions of languages are used, the benchmarks may be tested, if time allows, on any available configurations of other vendors' hardware to determine approximate run times to expect when the individual vendors demonstrate the proposed configuration. A few major procurement evaluation benchmarks have been tested to the extent that the real driver programs and their synthetic surrogates were both run on "other-vendor" equipment and measures like those shown in Table 6-4 collected to ensure that the representativeness carried across vendor lines. Such testing is seldom worthwhile unless equipment for several data centers is to be acquired based on a single benchmark demonstration.

The acceptable error for each synthetic program's resource usage parameters, when compared to the resource usage by the real program, should be limited to no more than 10% per parameter. The "total error" for all parameters of all programs should be no more than 5% using the "square root of the sum of the squares" method. This approach is sometimes referred to as the "standard error" in introductory statistics texts.

As a practical matter, it is better to look first at the total error before any adjustments are undertaken at the instruction level. Many times the entire benchmark jobstream will be very close to the real jobstream, say within 2%, even though there may be scattered individual parameters that are as much as 40 or 50% off of their intended values. The issue is usually how close the entire benchmark represents the entire workload, so adjustments may be unnecessary in spite of recognized errors within parts of the benchmark. Here again, the objective of the benchmark is the important consideration. If detailed performance information about one specific program is desired, then the synthetic program which represents that specific program would naturally have to be tuned as closely as possible to the real program's characteristics.

The run time of the entire benchmark on the existing equipment should be between about two and four hours. Nominally, this would allow from .25% to about .5% of a total month's running time to be represented (depending, of course, on the number of hours of running time at the installation in question per month). This benchmark run time is long enough to allow the benchmark to "settle down" and generate a load that truly represents the real workload.

This benchmark run time may also be broken into thirds with each third representing the characteristic workload of one shift. Terminal activity may then be directed substantially into the period that stands for the day shift while heavy batch processing may be required during the thirds that stand for evening or midnight shifts.

The final point that needs to be incorporated into each synthetic program is a feature for self-auditing. This is very simple to add during the development of the benchmark. If the self-auditing feature is left out until the benchmark is completed, it is extremely difficult to add it in without altering the way in which the benchmark executes and, therefore, its overall representativeness. The purpose of the audit trail is to show that each program and major portion of the program really did get executed during the manufacturer's demonstration. Simple counters may be incorporated in each program with the initial count determined by, say, a random number generator. Incrementing this count at each critical point would yield a single number for each execution of each synthetic program and the sum of all these counters would give a single number that indicates whether all of every benchmark part was in fact performed. Variations in individual counters from the expected totals would direct the analyst's attention to the specific part of the benchmark where question exists.

This random number initiator approach is also widely used to create the data upon which the benchmark programs will work during the demonstration. This allows the vendors to create the data base on their own equipment when they are doing pretests for purposes of configuring the right equipment, while the prospective buyer retains the ability to change all data at the time of the demonstration by providing a new "seed" for the random number generator. This use of an internal random number generator for initializing audit trail counters and data base information virtually guarantees that the actual benchmark will have to be performed and that no "prestaging" of results will be possible. The only preparation necessary on the part of prospective buyers is that the benchmark be run ahead of time at their own site by using the same seeds as will be given to the vendor at demonstration time. This means that all of the input and output of the benchmark job stream would be totally unintelligible, but completely predictable, data. This kind of input and output makes a very secure benchmark.

Benchmarking Proposed Systems

When the workload does not exist, benchmarking is still possible but it is a more technically demanding and complex job. First, the flow and structure of jobs that will account for about 50% of the proposed workload must be specified. This specification should be by program or job and it should be at the level of flow charts (even though flow charts themselves may not be needed). Descriptions of the activities of each program will be needed along with detailed definitions of all major files (or data bases) that are to be accessed by these programs and of all files that are to be accessed by more than one of these programs. These descriptions would normally be at the "task" level rather than at the instruction level treated for existing systems.

Once detailed design specifications are available for about one-half of the proposed workload, the proposed workload should be modeled by using either a simulation or an analytic modeling approach. (Generally, only the simplest systems may be treated by using analytic models, so most of the time a simulation capability will be needed to accomplish this step.) When the results of the modeling are available, they may be treated as though they were obtained from accounting data or software monitors and the procedure outlined for existing systems followed. That is, select the benchmark kernals based on predicted system usage and build the synthetic programs and total benchmark job stream. Validate the results of modeling this benchmark job stream against the models of the design specifications and adjust where necessary to bring the model of the benchmark within reasonable limits of the model of the system specifications.

The only difference in developing benchmarks for proposed systems as compared to those for existing systems is in the "total error" which is normally accepted. Since the modeling already represents a level of abstraction away from reality, the total acceptable error for benchmarks of proposed systems is usually considered to be about 20 or 30% rather than the 5% figure suggested for benchmarks of existing systems.

BENCHMARK LIMITATIONS

The advantages of using benchmarks have been stressed throughout this chapter. This is not meant to imply that there are no disadvantages. In fact, the disadvantages of using benchmarks can be overwhelming.

Cost

The major limitation of the use of benchmarks is that it can be very expensive. It requires a total dedication of at least one and possibly of several of the most knowledgeable technicians that are available or that can be obtained from outside sources. Probably no other CPE activity can cost as much as benchmarking except, in some cases, simulation. It is not unusual to have to spend five or six staff years to develop a benchmark that would be used for a procurement evaluation, and, no matter how talented the individuals involved, something like six months should be considered the minimum possible time in which such a benchmark can be developed and validated.

Representativeness

Benchmarks must be developed with extreme care and in a very methodical fashion to be certain that they really are representative of the workload that is to be benchmarked. Unless this care and attention are applied, benchmarks should not be used since they would not be representative. A benchmark that is anything less than representative will be misleading.

External Factors

Nearly every computer system requires periodic human intervention. This may be only to mount a tape or load another box of paper in a printer, but some intervention will ultimately be needed. Such external factors may be minimized during benchmark runs by making small compromises in the benchmark's representativeness to ensure that the system need never wait for a human action. With the exception of human intervention, external factors tend to be sudden and unexpected. For example, an equipment failure or a program bug may occur during a benchmark run. Such events tend to occur frequently when benchmarking. The normal approach to such problems is to restart the benchmark from the beginning. It is worthwhile to keep careful records of such occurrences during benchmark runs as they may ultimately point out weaknesses in the system that is being examined.

AN OBSERVATION

The field of benchmarking has changed more rapidly in the past few years than any other CPE tool or technique. This is unusual and was unexpected since benchmarking is by far the oldest established approach discussed in this book. The major reason for this change has been the recent addition of RTEs to the field of benchmarking—particularly for procurement evaluations. Remote Terminal Evaluators were proposed several years ago (in the late 1960s), then ignored, then developed vigorously, then ignored again, and so forth. It was not clear that they would ever become an accepted tool for examining the performance of computer systems. Finally, early in 1980, there seemed to be a rather wide acceptance of RTEs as a CPE tool that vendors would accept in competitive procurement situations. It is hoped that this situation lasts.

Because of the rapid evolution of benchmarking, it is strongly recommended that no source material prepared earlier than 1979 be relied upon as authoritative information. The information in this chapter is purposely made extremely general and brief. The reader with an interest in extensively using benchmarks is urged to examine current articles that are available at the time that the benchmarking project is needed. A complete bibliography of CPE articles, books, and other publications is presented annually in the March issue of *EDP Performance Review*.* This listing should be consulted and the referenced works on benchmarking should be read to determine where the field of benchmarking stands at any time.

---

* *EDP Performance Review*, a monthly publication of Applied Computer Research, PO Box 9280, Phoenix, Arizona 85068.

7
Simulation

The preceding chapters dealt with CPE tools and techniques which involve making direct measurements of existing systems. Situations often occur where performance measurements are needed for systems which do not exist or are not available for direct measurement. In these situations, the techniques of simulation may be applied. Simulation involves the creation of models of a system or subsystem to gather measurement-like data for use in making management decisions.

ESSENTIAL WORKING CONCEPTS

Two points are emphasized here that should be kept in mind throughout the discussion of simulation. First, the concept of *predictive measurement* is essential to the understanding and effective use of simulation. The second point has to do with the distinction between an "art" and a "science."

Simulation is a prediction technique, not a measurement technique. The purpose of simulation is to estimate what the measurements would be if the simulated system were to be measured directly. These predictive measurements are based on a conceptual view, or model, of a real system—even though the real system may not yet exist. When the simulated system does exist, actual measurements may be used to improve the quality of the simulation models and results. The output of the simulation, however, is a set of predictive measurements which depend on the quality of the model, not on the real system itself. To a great extent, the talent of the individual who analyzes the problem and creates and implements the simulation is most significant. This individual's "artfulness" determines how closely the model will approximate reality. Human judgment and interpretation are essential in using simulation. Because of this, inaccuracies will be introduced and should be anticipated.

Simulation might best be described as an *art of scientific application* rather than a science in its own right. It is a multidisciplinary endeavor whose practitioners bring together techniques from such diverse fields as system analysis, applied mathematics, operations research, computer design, computer architecture, and programming.

DEFINITION

A useful definition of simulation in the context of computer performance evaluation is as follows:

> *Simulation* is the use of numerical logic models of a system, concept, or operation to examine its expected behavior over time.

Computer system simulation is a methodology for performing experiments on dynamic systems through the medium of a computerized model or models which approximate the target system over a limited range of interest. In order to simulate automated systems, a computerized model is required. There are other means of implementing models. In some fields analogous systems are used—systems that exhibit dynamic properties similar to those of the target system but which can be handled more conveniently. Wind tunnels and scale models are examples of analagous models. In the computer field models are implemented through the use of computer programs. These programs are often executed on computers (called *host* computers) other than the computer system which is being simulated (called the *target* computer).

Rather than providing an exact replica of the target system, a simulation approximates a limited part of the real system. Inaccuracies are inherent in using simulation since a model is a conceptual representation of the system rather than a duplicate of the real system. Whenever simulation is used, highly qualified judgment is required to interpret any underlying assumptions, methods, and results.

Every computer system simulation deals with a limited range of interests. The initial definition of the scope and boundaries of these interests and identification of external but pertinent interacting factors are of crucial importance and effect. The scope of the model must be rigorously defined and understood. Decisions are needed about which elements of the process will be included in the model and which will be left out. Once the "world" of the model is defined, the interfaces with the external world must be delineated.

It is often convenient in defining simulation to use an analogy to clarify various aspects of the modeling and simulation process. The concepts of *approximation* and *range* as used above are quite easily understood by using the analogy of a supermarket.

Questions relating to scope or extent occur when determining whether a supermarket task model shall consist of shoppers driving in, parking, shopping, and exiting, or only shopping activity within the store. Models depicting the broader and finer scopes possible with this simple problem are suggested in Figure 7-1. The interfaces with the outside world are different in each case and different interpretations would be given to the inputs and outputs of each model.

Similarly, the modeler of a computer system must decide whether the model of applications (analogous to supermarket shoppers) shall be concerned solely with computation or shall span the terminal, transmission, and scheduling as well. Figure 7-2 shows the definition of very different scopes for this problem. The factors which would

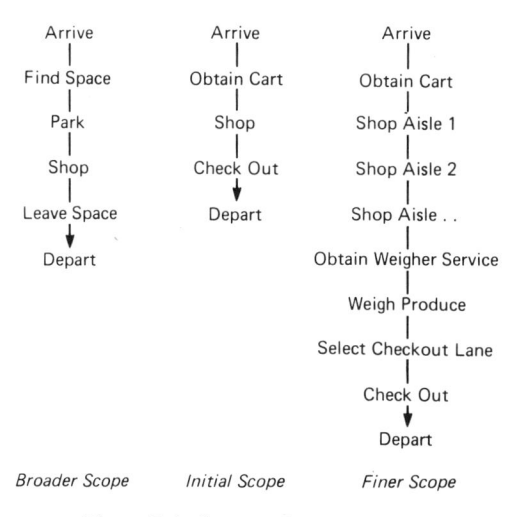

```
      Arrive              Arrive              Arrive
        |                   |                   |
    Find Space          Obtain Cart         Obtain Cart
        |                   |                   |
       Park                Shop            Shop Aisle 1
        |                   |                   |
       Shop            Check Out          Shop Aisle 2
        |                   ↓                   |
    Leave Space           Depart           Shop Aisle . .
        ↓                                       |
      Depart                              Obtain Weigher Service
                                                |
                                          Weigh Produce
                                                |
                                        Select Checkout Lane
                                                |
                                            Check Out
                                                ↓
                                              Depart

   Broader Scope       Initial Scope         Finer Scope
```

Figure 7-1. Supermarket user models.

138 COMPUTER PERFORMANCE EVALUATION

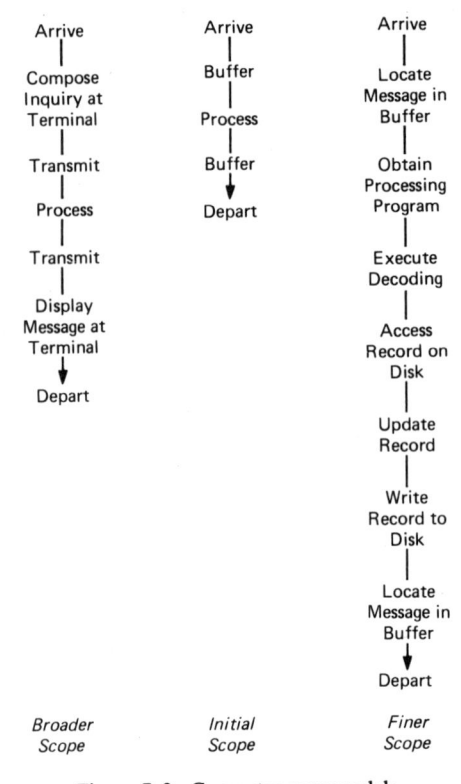

```
   Arrive              Arrive              Arrive
     |                   |                   |
   Compose             Buffer              Locate
   Inquiry at            |                 Message in
   Terminal            Process             Buffer
     |                   |                   |
   Transmit            Buffer              Obtain
     |                   ↓                 Processing
   Process             Depart              Program
     |                                       |
   Transmit                                Execute
     |                                     Decoding
   Display                                   |
   Message at                              Access
   Terminal                                Record on
     ↓                                     Disk
   Depart                                    |
                                           Update
                                           Record
                                             |
                                           Write
                                           Record to
                                           Disk
                                             |
                                           Locate
                                           Message in
                                           Buffer
                                             ↓
                                           Depart

   Broader             Initial             Finer
   Scope               Scope               Scope
```

Figure 7-2. Computer user models.

influence the choice of the model would include the importance of the functions included in the model and the ability to make reasonable assumptions about their effects on the system at its interfaces.

WHEN TO USE SIMULATION

In a broad context, simulation is used to obtain experimental data to gain insight into a system's operation. Characteristics of the target system provide the reasons or motivation for applying simulation techniques. Typical reasons are that the target system is: conceptual, unavailable, too expensive or too cumbersome to operate, or too complex to handle by means of analytic models.

The primary use of simulation is as a method for testing design hypotheses or demonstrating the performance or sensitivity of "paper" systems. Another use is to evaluate the performance of a system that exists but that is not available for direct experimentation. Computer systems that must operate around-the-clock may be simulated to test configuration revisions, alternate scheduling strategies, and so forth.

Another situation in which simulation is indicated is with a system that requires such a tremendous expenditure of resources as to preclude cost-effective, direct experimentation. The testing of a military weapon system, for example, can involve excessive consumption or destruction of resources. Other examples of target systems that have been simulated to avoid prohibitive expenditures include spacecraft docking operations and large communications networks.

Simulation may be the only viable method for evaluating the performance of cumbersome real-time, man-machine systems. Simulation may be useful to test those systems whose experimental operation would otherwise require oppressive accumulation of human and machine resources—a teleprocessing system, for example.

Simulation may also be feasible when a system is too complex to be conveniently represented by solvable mathematical formulations. The requirement for closed solutions is bypassed in simulation by avoiding the mathematics entirely or by providing a procedural analogy. Linear programming and symbolic models providing solutions via differential equations are not applicable in many situations where procedural models could be used. Techniques of analysis have been recently improved to the point where it is now feasible to apply analytic models in many situations (see Chapter 8). However, simulation using numerical logic models is still a feasible approach when solving models formulated by using queuing theory becomes prohibitive as events and interactions become increasingly complex. Whenever a computer performance problem can be sufficiently simplified to use analytic modeling approaches, analytic models should be used in preference to simulation.

Simulations of existing computer systems are usually performed in conjunction with, and as an extension of, other CPE tools and techniques. Input data can be derived directly from monitors and accounting data reduction programs. "Trace-driven" simulation employs various direct measurements to improve simulation results by using software monitor data as input to the models. Benchmarks can be used to calibrate simulation models. Once calibrated, the simulation may be used to evaluate expanded system configurations, new applications, and expanding workloads.

The general reasons given at the beginning of this section for using simulation may now be restated purely in the context of CPE. Computer systems should be simulated when the system is in the design phase, is not installed, or is not available, when measurement tools are not available or cannot be used, or when analytic models are insufficient for the problem.

THE PROCESS OF SIMULATION

Simulation should not be viewed as a self-contained task like writing a computer program. It is more accurate and far more useful to view simulation as a *process* or continuum of tasks. Figure 7-3 provides a diagram of the major tasks which constitute the process of simulation.

Define the Problem

Defining the problem, including its scope and boundaries, is often the most important and most difficult part of solving the problem.

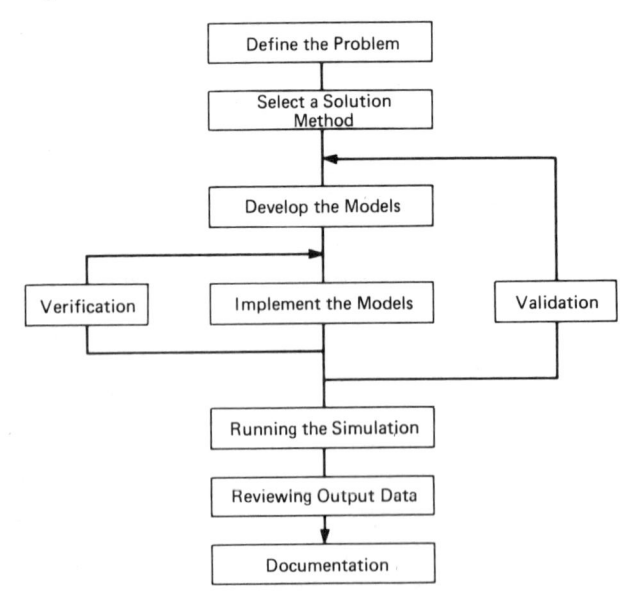

Figure 7-3. The simulation process.

The costs involved to develop a solution and the benefits to be derived from applying the solution depend directly upon how the problem is defined. Problems with computer systems may be grouped under four major topics. In simplified terms, these are:

Optimization. Could this system be made to perform better?
Upgrading. Could an existing system be made to handle new or different tasks?
Design. What new system should be created and implemented?
Justification. Would this system be missed if it didn't exist?

Generally, these problems are not encountered individually. Most real situations involve combinations of two or more of these four topics.

Management decisions involve selecting the best or most acceptable alternative solution from among several courses of action. Because of this, the simulation analyst should be careful to define the problem's scope broadly enough to yield a range of possible solutions from which management may choose a solution which is acceptable to all who are involved.

Before the problem definition task is completed, the simulation analyst should have addressed the following general and specific areas:

General
- Project objectives (what must be done?)
- Individuals responsible for area where problem lies
- Tools available to address problem
- Constraints on the solution (are there alternative solutions that are unacceptable?)

Specific
- Workload data available
- Workload data needed
- Schematics or listings of hardware or software involved
- Development status of system triggering problem

The final phase of this task consists of formally writing down the problem as defined by the simulation analyst along with as many insights into possible solutions as may be apparent at the outset. This formal definition should be reviewed and accepted as valid by the individual who will ultimately be responsible for accepting or rejecting the results of the project.

Select a Solution Method

This task might just as well be called, "Collect Data." It is best to commence collecting the data identified in the Problem Definition task with a view of other potential solution tools. Collecting the data needed to analyze most problems that appear to require simulation for their solutions will usually involve the use of all available solution tools. Often, the path to acceptable solutions becomes apparent early in the data collection process. In such cases, the method has selected itself.

When all necessary data have been collected and no obvious CPE approach has been identified as a possible solution device, then simulation would be the only remaining method. It is important to note that the decision to use simulation should only be made after rejecting all of the other, lower-priced alternatives. If the problem is like one that has been encountered and solved by using simulation before, a set of usable models or a "canned" simulation package may be available. The time and money saved by using such simulation approaches can be considerable. The skills needed to use "canned" packages are usually available in most programming departments. ("Canned" packages, or computer simulation program packages, are discussed later in this chapter under "Implement the Models.")

Solution method selection is quite straightforward when dealing with problems mentioned earlier under "When to Use Simulation." In these cases, it is pointless to search for possible applications of other CPE approaches. The one caution in this area is that if the problem can be reduced to one which can be addressed using analytic models, then this should be done.

Develop the Models

In this task the conceptual system is developed and described to the greatest possible extent. A flow chart of the system should be devised which shows the interrelationships of system functions and elements in a processing-sequence-oriented formulation.

It is important to realize that computer applications, rather than the computer equipment itself, are usually modeled. The object of the processing—execution of the job or segment or program—is the primary concern in modeling. The computer is not normally treated as the "object" entity, but rather as the "service" entity. That is, the computer is a collection of resources, facilities, and services which are used by the processing stream. The interconnections of computer resources and the competition for these resources are expressly considered where they influence the rules for allocating resources.

Models may be created at various levels of detail. At any given level of detail, the model is limited in scope. The clear identification of the boundaries of each model—what it includes and what it does not—is necessary. An explicit statement of the assumptions upon which the model rests is also important. Boundary selection is strongly influenced by the importance assigned to the functions that are included in the model and by the ability to make reasonable assumptions about the effects of these functions on the system at its interface with the outside world.

Implement the Models

The paper or conceptual models are translated into computerized form as part of the implementation task. This may be done by using any of four major categories of simulation implementation tools. These categories are: scientific programming languages (like FORTRAN and ALGOL), general-purpose simulation languages (SIMSCRIPT, SIMULA, GPSS, and so forth), computer-oriented simulation languages (ECSS, CSS), and computer simulation program packages (SCERT, CASE).

A few broad generalizations about differences in these categories of simulation implementation tools may be made. These generalizations regard the expertise needed to use each category of tool, the flexibility of the models created, and the compactness of expression attainable in each category. In general, as one moves from use of scientific programming languages through general-purpose and computer-oriented simulation languages to the computer simulation program packages, less expertise in simulation is required and models may be expressed more compactly, but the flexibility of implemented models decreases. These factors are shown graphically in Figure 7-4, "Comparing implementation tools." (These comparisons are at a conceptual level only. That one tool may be shown two or three times as far along an axis as another should not be taken to imply that either tool has two or three times the merit of the other with respect to that axis.)

It may also be observed that scientific programming languages contain no simulation constructs; therefore, there should be no model bias induced by this category of tool. Any scientific program—simulation or not—may be implemented by using a scientific language. This allows extreme flexibility when models are programmed with these languages. General-purpose simulation languages may be used to implement any type of simulation—whether a supermarket or a computer system. There are two main types of general-purpose simulation languages: statement-like and block-diagram-oriented. The statement-like languages (SIMSCRIPT, SIMULA) retain most features of higher-level scientific languages but incorporate specific syntaxes and vocabulary of modeling. They also incorporate simulation control features and

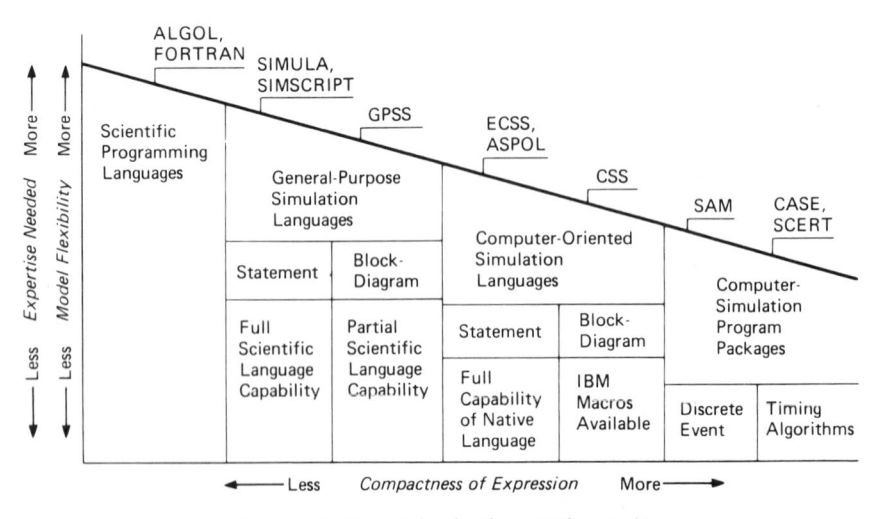

Figure 7-4. Comparing implementation tools.

queuing macros to ease the implementation and provide for more compactly expressed models. Just as with scientific programming languages, statement-like simulation languages require program writing, syntax checking, and compilation.

The block-diagram-oriented languages (GPSS, BOSS) incorporate many macros as do the previous general-purpose simulation languages but add model constructs. This feature enables the user to implement a model entirely through use of data-oriented code which is related to block-diagram notation for coding and modeling convenience. Because of this, the user relinquishes nearly all capability to elect some special "world view," but gains an extremely compact coding structure along with the capability to run in execution mode. This does away with the need to recompile each time a change is made to the model's structure or parameters.

Computer-oriented simulation languages are generally specialized adaptations of general-purpose simulation languages with built-in constructs and specialized vocabulary to ease the simulation of computer systems. Both ECSS and ASPOL are SIMSCRIPT-based languages while CSS resembles GPSS. It is usually possible to read the coding of a computer-oriented simulation language program and follow the details of the particular computer problem which is being simulated. In general, there are libraries of code to represent computer elements and functions which are available from users of individual languages. When the element or function of interest has already been coded by some language developer, it is relatively easy to implement a model by using one of the computer-oriented languages.

Computer simulation program packages are copyrighted commercial products which, by reputation or claim, are either algorithmic timing routines or discrete event simulators. (There is some discussion about which product is which type of tool. Most users appear to regard the product SAM as a discrete event simulator and the products SCERT and CASE as algorithmic timers. This distinction is primarily academic, so it is not pursued here.) Tools in this category are widely referred to as *canned simulators* or *canned packages*. The allusion to "canned" refers simply to the fact that these are available, off-the-shelf products which contain many facilities to make them easy to use. The major advantage of these facilities is that extensive libraries for each simulator are maintained by the vendor for use by the buyers of these packages. There has been widespread criticism of the fact that the internal constructs of the models used by such products are invisible to the individuals using the products. Although this is necessarily the case for proprietary products, a great deal can be learned about the capability and validity of each package when they are used. When such packages are used to implement a simulation project, the "Validation" and "Review of Output Data" tasks take on added importance.

Before leaving this discussion of available simulation implementation tools, a few other general comments should be made. Most people who are deeply involved in the use of these tools regard all *discrete event* implementation tools as suitable for extremely detailed modeling at the one-minute-or-shorter time interval. All categories except the algorithmic timers are discrete event simulation tools. (More will be said about discrete event simulation in the following major section: "Discrete Event Simulation.") When problems involve simulation of events which occur over a period of one day or longer, the algorithmic timers are usually considered appropriate tools. Unfortunately, most computer problems deserving simulation last longer than one minute but shorter than one day. In such cases, the approach to use is the one that is most familiar at the installation. In the final analysis, the best implementation tool to use seems to turn out to be the tool which the involved analyst wishes to use. When there is a preference, it is better to allow the individual who will actually do the modeling to choose the implementation tool than to select another approach for that person to use. If there is no preference on the part of the simulation analyst, it is probably best to start most projects with the tools which require the least amount of expertise: the algorithmic timers or canned packages. After such tools are exploited to their limits, the move up to one of the more flexible tools is quite natural and easy.

Verification and Validation

In the process of simulation, *verification* means checking the implementation of the models for consistency and reasonableness. The *programs* are tested and the question here concerns the correctness of the program's operation, not the correctness of the model. Verification can usually be accomplished by making a few selected hand computations of processes implemented by the program. When possible, it is best to have the verification task accomplished by an analyst who has not been involved in the design and coding of the simulation.

Validation is defined here as the attainment of the degree of accuracy deemed necessary for the particular simulation project being conducted. Validation is often overrated as a problem area in the simulation process. Perhaps this is simply a problem of semantics. "Accuracy" is a measure of the coincidence of some process with a corresponding, measurable reality. Accuracy is objective but it carries a connotation of relativeness. Validity is subjective and is always relative. It is entirely possible for some outcome to be inaccurate but valid. To test the validity of a simulation it is first necessary to establish some bounds of accuracy that will be *acceptable*.

When a simulation is made of a system which exists and can be measured, standards of accuracy should be established for determining when the simulation will be considered valid. The reason for simulating existing systems is usually to predict what effect changes will have on the system before the changes are made. It may be completely acceptable to set an accuracy of the initial simulation at within 20% of the measured system. Of course several factors of the system would normally be compared with the corresponding factors in the models, and accuracy standards might be set at different levels depending on the criticality of each factor to the overall experiment. Once the models have met the initial validity tests, they should be expected to behave reasonably in the simulation runs with the changes made to predict the *absolute* direction and *general* magnitude to expect from the changes when the changes are made to the real system.

For example, a set of programs was simulated by using two different simulation tools. The acceptable accuracy for processing time was set at plus or minus 5%. The initial simulations of the existing programs were within these bounds for both tools. A few changes were made in the models to represent increased disk blocking factors and overlapping runs of some of the programs. One tool indicated that processing time would decrease by about 20% and the other tool predicted a decrease of about 30%. The changes were then made to the real programs and a 25% decrease of processing time was measured. Both tools had produced valid models because they were within the initial bounds of accuracy and they had correctly predicted the absolute direction and general magnitude of the changes. No importance was attached to the fact that neither tool predicted the new run times precisely. If either tool were to have been used again with the altered set of programs serving as the existing system to predict the impact of some further changes, then the accuracy of the model would have to be brought back within the accuracy standards set for the new experiment. Adjusting various features of the model to make simulation results approach some known measures is called *tuning the model.*

When no system exists or it is otherwise impossible to validate using measurements, relative validity may be established by comparison with qualitative conceptual standards. There are two ways to create such standards. First, it is often feasible to obtain a mathematical or engineering estimate of the system's—or of major system components'—performance. When this is possible, these estimates may be compared directly to the simulation results. A second method for deriving qualitative conceptual standards may be possible by removing random and nonlinear quantities from the models and by comparing the fixed output with an analytic solution. One of these validation approaches should be applied soon after the models have been implemented to ensure that the simulation can produce reasonable results.

Finally, if it is not possible to develop absolute or conceptual standards, it is still possible to heuristically validate a model. Heuristic validation is done by finding a qualified simulation analyst who has no previous project involvement and by stepping through a detailed explanation of each part of the model and the underlying assumptions which were used in constructing and implementing the model. The outside analyst acts as a critic or "devil's advocate" during this process. Once the logic of the simulation implementation has been accepted by the outside analyst, it is considered to be heuristically validated. This validation approach amounts to trusting the capability of the original analyst after it is supported by an impartial second opinion.

Validation methods for simulations of nonexistent systems may seem to be insufficient tests of a model's predictive capacity. This is seldom the case. The results of most simulation projects support management decisions with regard to future alternatives. Most such decisions can be made with reasonable estimates of their expected impact. Simulation, when carefully used, gives exactly this: reasonable estimates of the expected impact of some specific course of action. When accuracy levels of 2 or 3% are required, simulation is seldom an acceptable tool. Simulation is best used for "go-or-no-go" decisions when only the direction of some approach is of interest. It is for this reason that simulation is almost never used in the final selection of a computer system. This is a decision where 2 or 3% can make a substantial difference. Used as a tool to estimate the performance of a nonexistent system, simulation should be considered as a 15 to 20% accurate approach. Most problems of CPE can be addressed within these bounds of accuracy.

Running the Simulation

This task is by far the easiest of all in the simulation process. It amounts only to execution of the programs which contain models of the system under study. Usually, running a simulation is no more of a problem than running any other new, one-time set of programs. If the proper tool has been selected, the models have been implemented and validated thoroughly, and the programs have been verified ahead of time, the simulation runs are simple and routine. Because of this, it is wise to look back into the preceding tasks of the simulation process when problems are encountered in running the models.

There are a few general comments in order regarding the run time of various possible simulation tools. These generalities probably have more exceptions than cases where they apply, but they may be worth considering in an environment where there are no practical bounds on the simulation tool which may be used. The run time of the simulation is usually an extremely small part of the cost of the project, so it is not wise to be very concerned with the computer costs associated with any particular simulation tool. If these costs are important, it is generally the case that the tools which allow the most flexibility in the models run the longest for any given problem, while those with less flexibility run the fastest. The numerous exceptions to this generality seem to occur when one of the available simulation tools is used in an area where it probably does not belong; for instance, using an algorithmic timer to examine very detailed and short duration phenomena or writing a FORTRAN simulation of several weeks of a total workload should produce exceptions.

Reviewing Output Data

By the time that the process of simulating a problem has gotten to the point where output begins to flow, there is normally a thorough grasp of which parts of the output are important. All factors considered during the validation of the models should be reexamined when they are available as a part of the total output. In addition, those less important variables must be examined to ensure that there are not remarkable variations which may cause the total validity of the models to be questionable.

There are three general types of outputs from most simulations—system performance information, system resource usage statistics, and system history or trend information—and they are treated in the following section ("Discrete Event Simulation"). Each of these categories must be examined to ensure that the data produced by the models are reasonable and acceptable, and that the data are suitable for use in the project which is underway.

Once all tests of the output have been made, application of the output is necessary. No generalizations can be made in this regard. The aim of the specific project must be reviewed in light of the insights provided by the simulation outputs and decisions must be formulated by taking the available output as the guideline.

Documentation

Documentation is given as the final task in the simulation process only because no project can be considered complete until the analysts have prepared and presented the results to management for their action. In fact, documentation should begin at the outset of the simulation project and continue through each task. This ensures that a complete record of all important actions, decisions, and assumptions are in hand when the project is finished. Documentation that is kept in this way is very valuable.

The documentation maintained should be of sufficient depth to serve as detailed reference material in the case that some portion of the project must be changed substantially or redone completely. At this level, the documentation may be maintained at a highly technical level as it would probably only be used by the analysts that were directly involved thoughout the project.

A higher level of project documentation should be maintained that can be referenced during future projects. Such documentation can prevent the reinvention of a simulation approach when similar problems arise later on. The level of detail that is generally acceptable for this type of document may be compared to the level of a technical article that is publishable in a special-interest group newsletter read by practioners of simulation. Such an article would include a description of the problem that was addressed, information on the assumptions that were needed and the general approach that was used, examples of the programming techniques or special tools used, and a description of the results which were obtained. When significant problems were encountered, these should also be discussed along with the way these problems were solved. If the recommendations which were offered as a result of the project are implemented, it is also very useful and interesting to describe their actual impact in this documentation.

The highest level of documentation should be the project report which is prepared for management. This document should be written at a "layman's" level to the greatest possible extent. It is usually enough to report only the recommendations and expected impact of each recommendation in detail. The balance of the report should briefly cover specific assumptions made which could be of management interest and any related problem areas which were not specifically addressed during the project and in which management may have further interest. These reports to management should contain graphic descriptions which convey the meaning of each recommendation whenever possible and these reports must be kept as short as possible. If the report is more than a dozen or so pages, a paragraph that summarizes the recommendations should be prepared for the beginning of the report and the analyst should recognize that this single paragraph is all that most management-level report recipients will ever read. Unless specifically requested, these management reports should never contain descriptions of such things as problems which were encountered, addressed, and solved during the conduct of the project, nor should the day-to-day details of the project's progress be discussed.

An important fact to note is that documentation can be the "Achilles' Heel" of the simulation process. Many modeling projects have failed simply because adequate documentation was not kept to support the conclusions of the project. It is not difficult to document a simulation project, although it may not always be easy to find the time needed to prepare as thorough a set of documentation as may be desired. The time required to produce sufficient documentation to support any simulation project is always worth finding.

DISCRETE EVENT SIMULATION

A discrete event model represents a process in which the system state changes in distinct steps. These state changes are usually characterized by the advance of time. Systems that can be described by discrete event models are those in which resource contention and allocation occurs. Queuing and probabilistic behavior are important phenomena which are encompassed by discrete event models. Computer systems exhibit such behavior and are excellent subjects for discrete event simulation.

Figure 7-5 is an example of a discrete event model for three system states (idle, busy, and queued) with regard to some fixed resource to serve three users. Initially (at the time T0), the system is idle. The first discrete event occurs at time T1 when users 1 and 2 arrive and cause the resource state to become both busy and queued. This is a change from state A to state C. At time T2, the state changes again from C to B, and so on as arrivals of users cause demands to be made on the resource. Note that at time T4 the system is in state C and that at time T5 a set of discrete events occur which change the system state to state C again. In other words, even though no apparent change of state has occurred, discrete events have occurred which are tracked by this simple model. Also note that when the system changes from state B to state C, or from C to B, there is no change in the use of the resource: it is busy in either case. The points which are of interest in a discrete event model are the changes which occur at state transitions and the duration of time from one change to the next. The discrete event model shown in Figure 7-5 could be

System States	A	C	B	A	C	C	B

Resource: Idle / Busy / Queued

User #1: Waiting / Served
User #2: Waiting / Served
User #3: Waiting / Served

T0 T1 T2 T3 T4 T5 T6 ....
Time →

System States
A - Resource is idle
B - Resource is busy
C - Resource is busy and queued

Discrete Events:
T0 - No event
T1 - Users 1 and 2 arrive; #1 served, #2 queued
T2 - User 1 done; #2 served
T3 - User 2 done
T4 - Users 1 and 3 arrive; #3 served, #1 queued
T5 - User 2 arrives; #2 queued, #3 done, #1 served
T6 - User 1 done, #2 served

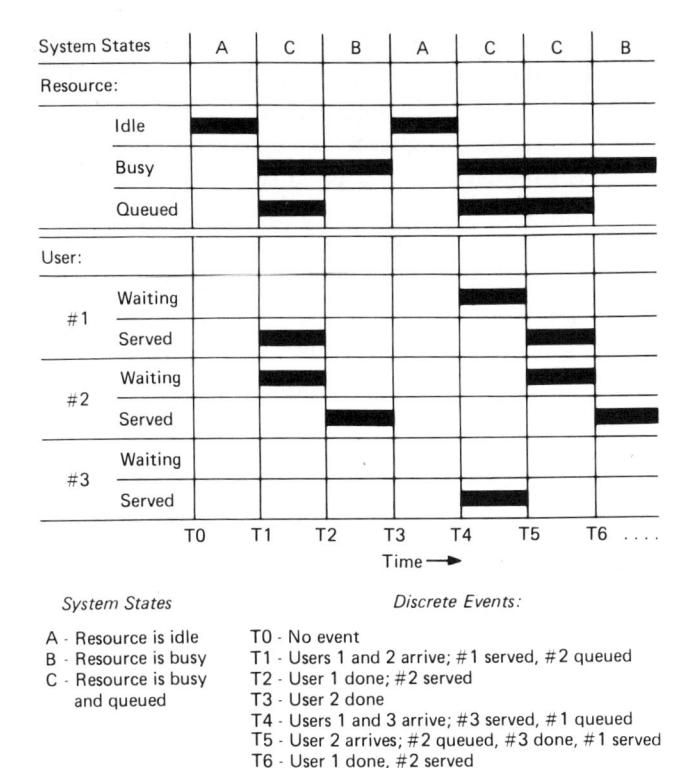

Figure 7-5. A discrete event model operating.

expanded and modified to represent, for example, an interrupt-driven multiprogramming system contending for several resources such as a processor, memory, and channels over some execution time.

Characteristics of System Variables

System variables are either deterministic or probabilistic. Deterministic variables are those with specific, defined values. Probabilistic (or stochastic) variables have values which reflect random variations and are defined by a statistical distribution or population. Some system properties may only be described through the use of a probability distribution. This may be due either to uncertainty about the behavior of the property or to lack of information regarding the property.

One common case where a system variable exhibits uncertain behavior is the rotational latency time which is needed to find the start of a record on a particular disk track. At any moment, the beginning of the record might be beneath the location of the read head so that no time would be needed to find the record start, or it may have just passed the read head and require the time needed for one complete revolution before the read operation could begin. Of course, the start of the record might also be anywhere between these two extremes. The equipment specifications may be used to parameterize this model. The time to find the beginning of any record, or latency time, is usually given as the time for a disk to complete one-half of a complete revolution. So the model for this portion of a disk access for a disk with a specified latency of 41 milliseconds would be a random selection of a time from a square or uniform distribution with a minimum value of one millisecond (assuming that one millisecond is the minimum time unit used in this model) and a maximum value of 82 milliseconds. This time would normally be modified to include the time needed to move the head to the proper track and the time to transfer the record if these were factors of interest in the simulation.

A probabilistic variable could also be used to encode a modeler's uncertainty about the value of some process or element in the simulation. This is often necesary to specify the execution time of a program or set of programs and it may also be used to describe the numbers of records, units, or other system elements for a particular execution. There are many cases where a statistical approach is the only reasonable way to characterize a particular property.

Random processes are easily implemented by using simulation. The computer enables a simulation to be rerun many times so that the analyst may observe the effect of random input changes on the output of the models. This is termed *Monte Carlo* simulation. The result of running in this fashion is statistical quantification of system performance. In fact, without the capability to perform Monte Carlo simulation, systems with statistically varying properties might well be precluded from observation. Hand-computed statistical solutions may be mathematically impossible, or, if possible, less accurate due to the necessity for coarsening assumptions needed to effect all but the simplest of situations.

Elements of Discrete Event Models

The major elements of a typical discrete event system or subsystem model are: *resources, flow-of-events,* and *demand.* Resources and flow-of-events are termed *entities.* The characteristics of entities are called *attributes.*

Resources are the facilities of a system. They represent those elements which the system allocates to its users and for which the users compete. Resources may carry attributes such as group identification and queue servicing rules.

Flow-of-events represents the sequential and logical ordering of user operations in the system. The flow-of-events involves both the resources and time consumed by the user as the user's state changes. In this process, users are created, operated upon, and destroyed. Each flow-of-events may carry such attributes as priority ranking.

Demand represents the schedule of use of the system facilities. This is usually expressed as the creation or arrival of users at the system's interface with the outside world.

The level at which flow-of-events and resources are described is of specific interest. The level for the flow-of-events denotes the fineness (measured in time) in compartmentalization or granularity between event transitions or steps. For resources, level connotes the fineness in differentiation of attributes and multiplicity.

The names given to elements of a model differ in the various simulation languages. Figure 7-6 shows the elements of discrete event models and general terminology associated with them in many simulation languages. This figure also breaks down the elements into the terminology which is normally encountered in both the supermarket and the computer system simulation examples.

Individual events are a subset of the flow-of-events. When the process being modeled is complex, a flow-of-events may be embedded in some larger or more general flow-of-events. This is analogous to the idea of a subroutine in a computer program.

The basic events of a model are characterized by the attribute of time. Time is expressed as a multiple of the simulation's Minimum Time Unit (MTU). The MTU is the smallest segment of time which may be used for describing events. The duration of the MTU for a model is specified based upon the modeler's judgment.

Elements	General Terminology of Simulation Languages
Resources	Elements, Servers
Flow-of-Events	Processes, Users, Applications, Transactions
Individual Events	Task, Service, State Change, Operation
Demand	Schedule, Arrival Rate, Loading

	Supermarket	Computer System
Resources	Carts	CPU
	Clerks	Buffers
	Aisles	Memory
Flow-of-Events	Shoppers	Applications
	Manager	Jobs
		Operating System
Individual Events	Securing Cart	Transimission
	Shopping	Scheduling
	Checkout	Processing
	Depositing Cart	I/O
Demand	Shoppers Interarrival Rate	Message Interarrival Rate
	Manager Schedule	Job Mix and Schedule

Figure 7-6. Discrete event model elements.

Resources are the elements which are allocated to users, retained by users, and competed for among users. Some resources are movable and others are fixed. Movable resources are those which may be shifted from place to place in the system by the users; fixed resources are used in place. Computer systems are largely composed of fixed resources like processors, channels, buffers, and so on. Examples of movable resources or a computer system are code and data which may be moved from one storage device to another, and the personnel of a facility which might move to various locations within the installation. These examples of movable resources also serve to illustrate opposite ends of a modeling spectrum—the coarse model encompassing people and machinery and the finer model including the effects of such things as software segment residence. Another significant feature of models of computer systems is the interconnectivity of resources. *Interconnectivity* describes paths or routes which must be followed through other resources in order to use some specific resource. Interconnectivity is an important consideration in discrete event models of computer systems because the accessibility of many resources is dependent upon the accessibility of other resources—

e.g., the accessibility of a processor is usually dependent on the accessibility of memory, and an I/O device on a channel, and so forth.

Consideration of the flow-of-events requires, as well as the scope and level appropriate for the model, identification of the dynamic processes to be simulated. Applications are the system users so that, in mapping their flow-of-events, attention must be paid to the structure or dynamic processes of the applications and to the level of detail needed to describe each application. The characteristic steps in models of each application might be at the level of code execution, application program execution, or entire job execution. At one level, execution steps could be identified as: I/O operations, execution processing, and overhead scheduling. At a finer level, the I/O processing could be differentiated into I/O setup overhead processing, I/O record access, record read/write time, and so forth. Figure 7-7 depicts a detailed flow-of-events for processing an application program showing the resources bound to each operation. (Different computer system architectures would usually require that the resources bound and the times shown as representative in Figure 7-7 be changed.)

The representative times shown in Figure 7-7 are only those times which can be predefined. Increased demands for resources which would occur as the flow-of-events of some other application began to interact with the flow shown in this figure would cause queuing to occur. These queue times would need to be allowed for in the overall discrete event model. Taking this into account, processing time would equal the service times plus the queue times.

The demand description in a model of a computer system would give the starting specifications for each application or other request on the system in question. For example, a typical real-time computer demand specification could indicate that a particular "update" application has exponentially distributed interarrival times with a mean of three hundred milliseconds. An error-checking application might occur at a regular interval each five hundred milliseconds as its specification. A typical batch application demand specification would call for use of a "sort" routine on an hourly basis (or daily, weekly, etc.). Other applications may have a demand specification as a continuously occuring process—one which either never ends during

158 COMPUTER PERFORMANCE EVALUATION

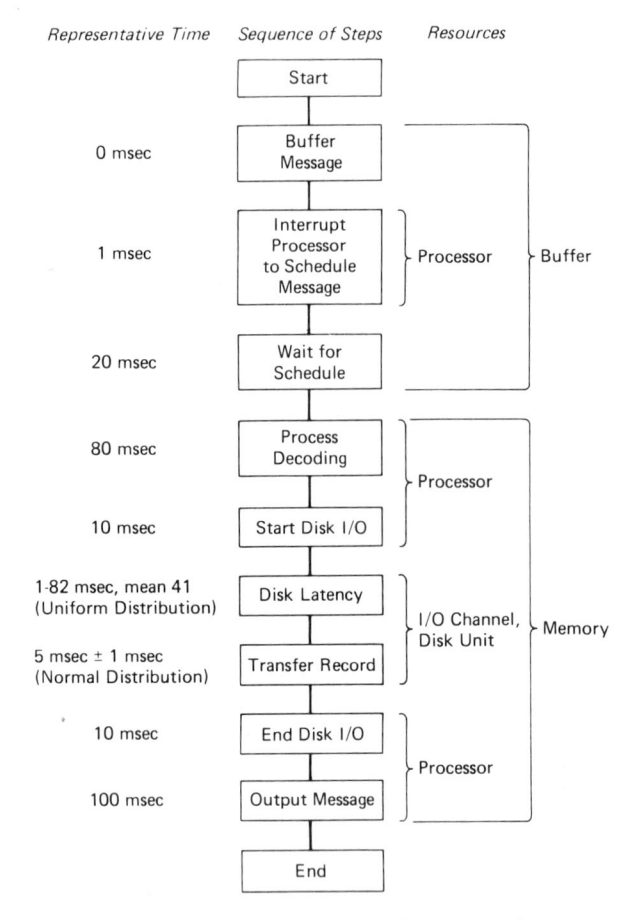

Representative Time	Sequence of Steps	Resources
	Start	
0 msec	Buffer Message	
1 msec	Interrupt Processor to Schedule Message	Processor — Buffer
20 msec	Wait for Schedule	
80 msec	Process Decoding	Processor
10 msec	Start Disk I/O	
1-82 msec, mean 41 (Uniform Distribution)	Disk Latency	I/O Channel, Disk Unit — Memory
5 msec ± 1 msec (Normal Distribution)	Transfer Record	
10 msec	End Disk I/O	Processor
100 msec	Output Message	
	End	

Figure 7-7. Flow-of-events and resources for a computing process.

the time considered in the simulation or which regenerates itself upon each completion. Examples of this type of demand include background jobs and processes. Some processes could require demand definitions using combinations of these four demand types (random, nonrandom, periodic, and continuous).

Output of Discrete Event Models

It has been mentioned that the output of simulation may be grouped into three major categories: system performance, system resource usage, and system history. These categories apply to the output of discrete event models and they will be described here in further detail.

System performance is usually given in user-oriented terms: the number and types of users served, the time statistics for processing users, and queuing statistics for user congestion. System performance for the supermarket model would include such things as the number and type of shoppers and the average time to process each type of shopper. For the computer example, system performance outputs would describe the number and types of messages processed, the ratio of message initiations to message completions, or the queuing incurred for various types of messages.

System resource usage output would reflect such things as the number and duration of uses of individual resources and the congestion or queues associated with those resources. Output for a computer model would show usage of processors, channels, segments, etc., along with the queues at each resource. The supermarket model would show such things as average use of carts, cash registers, clerks, and so forth.

System history output traces the significant system events and their changes of state to characterize particular activities in detail. History outputs are different from performance and usage output in that both performance and usage data are given as summary statistics showing the ending conditions of events while history data trace the various situations encountered throughout the processing of an event. Models of computer systems typically provide system history outputs at the level of a "program trace" for the execution of any application of interest. System history output for a supermarket model might be concerned with breaking an event like "select canned goods" into information about the number of cans of a specific product examined and delays encountered in so doing. System history output is quite valuable in the initial verification and validation, or "trouble-shooting" phase of model development as intermediate statistics are made available to the analyst at a detailed level.

APPLICATIONS IN THE COMPUTER SYSTEM LIFE CYCLE

In Chapter 1 the life cycle of a computer system was discussed in four user-oriented phases. These phases were procurement, installation, operation, and transition. These phases represent a continuously evolving process from the conceptual design of a system through its acquisition, use, old age, and rejuvenation or replacement. This life cycle viewpoint provides a contextual backdrop for discussing the application and utility of the simulation process. One further area which needs to be a part of this discussion is the application of simulation in the design and manufacture of computer systems.

During the procurement phase, simulation is the principal CPE tool. Simulation is used to aid in designing and specifying the workload which will be supported by the planned system. The wide diversity of the work which may be performed by today's computer systems represents a major challenge to analysis by any means other than simulation. As models of the diverse workload are developed, tremendous insight may be gained by running these models against models of a range of possible systems and configurations to establish ranges of performance effectiveness by equipment classes. Such an exercise is known as *sizing* the configuration. The information obtained during a sizing project allows major long-term projections to be made of such important items as system cost, space and utility requirements, and estimates of the number of personnel needed to operate the anticipated equipment. Initial sizing efforts can produce invaluable planning data even though the simulation models only require order-of-magnitude accuracies.

As the procurement phase matures, the information about the intended workload will be refined and this information can be used to improve the models of the total system. The results from such refined models may be used to produce detailed specifications for use in requests for proposals from equipment suppliers. Only in the final step of the procurement phase—equipment selection—does simulation become inadequate for the task. Although it is sometimes possible to select very small or purely batch-oriented serial systems using the results of simulation, equipment selections are usually based on comparisons of differences in performance that are simply too small to be within the bounds of the accuracy of the modeling process. Selections are better accomplished by actual observations of competing configurations running benchmarks of the intended workload (see Chapter 6).

The installation phase of a systems's life cycle is almost entirely hardware-oriented. It involves the energizing, connection, checkout, and acceptance testing of the selected configuration. The operating system and initial applications will be brought to operational status and the total system will be readied for useful production. There are seldom any opportunities to use simulation during the installation phase.

Once the operational phase begins, simulation again becomes a useful tool for obtaining data. In some cases the computer manufacturer will provide simulation models of the system to the purchaser to aid in activating system applications in an orderly, effective manner. Such an application is helpful when the system must be in operation nearly all of the time so that tests of such things as new scheduling approaches or data management techniques cannot be done directly. In these cases, simulation can be used to test and screen the effects of enhancements, so that any available test time may be used for the most promising enhancement trials. Simulation experiments can determine such things as the optimum location of programs in main storage or the best distribution of records in direct access storage. Simulation is also sufficiently accurate to determine whether new components like processors or memory modules are required, or whether proposed new workloads can be accommodated. As the system ages, simulation is an extremely useful tool for projecting workload growth and predicting the time when the equipment will no longer handle the total load.

The transition phase is quite like the procurement phase in that it is a time of preparation and planning. Simulation is the primary CPE tool throughout the transition phase at the end of a system's life cycle. Simulation applications provide data to justify the expansion or replacement of the existing equipment based on the recognized growth or change of the current workload. Simulation is often valuable late in a system's life by showing ways of redistributing or eliminating work to delay the time when new equipment must be purchased. The transition phase of an existing system is heavily overlapped with the procurement and sometimes the installation phases of the replacement system. This causes severe demands on the available simulation analysts and many of the potential benefits which might be obtained during the transition phase are lost due to necessary concentration on the follow-up system. It is seldom worthwhile to try to staff to cope with all of the potentially profitable uses of simulation during the infrequent times when transition/procurement/installation are encountered. This is an ideal time to use outside consultants to meet the unusual peak demands for scarce CPE talent.

Computer system manufacturers are probably the largest individual users of simulation. Their applications are generally invisible to computer users unless the users know to ask for assistance from their equipment manufacturers when simulation projects are contemplated. Manufacturers rely heavily on simulation in the design of each new architecture and most new components. They also use simulation to aid the development of control programs and major utility programs. The vast experience and understanding of their equipment gained during design and development projects is put to use when they market their systems. Usually the marketing staff of a computer manufacturer has a highly skilled simulation group which is relied upon to make the initial estimates of configurations needed to successfully respond to requests for proposals from potential buyers. These simulations go beyond estimating the proper number of specific components and their interconnection, to such details as the dynamic properties of multiplexors and transmission line controllers under loads stated by the prospective buyer. At times, manufacturers employ simulation on a much broader scale to assess the effect of automating manual operations to prepare proposals for major changes in the operational approach of potential customers. Computer users who employ simulation should make the effort needed to become acquainted with the simulation analysts of the manufacturer of their brand of equipment. These groups probably represent the richest source of information about and assistance with the details of applying simulation to their systems.

LIMITATIONS AND STRENGTHS

The major drawbacks to the use of simulation are that it is both expensive to use and very time-consuming. Simulation results may be misleading or wrong if the models are not checked thoroughly and validated. Beyond these application-oriented limitations there may also be personnel-oriented problems. There is sometimes a tendency for an "ivory tower" atmosphere to develop around the simulation technicians that could inhibit the group from doing useful work by creating a barrier between the simulators and other individuals with whom they must interact. People who are really good at using simulation are usually highly creative and independent-minded. Because of this, they are more difficult to manage as a group than are most other technical teams. Finally, every good simulation team is subject to continuous proselytism by other departments and employers. Managing a simulation group is a significant challenge for most first- and second-level managers.

The major advantage to the use of simulation is that simulation gives answers to even the most difficult problems. Simulation provides an artificial laboratory for dealing with complex, large, unknown, or expensive subjects where even the most exotic alternatives may be examined without harmful consequences. The high cost of using simulation is generally paid back several-fold in savings from improvements to existing systems, from developing better new systems, and from learning ahead of time not to create bad systems. The methodology of simulation makes management decisions easier by revealing the important elements of a problem along with alternative solutions to the problem.

8
Analytic Models

There are more similarities between analytic modeling and simulation than there are differences. Analytic models might be considered as a subset or special case of simulation. The key difference between the two as they are used in CPE is that analytic models are deterministic while simulation models are nondeterministic. That is, the input to an analytic model produces a single, repeatable set of outputs. A simulation model usually produces a range of outputs for any set of inputs; rerunning a simulation model with the same inputs may produce slightly different values as output.

Analytic models are recent additions to the tools available for CPE projects. Even though analytic modeling predates computers by many years, it was believed that computer systems were too complex to be handled by so simple an approach as analytic modeling. Oddly enough, this approach has proven most valuable in analyzing on-line, transaction-oriented systems which are most difficult to examine by using simulation or other analysis methods. Many simplifications are necessary to apply analytic models, but, for the most part, these do not severely restrict the modeler, nor do they limit the usefulness of the results. Analytic models give extremely fast, reasonably accurate, and acceptably detailed solutions to many common problems.

Credit for making analytic models a practical tool for CPE projects belongs to Dr. Jeffrey P. Buzen. Material in this chapter is based in large part on several papers which he authored. A few of Dr. Buzen's significant publications are listed in the Analytic Models section of the Suggested Readings at the end of this book for individuals wishing further information on this topic.

DEFINITION

Analytic models of computer systems are sets of mathematical equations whose independent variables (inputs) produce a single set of dependent variables (outputs).

The definition given of simulation at the beginning of the previous chapter could be adapted for analytic models simply by dropping the last two words, "over time". Analytic modeling is most useful during the operations phase of a computer system's life cycle for testing the effect of relatively small changes to various components of the equipment configuration. Analytic modeling is also useful for estimating when bottlenecks will occur and which parts of the configuration will be the likely causes of these bottlenecks.

Since analytic models are quite simple and since they are not normally understood by most managers, analytic models will be described here in detail by using examples of actual models. This approach necessarily requires the use of some mathematical notation but no more than basic arithmetic should be needed to follow through any of the examples. As used for CPE projects, analytic models rely on a branch of mathematics known as "queuing theory." It is not necessary to understand queuing theory to understand how analytic models are used; however, the individual who actually applies analytic models should have a reasonable understanding of queuing theory. This topic is considered to be outside the scope of this book and is only mentioned as an area which should be in the background of the individual who creates and uses analytic models.

QUEUES

Queuing means waiting in line for some service. There are many types of queues. Figure 8-1 shows a single-server queue. This queue could be used to model a tool booth, a box office window, a check-

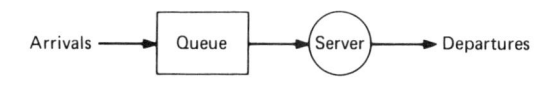

Figure 8-1. A single-server queue.

166 COMPUTER PERFORMANCE EVALUATION

out counter, a typist, a central processor, a disk drive, or any number of other physical situations.

There are many other kinds of queues which should come to mind, but this simplest of queues is sufficient for introducing the application of analytic models. Queues may be in series where the departures from one queue become the arrivals at another queue. They may also be in series with branches so that departures from the first queue (or queues) become arrivals at two or more other queues, and these series may be iterative. That is, any arrival may have to go through several queues more than once before finally departing from the system. Figure 8-2 shows a series of single-server queues that branch and are used iteratively.

The question that faces every arrival at a queue or series of queues is: "How long will it take to become a departure?" Only two things need to be known to answer this question: the service time for each server and the arrival rate at each queue. These are normally abbreviated *s* and *a*, respectively. These are the *independent variables* of the portion of queuing theory discussed here. The *dependent variable* which answers the above question is called *R*, for *response time*. A second dependent variable which is often useful may also be calculated for any set of independent variables. This variable is called *U*, for *utilization of the server*.

The queuing equations, or analytic models, for the single-server queue are as follows:

$$U = a \times s,$$ or utilization equals arrival rate multiplied by service time

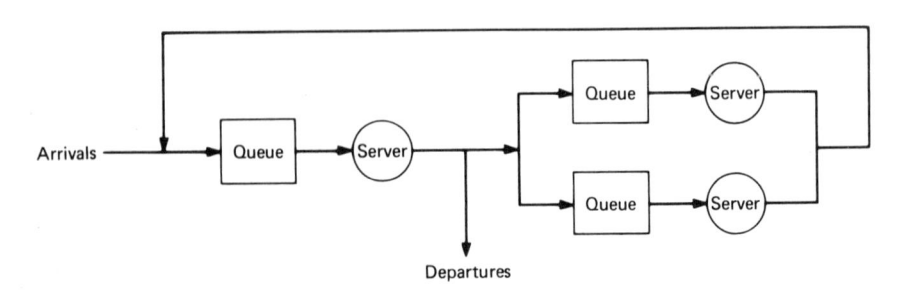

Figure 8-2. A series of single-server queues.

and
$$R = s/(1 - a \times s)$$ or response time equals service time divided by one minus utilization

which is also written as
$$R = s/(1 - U)$$

The second way of writing the equation for R contains U as though U were an independent variable. It is not; it is simply written this way since the value of a times s, or U, is conventionally solved first and there is no point in repeating the multiplication when the value of U is already known. At this point, enough is known of queuing theory to solve some interesting and rather complex problems about computer performance.

A MODEL OF A COMPUTER SYSTEM

Suppose that the single-server queue shown in Figure 8-1 represents an entire computer system. If it were known that, on the average, ten jobs were introduced to this system every hour and that an average job required three minutes (.05 hours) of system time, then the question about how long it would take for an average job to be completed could be answered with the stated analytic models:

$$U = a \times s$$
$$= 10 \times .05$$
$$= .50 \text{ (or the system would be 50\% busy)}$$

and
$$R = s/(1 - U)$$
$$= .05/(1 - .50)$$
$$= .10 \text{ hours (or six minutes for an average job)}$$

Note that even in this very simple example, the effects of queuing for resources in the total system are observable. The average job requires only three minutes of system time but it takes six minutes to go from being an arrival to being a departure. The other three minutes would be explained as time spent in the queue waiting for system resources to become available. At this level of modeling it is not possible to say which system resources cause the queuing or even whether waiting could be attributed any more to one resource than to another.

Refining this model, suppose that the series of single-server queues shown in Figure 8-2 were redrawn and labeled as parts of a computer system. Figure 8-3 shows such a change with a CPU in place of the first server and DISK #1 and DISK #2 as the second two servers. The arrivals and departures are also relabeled as the familiar "INPUT" and "OUTPUT" of a computer system. In accomplishing this refinement of the model it is necessary to know a little more about the working of the system. For the sake of explanation, the number of times that an arrival visits any one of the servers, or resources, of the system is referred to as $v(1)$, $v(2)$, and $v(3)$, where $v(1)$ is visits to the CPU, $v(2)$ visits to DISK #1, and $v(3)$ visits to DISK #2. Similarly, $s(1)$, $s(2)$, and $s(3)$ represent the service times at the CPU, DISK #1, and DISK #2, respectively.

The Equations

It should be mentioned before going further with the examples that the analytic models being used are dependent on a few assumptions of queuing theory. It is sufficient to say that these assumptions are generally satisfied by the behavior of a computer system, particularly an online transaction processing system. It is generally easier to apply queuing theory in analytic models without concern over whether the assumptions are met and then to *validate* the results of the model against actual measured data than to spend time trying to prove that the assumptions of queuing theory are met. If the model's results compare favorably with measured data, the assumptions may be considered to have been fulfilled. This may not be a mathematically pure approach, but it usually works in modeling computer systems.

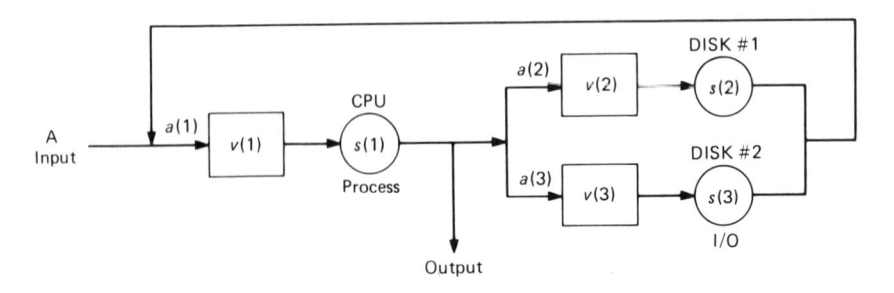

Figure 8-3. A model of a computer system.

ANALYTIC MODELS   169

In CPE projects it is the results that matter, not the purity of the method. The assumptions are concerned with the randomness of both the arrivals and the service times. Most internal functions of computer systems are sufficiently close to random to apply queuing theory without worrying over such factors.

There are also a few conventions of mathematics which will be used to simplify writing the expanded equations needed to describe this system. These conventions may need explanation. When variables are written using the same letter but followed by numbers to distinguish one variable from another, like $s(1)$, $s(2)$, and $s(3)$, above, they are referred to collectively as "the variables $s(i)$." Often this would be followed by the explanation, "for $i = 1, 2, 3$." Entire sets of equations can be written very quickly by using this convention. For example:

$$U(i) = a(i) \times s(i), \text{ for } i = 1,2, \ldots n$$

means that there are any number, n, sets of independent variables a and s, and that there are an equal number, n, of dependent variables, U, that correspond to these variables. If n were 100, then the above would be the same as writing 100 sets of equations of the form $U(1) = a(1) \times s(1)$, etc. There is no relationship implied or intended between variables using the same letter, say a, and different numbers or "subscripts." That is, $a(3)$ and $a(8)$ are not necessarily related in any way other than that they are both arrival rates. One arrival rate could be two per hour and the other fifty per millisecond.

Using this convention, the analytic model of the system shown in Figure 8-3 can be represented by the *six* equations:

and
$$U(i) = a(i) \times s(i)$$
$$R(i) = s(i)/(1 - U(i)), \text{ for } i = 1,2,3$$

These equations are in the form that will be used for all subsequent examples. There are *six* equations because, when the values of i are substituted, three equations for U ($U(1)$, $U(2)$, and $U(3)$) and three equations for R ($R(1)$, $R(2)$, and $R(3)$) would result.

The Parameters

Knowing the equations that must be solved to model a computer system, the remaining items that must be determined are the specific values of the independent variables, a and s. The service times, or $s(i)$, may be measured directly by some available tool like a software or hardware monitor. Typically, this would require collection of the time that each "server" was busy and a count of the number of transactions entered into the system and of the number of I/Os at each disk unit. This is a relatively simple process and will be dealt with in a moment. Determining the arrival rates, or $a(i)$, for each server is generally somewhat more difficult. In the system shown in Figure 8-3, it may be reasoned that the processor is "visited" the same number of times as the disks, *plus one*. The final visit would be the one before the "output" for this system. Mathematically, this may be written as:

$$v(1) = v(2) + v(3) + 1$$

Or the number of visits to the CPU is equal to the number of visits to disk #1 plus the number of visits to disk #2 plus one. This fact will be used later to avoid the more difficult problem of making a precise count of the use of a CPU when the generally easy count of the use of disks may be used just as well.

Each transaction, or arrival, would be expected to cause some number of "visits" to each resource in the system. These visits would be broken down to determine arrival rates for each queue shown in Figure 8-3. The arrival rate for the CPU, $a(1)$, would be found by multiplying the observed number of transactions per second, a_T, by the number of visits to the CPU, $v(1)$. The disk arrival rates would be found in the same way. The formulas would be:

$$a(i) = a_T \times v(i), \text{ for } i = 1, 2, 3$$

Call this set of equations "Set #1".

Determining the service times, or $s(i)$, involves only a measurement of the time that each resource is used and the count of the uses of the I/O devices. Here, this amounts to accumulating CPU time, disk times, and a count of the I/Os on each disk. Suppose that the time each resource is used is represented by $B(i)$, for $i = 1, 2, 3$, and that the number of I/Os to each disk is abbreviated $I(i)$, for $i = 2, 3$. The total numer of transactions during the period may be called A. (Don't confuse this A with a_T, which is the arrival rate, not the total number of arrivals.) If the period of interest is called T, then:

$$a_T = A \div T$$

The service times for each resource would be found by using the following formulas:

$$s(i) = B(i)/(A \times v(i)), \text{ for } i = 1, 2, 3$$

Call this set of equations "Set #2".

Data Collection

At this point only a few easily measured pieces of data need to be collected to use the analytic models: the length of the measurement period (T), the total number of transactions which occur during this period (A), the busy time of the CPU and each disk ($B(i)$, for $i = 1, 2, 3$), and the number of I/Os for each disk ($I(i)$, for $i = 2, 3$). Suppose that the following measurements were collected for each of these items:

T = 30 minutes (or 1800 seconds)
A = 9000 transactions
$B(1)$ = 486 seconds of CPU busy time
$B(2)$ = 360 seconds of disk #1 busy time
$B(3)$ = 900 seconds of disk #2 busy time
$I(2)$ = 9000 I/Os for disk #1 and
$I(3)$ = 36000 I/Os for disk #2

In addition to the data needed to apply the models, it is also reasonable to collect enough information to validate the results of the model. In this example, and in most real applications, the utilization of each resource ($U(i)$, for $i = 1, 2, 3$) is directly available from data collection tools. From the above data, utilizations are easily calculated from busy times ($B(i)$, for $i = 1, 2, 3$) divided by elapsed time (T):

$$U(1) = 486/1800$$
$$= .27 \text{ or } 27\% \text{ busy}$$
$$U(2) = 360/1800$$
$$= .20 \text{ or } 20\% \text{ busy}$$
$$U(3) = 900/1800$$
$$= .50 \text{ or } 50\% \text{ busy}$$

The overall system response time ($R(T)$) is usually of primary interest rather than the response time of each server ($R(i)$, for $i = 1, 2, 3$) and it is not normally as easy to measure the server response times as it is to measure the overall system response time. Suppose that this additional measure was made solely for purposes of validation later and showed that:

$$R(T) = 0.330 \text{ seconds per transaction}$$

Determining the Independent Variables

The number of visits to disks #1 and #2 per transaction may be determined by dividing the number of I/Os for each disk by the total number of transactions:

$$v(2) = I(2)/A$$
$$= 9000/9000$$
$$= 1 \text{ visit per transaction for disk \#1}$$
$$v(3) = I(3)/A$$
$$= 36000/9000$$
$$= 4 \text{ visits per transaction for disk \#2}$$

The number of visits per transaction to the CPU ($v(1)$) may be found by recalling that it was established earlier that:

$$v(1) = v(2) + v(3) + 1$$
$$= 1 \quad + 4 \quad + 1$$
$$= 6$$

The average transaction rate (a_T) would be the total number of transactions (A) divided by the elapsed time (T):

$$a_T = A/T$$
$$= 9000/1800$$
$$= 5 \text{ transactions per second}$$

Now the independent variables ($a(i)$ and $s(i)$, for $i = 1, 2, 3$) may be calculated using the equations developed above and called "Set #1" and "Set #2":

$$a(1) = a_T \times v(1)$$
$$= 5 \times 6$$
$$= 30 \text{ arrivals per second for the CPU}$$
$$a(2) = a_T \times v(2)$$
$$= 5 \times 1$$
$$= 5 \text{ arrivals per second for disk #1}$$

and

$$a(3) = a_T \times v(3)$$
$$= 5 \times 4$$
$$= 20 \text{ arrivals per second for disk #2}$$

And the service times:

$$s(1) = B(1)/(A \times v(1))$$
$$= 486/(9000 \times 6)$$
$$= .009 \text{ seconds}$$
$$s(2) = B(2)/(A \times v(2))$$
$$= 360/(9000 \times 1)$$
$$= .040 \text{ seconds}$$

and

$$s(3) = B(3)/(A \times v(3))$$
$$= 900/(9000 \times 4)$$
$$= .025 \text{ seconds}$$

The analytic models may be solved at this point:

$$U(1) = a(1) \times s(1)$$
$$= 30 \times .009$$
$$= .27 \text{ or } 27\% \text{ CPU utilization}$$

$$U(2) = a(2) \times s(2)$$
$$= 5 \times .040$$
$$= .20 \text{ or } 20\% \text{ disk \#1 utilization}$$

and

$$U(3) = a(3) \times s(3)$$
$$= 20 \times .025$$
$$= .50 \text{ or } 50\% \text{ disk \#2 utilization}$$

And the response times for each component are:

$$R(1) = s(1)/(1 - U(1))$$
$$= .009/(1 - .27)$$
$$= .0123 \text{ seconds for the CPU}$$
$$R(2) = s(2)/(1 - U(2))$$
$$= .040/(1 - .20)$$
$$= .050 \text{ seconds for disk \#1}$$

and

$$R(3) = s(3)/(1 - U(3))$$
$$= .025/(1 - .50)$$
$$= .050 \text{ seconds for disk \#2}$$

The total system's response time $R(T)$ in this particular structure would be found by adding up the time spent on each resource for one average transaction. This amounts to multiplying the number of visits to each resource by the time spent at that resource:

$$R(T) = v(1) \times R(1) + v(2) \times R(2) + v(3) \times R(3)$$
$$= 6 \times .0123 + 1 \times .050 + 4 \times .050$$
$$= .0738 + .050 + .200$$
$$= .324 \text{ seconds per average transaction}$$

Validation

It was pointed out earlier that validation is necessary when using analytic models for computer systems. This is so because queuing theory is based on assumptions and these assumptions may not be satisfied by the system at the time when it is being examined. Carrying out the validation also gives the modeler confidence that the models should make correct predictions of the impact of changes—

which cannot be validated ahead of time. Validation requires no more than a direct comparison between the calculated values and the corresponding measured values. The data derived above and measured earlier is set forth below in tabular form to make such a comparison.

	calculated	measured	error
$U(1)$	.27	.27	0
$U(2)$	.20	.20	0
$U(3)$	.50	.50	0
$R(1)$	.0123	——	–
$R(2)$	.050	——	–
$R(3)$	.050	——	–
$R(T)$	.324	.330	.006 or about 2%

Based on this comparison it could be concluded that the models are sufficiently valid for most practical applications. If the 2% error in total response time was declared unacceptable, more detailed measurements of the CPU and disk times would be needed. Based on these more detailed measures, small adjustments could be made in the independent variables to bring the final calculated result as close to the measured value as considered necessary.

APPLYING THE MODEL AS A PREDICTIVE TOOL

The primary purpose of modeling is to determine how a system would perform under various changes. The kinds of changes most often encountered at computer installations are workload increases and equipment modification. Even with the very simple model explained above, both of these kinds of changes may be assessed.

For example, suppose that the workload of the system modeled could be doubled. Would this equipment handle the increased workload? In terms of the models, the question may be restated as: Would doubling the arrival rates with the same service times produce acceptable response time?

$a(1)$ = 60 arrivals per second
$a(2)$ = 10 arrivals per second   double previous $a(i)$
$a(3)$ = 40 arrivals per second

176 COMPUTER PERFORMANCE EVALUATION

and
$$s(1) = .009 \text{ seconds}$$
$$s(2) = .040 \text{ seconds}$$
$$s(3) = .025 \text{ seconds}$$

no change in $s(i)$

Then the analytic models may be applied:

$$U(1) = 60 \times .009 = .54$$
$$U(2) = 10 \times .040 = .40$$
$$U(3) = 40 \times .025 = 1.00 \text{ (not allowed, } 0 \leq U < 1)$$

and
$$R(1) = .009/(1 - .54) = .0196$$
$$R(2) = .040/(1 - .40) = .0667$$
$$R(3) = .025/(1 - 1) = ?? \text{ (no solution)}$$

Therefore, the current equipment would not handle a doubled workload and disk #2 would be the limiting resource.

Suppose it was possible to move one-fourth of the I/Os from disk #2 to disk #1. Would the double workload then fit?

	old	new
$a(1)$	60	60
$a(2)$	10	20
$a(3)$	40	30

The service times ($s(i)$) would still be unchanged. Inserting the new arrival rates into the analytic models and solving:

$$U(1) = 60 \times .009 = .54$$
$$U(2) = 20 \times .040 = .80$$
$$U(3) = 30 \times .025 = .75$$

and
$$R(1) = .009/(1 - .54) = .0196$$
$$R(2) = .040/(1 - .80) = .2000$$
$$R(3) = .025/(1 - .75) = .1000$$

and
$$R(T) = 6 \times .0196 + 2 \times .2000 + 3 \times .1000$$
$$= .8176 \text{ seconds per transaction}$$

Here the models predict that the doubled workload would be handled by this equipment with the shift of I/Os from disk #2 to disk #1 and the resulting response time would be about 2½ times longer than the original workload (.8176 versus .324 seconds per transaction).

Another type of problem that is quite common at computer installations is that of estimating the effect of equipment changes. Suppose that the original workload level and distribution of disk activity was not expected to change but that a processor of one-half of the original processor's speed might be obtained. Would the new CPU support the workload?

In this case all arrival rates would remain unchanged as would the service times for the two disks, but the service time for the CPU would be doubled from .009 to .018 seconds per visit. Solving the models with this one changed independent variable:

$$U(1) = 30 \times .018 = .54$$
$$U(2) = 5 \times .040 = .20$$
$$U(3) = 20 \times .025 = .50$$

and

$$R(1) = .018/(1 - .54) = .039$$
$$R(2) = .040/(1 - .20) = .050$$
$$R(3) = .025/(1 - .50) = .050$$

and

$$R(T) = 6 \times .039 + 1 \times .050 + 4 \times .050$$
$$= .484 \text{ seconds per transaction}$$

The slower CPU is predicted to slow response time by about 50%.

If some option became available that increased the effective speed of the disks by 10%, what would happen to response time if the option were bought? That is $s(2)$ decreases from .040 to .036, and $s(3)$ from .025 to .0225.

$$U(1) = 30 \times .018 = .54$$
$$U(2) = 5 \times .036 = .18$$
$$U(3) = 20 \times .0225 = .45$$

and

$$R(1) = .018/(1 - .54) = .039$$
$$R(2) = .036/(1 \times .18) = .044$$
$$R(3) = .0225/(1 - .45) - .041$$

and

$$R(T) = 6 \times .039 + 1 \times .044 + 4 \times .041$$
$$= .442 \text{ seconds per transaction}$$

The faster disks would be expected to decrease response time by about 9%.

The alternatives that may be tested with this very simple model seem almost endless. Without showing the calculations, suppose the workload were to be doubled with the slower CPU and the faster disks. In this case, the CPU would be the bottleneck and the doubled workload would not fit. If the original, faster processor and the new faster disks were possible, the doubled workload would fit but response time would more than triple to 1.074 seconds per transaction (versus the original .324).

Effects of changes in programming may also be predicted. Suppose that one I/O on disk #2 could be eliminated by, say, making the index portion of one of disk #2 files memory-resident. The immediate effect of this change would be a reduction of $v(3)$ from 4 to 3. There would be no change in $v(2)$ (it would still be 1 visit per transaction) but $v(1)$ would change from 6 to 5 (because $v(1)$ still equals $v(2) + v(3) + 1$). Such a modification would have other effects as well and estimating these requires that the modeler use judgment based on an understanding of the system under study. Observing that $s(1)$ is the average amount of CPU time between I/Os and that there is now one less I/O per transaction, then the necessary CPU time would have to be spread over the reduced number of visits to the CPU. That is, originally $s(1) = .009$ seconds and $v(1) = 6$, so the total CPU time per transaction was .054 seconds (.009 × 6). With the change in $v(1)$ to 5, an initial estimate of $s(1)$ would be .0108 seconds (.054/5). This estimate ignores a potentially important fact: making the file index memory-resident not only saves an I/O operation, it also saves the CPU overhead needed to initiate that operation. If this overhead is measured or estimated at .003 seconds per transaction, the total CPU time per transaction would be .051 seconds. Then a better estimate of $s(1)$ would be .0102 seconds (.051/5). Another factor to consider is whether $s(3)$ would change. Since the index has been removed from the disk, the distribution of seek times may also change. In this case it is usually best to make an upper and lower estimate on the new $s(3)$ and solve for a range of solutions with these two values as the expected limits. If the bounds were estimated as plus or minus 10% from the original service time for disk #2, then the two new $s(3)$ values would be .0225 (.025 − 10%) and .0275 (.025 + 10%) as the lower and upper limits, respectively. Note also that, since $v(3)$ is now going to be 3 instead of 4, a reduction of disk #2 busy time should be expected (from 900 seconds to 675 seconds in an 1800 second measurement period).

Taking all of these estimates into account the new independent variables are tabulated below along with the original example's independent variables.

	original	estimated
$v(1)$	6	5
$v(2)$	1	1
$v(3)$	4	3
$a(1)$	30	25
$a(2)$	5	5
$a(3)$	20	15
$s(1)$	.009	.0102
$s(2)$	.040	.040
$s(3)$	.025	.0225–.0275

Solving the analytic models indicates that the altered program's new response time should be between .220 and .259 seconds per transaction. This would represent a reduction in response time of from 22 to 30% by making disk #2's index memory-resident. The reader is encouraged to try doubling the workload with the altered program's estimates to see whether the existing equipment would now handle this increase. (Only the $a(i)$ change—they double; the $s(i)$ remain unchanged from the estimates.)

Modeling Skills

The preceding examples illustrate the types of skills that are necessary to apply analytic models to practical problems. These skills are very different from those which are required to derive the basic equations or to carry out extensive research with queuing theory. The essential skills for application of analytic models are those needed to carry out modification analyses. These are best seen in the last example regarding the program modification to make one disk's index memory resident. The analyst must be able to determine the impact of proposed changes on the independent variables of the models and must be prepared to introduce additional assumptions to clarify or define the meaning of a proposed modification. The more the analyst knows about how the system operates, the more accurate these determinations become.

A further point that should be illustrated by going through the preceding examples is that the derivation of the equations is only of secondary importance in modeling applications. As models become more elaborate, the equations given above are replaced by computer programs which often include queuing equations of much greater complexity. Such programs have recently become available as commercial products. However, the skills needed to apply even much more sophisticated analytic models are the same as those mentioned above. These skills depend primarily on knowledge of the system being modeled and this knowledge is the most crucial ingredient for successful application of analytic models in CPE projects.

Model Extensions

Many problems may be addressed by relatively simple changes or additions to the basic models shown earlier. In many cases the basic equations for U and R remain unchanged while further sophistication is incorporated by more elaborate analysis or by finer breakout of the system components described by the models. Figure 8-4 shows a diagram for enlarging the system shown in Figure 8-3 or it may be that Figure 8-4 is simply a more detailed picture of the system studied in the examples. Further measurement would be needed to determine the distribution of "visits" to the resources shown in Figure 8-4, but the basic equations, $U(i) = a(i) \times s(i)$ and $R(i) = s(i)/(1 - U(i))$, for $i = 1, 2, 3, 4, 5, 6$, would still apply.

ANALYTIC MODELS   181

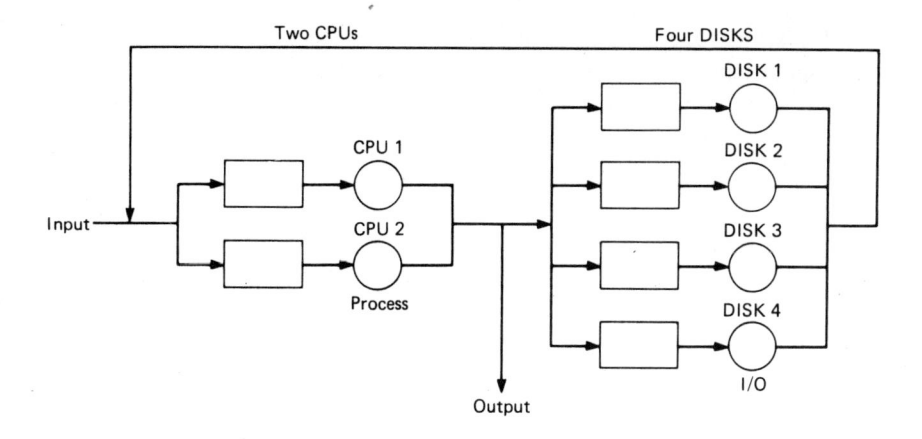

Figure 8-4. An enlarged system.

Analytic models may also be applied to different architectures. Figure 8-5 shows one type of architecture that incorporates an "I/O Processor." Such a system could still be analyzed using the models for single-server queues as expressed by $U(i)$ and $R(i)$. In this particular example, i would range from one through eight to include each of the eight separate resources shown in Figure 8-5. Again, detailed analysis of the workload and its characteristics on this architecture would be needed before the models could be solved.

There are also methods for incorporating different types of workloads into analytic models of computer systems. Typically,

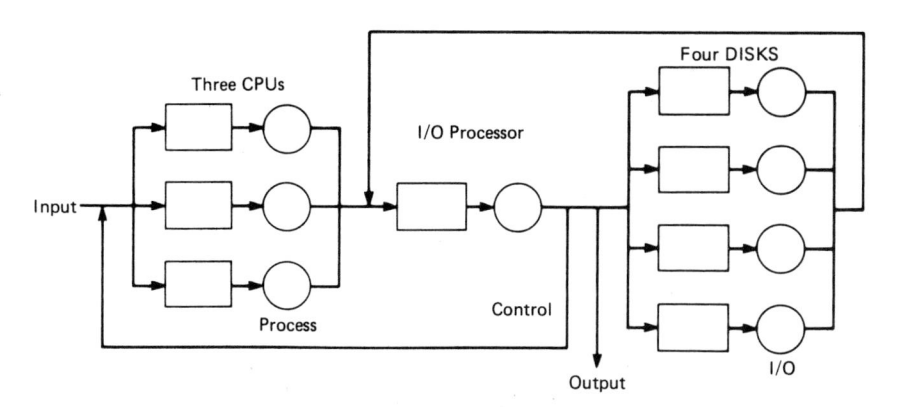

Figure 8-5. A different architecture.

most systems are simultaneously used for batch programs, transaction processing, and time sharing applications. Models can be developed which accomodate these kinds of loads. Further, such things as processing priorities, resource sharing, and contentions may be handled by more elaborate analytic models. In some cases, analytic models are implemented as online programs so that the analyst may interact directly to arrive at some set of feasible solutions as might be obtained from a simulation model. Incorporating many of these types of extensions can cause the use of analytic models to become very cumbersome. In most cases, it is far cheaper to acquire a package with a full range of these features than it is to try to develop these capabilities at an individual installation.

STRENGTHS AND LIMITATIONS
Strengths
The major advantage of analytic models over simulation is that analytic models may be applied quickly. The models can be created in a very short time and they require very little computer time to be run. Beyond this strength, it is often possible to solve analytic models manually using a small calculator. There are no language limitations when analytic models are programmed to be run on computers as they are simply sets of reasonably simple mathematical equations which can be handled by nearly any programming language. Finally, analytic models are more easily understood than are simulation models by most analysts and managers.

Limitations
The crucial disadvantage of analytic models is that the system under study may not be deterministic. Because of this it is usually unwise to try to apply analytic models in situations where validation against actual measurements is impossible. A second limitation is that the system may require study at such a fine level of detail that the system becomes too complex to solve by using analytic models. When "unrealistic" changes have to be made of the independent variables in order to validate the model, the system may be too complex for examination using analytic models. In most cases, models must be rerun for each condition which is of interest. When there are large

numbers of conditions that must be examined, these reruns may be prohibitive. Finally, when elaborate models are created "from scratch" a thorough knowledge of queuing theory is necessary. This limitation may be avoided by using a commercial package developed by individuals with the necessary queuing theory background.

As a general rule, analytic models should be used rather than simulation in cases where either could be applied.

9
Software Physics

The term "software physics" is relatively new but, unfortunately, it has already been applied in more than one way and has meant very different things. Here, software physics is used as described by Kolence* in his work with the Institute for Software Engineering. In this context, software physics provides a theoretical framework for examining the performance of computing equipment when it is subjected to various software workloads. The word "software," throughout discussions of software physics, means any instructions which may execute on a computer system regardless of whether they are all or part of user programs, operating system, utilities, and so forth.

Software physics, as any other new topic, has not been accepted as a legitimate approach without substantial controversy. Software physics is discussed in reasonable detail here because it has been used in critical environments by several CPE practitioners and has been found to be a useful and valid technique in their applications. Beyond this reason, software physics appears to provide a totally encompassing, rigorous, mathematical foundation for addressing most of the technical problems encountered in typical CPE projects. Whether this foundation will stand all tests, only time will tell.

The material presented here is introductory and should not be taken as an exhaustive description of software physics. The intent here is to explain enough about software physics, its basic units, and its simpler uses so that the reader will know what software physics is and where it might be applied. Those with deeper interest in this topic are referred to Kolence's work.

* Kolence, Kenneth W. *Introduction to Software Physics,* Institute for Software Engineering, Palo Alto, California, 1976.

SOFTWARE WORK AND SOFTWARE POWER DEFINITIONS

A basic requirement for a theory such as software physics is that the theory serve some practical purpose. The theory must provide mathematical derivations for all necessary measures, and it must formalize effective methods of using these measures with a limited number of basic measurable properties. The theory of software physics asserts that only three basic measurable properties are needed: software work, time, and storage occupancy. Software work is considered the key property since it characterizes the workload without being dependent on specific equipment or configuration characteristics. Storage capacity usage (seconds of storage occupancy) can also be converted to units of software work.

One unit of *software work* is done by a processor on some storage device when the processor transfers one 8-bit byte to that storage device. For example, a tape drive or disk drive writing a 2000-byte block does 2000 units of work on the tape or disk pack. If the same block is read, the drive does 2000 units of work on main storage. A printer does 132 units of work whenever it prints a 132-character line. A card reader does 80 units of work on main storage for each card read. A card punch does the same amount for each card punched. The central processor does a unit of work on main storage for every byte transferred into real storage. It also does a unit of work on the CPU registers for each byte accessed from main storage. The total CPU work is the sum of these two types of work. For the sake of brevity, one "unit of software work" is referred as one "work" in discussions using the terminology of software physics.

Software work can be calculated from the normal types of measurements collected by some accounting data collection routines. For peripheral drives, the software work performed is:

work = (#I/O actions) × (average block size in bytes)

For a processor, it is usually necessary at first to measure the average work per second (called *software power*) with a hardware monitor. Taking this average power value as a constant for a given processor, the common measure "CPU seconds" is easily converted to units of software work. The basic equation for software power is:

$$\text{software power} = \frac{\text{software work}}{\text{execution time}}$$

or:

$$\text{CPU work} = (\text{average CPU power}) \times (\text{CPU seconds})$$

There are many measurement tools which can be used to determine the software work for a workload, application, or other workload component. Most accounting data collection routines provide the data needed for batch and some online work. Hardware monitors can directly measure the work of the full workload or of selected portions of the workload. Software monitors can also provide much of the needed data. Together, these tools are able to collect all data needed for applications of software physics.

There are two basic ways to describe the software work done by a workload or workload component. One way is to determine the work done by subconfiguration (CPU and channel, control unit, or device). Although useful for several purposes in software physics, this characterization is not independent of the configuration. A more widely useful form is by *equipment class* for any given workload or workload component. That is, a workload or workload component is generally characterized by the work done by the CPU, by disks, by tapes, by terminals, by printers, and so forth. When this is done, the workload description is called a software work vector. A software work vector is a list of work done in each equipment class. For example:

$$\text{Software work vector} = (\text{software work of CPU,}$$
software work of disks, software work of tapes, and so forth)

Software work, and particularly the software work vector by equipment class, should be constant for a given job, application, or other workload component processing a given set of data, regardless of equipment configuration or workload job mixture. The rate at which the work is performed (the software power used) would vary as the configuration varied showing the effect of each configuration relative to the capacity requirements of the workload.

The software work vector's independence of equipment and workload mix permits the vector to be the basic method for quantitatively representing all or part of any workload. Software work is simply a statement of the capacity requirement of the workload and this expression can be applied in the many capacity management functions which require workload characterizations.

Since all other plans and planning activities depend on the forecast, the workload forecast is the basic planning function. Workload forecasting methods in software physics depend on the use of a special form of the software work vector, called the *software unit vector*.

Example 1

Generally, the software work vector contains elements or numbers representing the work performed in each equipment class. However, a simplified vector composed of just the work by the CPU, disks, and tapes can be used to illustrate the technique. For a given application, job, or other workload component of interest, work can be measured by equipment class and represented by a software work vector as below:

$$\text{software work} = \begin{bmatrix} \text{CPU work} \\ \text{disk work} \\ \text{tape work} \end{bmatrix}$$

Assume the job does 600 units of CPU work, 200 units of disk work, and 100 units of tape work. The total work is the sum of the work done in all equipment classes (here, 900 units). This may be written in vector notation as above and subjected to mathematical operations:

$$\text{software work} = \begin{bmatrix} 600 \\ 200 \\ 100 \end{bmatrix} = 900 \times \begin{bmatrix} 600 \div 900 \\ 200 \div 900 \\ 100 \div 900 \end{bmatrix}$$

$$= 900 \times \begin{bmatrix} .67 \\ .22 \\ .11 \end{bmatrix}$$

$$= (\text{total software work}) \times (\text{the software unit vector})$$

The vector quantity (0.67, 0.22, 0.11) is called the software unit vector. It is called a unit vector because the sum of the elements is equal to 1.00. This vector is found by dividing each individual element by the sum of all original elements.

For many workload components, the software unit vector is constant regardless of the quantity of total work performed. (Those that are not constant can also be handled but are not covered here.) The constancy of the software unit vector means that for a given run or set of runs of a workload component, the only quantity which will vary will be the total work. This can be verified in most installations by taking some major batch application for which accounting data is available, and calculating the work for several different months using assumed block sizes, I/O counts, and an assumed CPU power. The total quantity of work may vary, but the software unit vector will generally remain quite stable.

The stability of the software work unit vector may be used in two different ways to prepare workload forecasts of software work by equipment class. The first way is in forecasting trends where the total work over time is plotted historically and projected into the future. The projected work by equipment class is obtained by multiplying the projected total work by the software unit vector.

Example 2

Assume the projected total work in some month will be 1500 units for the job whose unit vector is (.67, .22, .11). Then the projected work by equipment class will be:

$$\text{projected work} = 1500 \times \begin{bmatrix} .67 \\ .22 \\ .11 \end{bmatrix} = \begin{bmatrix} 1005 \\ 330 \\ 165 \end{bmatrix}$$

That is, 1005 units of CPU work, 330 units of disk work, and 165 units of tape work are projected.

This trend forecasting technique is similar to other techniques but it has the advantage of requiring that only total work be forecasted.

SOFTWARE PHYSICS 189

A better technique that may be used is one which is based on each user's projection of requirements in the units most natural to the purpose of the application. For example, a payroll application is most naturally forecasted in terms of the number of paychecks to be produced per month. An order-processing application is most naturally projected in units of orders received. All such business-oriented "projection units" are called Natural Forecast Units (abbreviated NFUs).

If the total software work done by an application is divided by the number of NFUs processed or produced (e.g., checks, orders, etc.), the work per NFU is usually found to be constant. In these cases, an NFU projection is easily converted to a software work projection by equipment class.

Example 3

Assume that 50 orders were processed in Example 1 when the total work was 900 units and that "orders" is an NFU for the application. Dividing 900 by 50 gives 18 units of software work per order. In Example 2, with 1500 as the total work, one would expect to have processed 83.3 orders (1500 ÷ 18). Since orders are normally integer quantities, 83 or 84 orders would actually be observed with the difference considered as observational error. If a user projected 20,000 orders per month, then this could be converted to software work by equipment class using the unit vector developed in Example 1:

$$\text{projected work} = 20{,}000 \text{ orders} \times 18 \text{ works per order} \times \begin{bmatrix} .67 \\ .22 \\ .11 \end{bmatrix}$$

$$= 360{,}000 \times \begin{bmatrix} .67 \\ .22 \\ .11 \end{bmatrix}$$

$$= \begin{bmatrix} 241{,}200 \\ 79{,}200 \\ 39{,}600 \end{bmatrix}$$

That is, 241,200 units of CPU work, 79,200 units of disk work, and 39,600 units of tape work are projected.

Measurements of the applications software work by equipment class are used initially to determine the work-per-NFU forecasts and analyzed to prepare actual workload projections for each application. The observed total work and the software work unit vector may then be compared to these projections for management review and control purposes.

In the sense that "repeatability" is normally used for job accounting or billing purposes, software work is the repeatable quantity of software physics. Rates based on projected software work and equipment class costs may be used to develop a cost accounting system and charging formulas. Combining this cost and charging methodology with the concept of NFUs permits charges on a "per transaction" basis through the use of a standard charge per NFU processed. In cases where more detailed costing data are needed, charges based on software work vectors (actual resource usage) may also be used although NFU charges (charges per transaction) are preferred by most users.

SOFTWARE POWER AS A MEASURE OF THROUGHPUT

Software work represents the quantity of work to be done. The property of time must be introduced to determine the speed at which this quantity of work can be completed. Since software work divided by time is the definition of *software power,* discussions of how long it should take to do a particular workload are in terms of software power. The software power used by a workload is limited by the software power available from a configuration. The power usage levels can be measured directly but the power available must be determined by calculations based on software physics theory. That is, *usage* is real while *availability* is theoretical. In practice, equipment planning and workload balancing means striving for the closest possible match between the workload power usage requirements and the theoretical capacity available from the equipment.

Full configuration software power usage by the workload is equivalent to throughput (the number of jobs processed per unit of time) multiplied by the software work for an average job. A mathematical demonstration of this equivalence is given below. A practical and important advantage of using software power instead of throughput is that it permits direct comparisons between various configurations of the same equipment or between entirely different systems.

To demonstrate that the throughput multiplied by the average job's software work is equivalent to full configuration software power, consider several different jobs called $S(1)$, $S(2)$, ... $S(n)$ (where n is the number of jobs). The throughput is obtained by dividing the number of jobs (n) by the elapsed time (T) to process these jobs:

$$\text{throughput} = \frac{n}{T} \quad (1)$$

The software work done by each job can be expressed as $W(1)$, $W(2)$, ... $W(n)$ (where $W(i)$ is the software work for job $S(i)$). The total work is the sum of the work by job, so the software usage level associated with processing the n jobs is:

$$\text{software power usage} = \frac{W(1) + W(2) + \ldots W(n)}{T} \quad (2)$$

The average work per job ($\overline{W}$) is the total work divided by the number of jobs (n):

$$\overline{W} = \text{average work per job} = \frac{W(1) + W(2) = \ldots W(n)}{n}$$

or

$$n \times \overline{W} = W(1) + W(2) + \ldots W(n) \quad (3)$$

Substituting $n \times \overline{W}$ in equation (2), the software power used can be expressed as:

$$\text{software power usage} = \frac{n \times \overline{W}}{T} = \frac{n}{T} \times \overline{W}$$

software power usage = (throughput) × (av. work per job)

If throughput is used alone, the fact that jobs are different sizes causes the measure to be inconsistent over time even within the same installation. This problem may be avoided by determining the average work per job ($\overline{W}$) over several months for the installation. Then throughput may be expressed in terms of a "standard job" as follows:

Let W equal the total work performed over any elapsed time T:

$$W = W(1) + W(2) + \ldots W(n) \qquad (4)$$

Let $\overline{W}$ equal the work done by the installation's standard job:

$$\overline{W} = \frac{W(1) + W(2) + \ldots W(n)}{n} \qquad (5)$$

Substituting W from equation (4) for its value in equation (5) shows that:

$$W \div \overline{W} = n \qquad (6)$$

where n is the number of equivalent standard jobs represented by the total work performed during time T.

Using equations (1) and (6) shows that:

$$\text{throughput} = \frac{n}{T} = \frac{W \div \overline{W}}{T} = \frac{W}{T} \div \overline{W}$$
$$= \textit{(software power usage)} \div \text{(standard job work)}$$

These relationships may be used to compare standard jobs between installations, and to compare the standard jobs found in different workloads in the same installations. The variability of the throughput measure as defined with job size is a function of the "standard job" work. It is more accurate to view the jobs-per-hour throughput measure as a conversion factor and to use software power as the basic and more practical throughput measure. The software physics throughput measure is called *throughput power* to distinguish it from the jobs-per-hour throughput measure.

Throughput power is the total work done by a configuration for a subworkload in a unit of time. It represents the rate at which total work is done on the full configuration.

As shown earlier, software work may be expressed in vector form by equipment class. Throughput power may also be expressed as a vector of the work done by the CPU, disks, tapes, and so forth. Using software work as expressed in Example 1:

$$\text{throughput power} = \frac{\text{software work}}{Te} = \frac{\begin{bmatrix} \text{CPU work} \\ \text{disk work} \\ \text{tape work} \end{bmatrix}}{Te}$$

The symbol Te denotes the elapsed time for the entire configuration. Dividing Te into each vector element gives:

$$\text{throughput power} = \begin{bmatrix} \text{CPU work} \div Te \\ \text{disk work} \div Te \\ \text{tape work} \div Te \end{bmatrix}$$

Each of these vector elements represents the average power used within the equipment class over the elapsed time Te.

This is called the *relative power usage* of the equipment class because the time is relative to the full configuration, not to the equipment class. The *absolute power usage* is calculated by taking the execution time (Tx) of the equipment class. For example if the CPU is in execution for time $Tx(\text{CPU})$, then the absolute CPU power usage will be:

$$\text{absolute CPU power used} = \frac{\text{CPU work}}{Tx(\text{CPU})}$$

Similarly,

$$\text{absolute disk power used} = \frac{\text{disk work}}{Tx(\text{disk})}$$

$$\text{absolute tape power used} = \frac{\text{tape work}}{Tx(\text{tape})}$$

Throughput power can be related to the absolute powers of equipment classes very simply.

$$\text{throughput power} = \begin{bmatrix} \dfrac{Tx(\text{CPU})}{Te} \cdot \dfrac{\text{CPU work}}{Tx(\text{CPU})} \\ \dfrac{Tx(\text{disk})}{Te} \cdot \dfrac{\text{disk work}}{Tx(\text{disk})} \\ \dfrac{Tx(\text{tape})}{Te} \cdot \dfrac{\text{tape work}}{Tx(\text{tape})} \end{bmatrix}$$

Quantities of the form $Tx(\text{CPU}) \div Te$ are equivalent to the CPU percent utilizations obtained by hardware and software monitors. This similarity does not hold for tapes or disks because the quantities $Tx(\text{disk})$ and $Tx(\text{tapes})$ represent the times that any disk or any tape is in execution, not the channel utilization times which are normally obtained. Other forms of the software work vector which relate more directly to the configuration can also be used. These involve percent utilization factors comparable to standard channel utilization percentages.

The sum of the utilization percentages represents the degree of multiprocessing (MP) occurring in the configuration. Mathematically:

$$MP = [Tx(\text{CPU}) + Tx(\text{disks}) + Tx(\text{tapes})] \div Te$$

Similar relationships are derivable for multiprogramming levels. The distinction between relative and absolute power is quite important for many practical applications of software physics because the theoretical power of a configuration is derived in terms of absolute power; and the balance or match between a workload and a configuration is reflected in the extent by which relative power differs from absolute power, and in the extent by which observed absolute power differs from the theoretically possible absolute powers.

SOFTWARE POWER FOR CAPACITY CALCULATIONS

A workload or workload component is the amount of software work to be done and the capacity of a system or system component is its ability to perform work. In practice, a system's ability to perform work is measured against a theoretical rate. This theoretical rate corresponds to the level of power usage which would be measured if an "ideal workload" were to be run on the system. Given a workload,

SOFTWARE PHYSICS 195

it is always possible to specify an ideal configuration to process that workload. Conversely, given a configuration, an ideal workload may be specified to be run on it. The practical problem is to bring *both* the workload and configuration into balance for as much time as possible. Since workloads are neither simple nor constant, compromises must always be made. A knowledge of what the ideal balance should be permits these compromises to be made in intelligent and cost-effective ways.

The capacity characteristics of a complete system depend on both the individual devices' characteristics and the devices' configuration in the system.

Example 4

A tape drive's absolute power is easily calculated for any block size using equipment specifications available from the drive's manufacturer. The formula for determining the execution time (Tx(tape)) for an IBM 3420 Model 3 is:

$$Tx(\text{tape, 3420-3}) = (8 + \frac{1}{120} \times (\text{block size} + 82)) \times 10^{-3} \text{ seconds}$$

$$= (8.68 + .00833 \times \text{block size}) \times 10^{-3} \text{ seconds}$$

The constants in this formula relate to the start, stop, and transfer times which characterize this particular tape drive. Since block sizes are expressed in eight-bit bytes in this formula, software work (W) may be used in place of block size. And since software power is software work divided by execution time, the formula for calculating tape drive power may develop as follows:

$$P(\text{tape, 3420-3}) = \frac{W}{Tx(\text{tape, 3420-3})}$$

Substituting execution time from above:

$$P(\text{tape, 3420-3}) = \frac{W}{(8.68 + .00833W) \times 10^{-3} \text{ sec}}$$

$$= \frac{W}{(8.68 + .00833W)} \text{ K work/sec}$$

The values of this equation for several block sizes are shown in tabular form and plotted in Figure 9-1.

Tape drives of this type normally come in sets of up to eight drives per control unit. Therefore, the capacity or theoretical software power of a tape drive *control unit* subconfiguration must be determined. Since the control unit is in execution whenever a tape drive is in execution, only one tape drive can be in execution at a time within a tape drive control unit. This means that the capacity of an entire tape drive control unit subconfiguration is equal to the absolute power of only a single drive, even though there may be several tape drives in the subconfiguration.

Similar logic leads to the conclusion that a *channel* subconfiguration containing only one tape drive control unit subconfiguration would also have a maximum absolute software power equal to that of a single tape drive. For these conditions, Figure 9-1 represents the tape power of a single tape drive, a control unit subconfiguration, or a channel subconfiguration regardless of the number of drives attached. The line labeled "Asymptotic Power" in Figure 9-1 is the maximum theoretical power of this type of tape drive (120 Kw/s or 120,000 bytes/second).

The reason that the power available from sets of tape drives is equal to that of a single drive in this case is that overlapped execution cannot occur. Within disk control unit subconfigurations, it is possible for *seek* and (in some instances) *search* times to be overlapped. The extent of possible overlap determines the total execution time required to complete a set of disk I/O commands.

Example 5:

Figure 9-2 shows how IBM 3330 disk drives operating in a non-RPS (rotational position sensing) mode can be overlapped. The general formula for the minimum execution time to process a set of N disk I/Os applies when one I/O command per spindle is being executed.

Therefore, N represents the number of spindles in the subconfiguration. Again, let W equal the average block size in bytes (which is numerically equivalent to the average software work per

SOFTWARE PHYSICS 197

Tabular Values: $P(tp, 3420\text{-}3) = \dfrac{W}{8.68 + .00833\,W}$ kw/s

Block Size (bytes)	Execution Time (10^{-3} sec)	Tape Power (kw/s)	% Block Size Efficiency
80	9.35	8.6	7.4
250	10.77	23.2	19.3
500	12.85	38.9	32.4
1000	17.02	58.8	49.0
2000	25.35	79.2	66.0
3000	33.67	89.1	74.2
4000	42.02	95.2	79.3
5000	50.35	99.3	82.8
6000	58.69	102.2	85.2
7000	67.02	104.4	87.0
8000	75.35	106.2	88.5
9000	83.69	107.5	89.6
10,000	92.02	108.7	90.1
100,000	841.98	118.8	99.0
1,000,000	8341.68	119.9	99.9

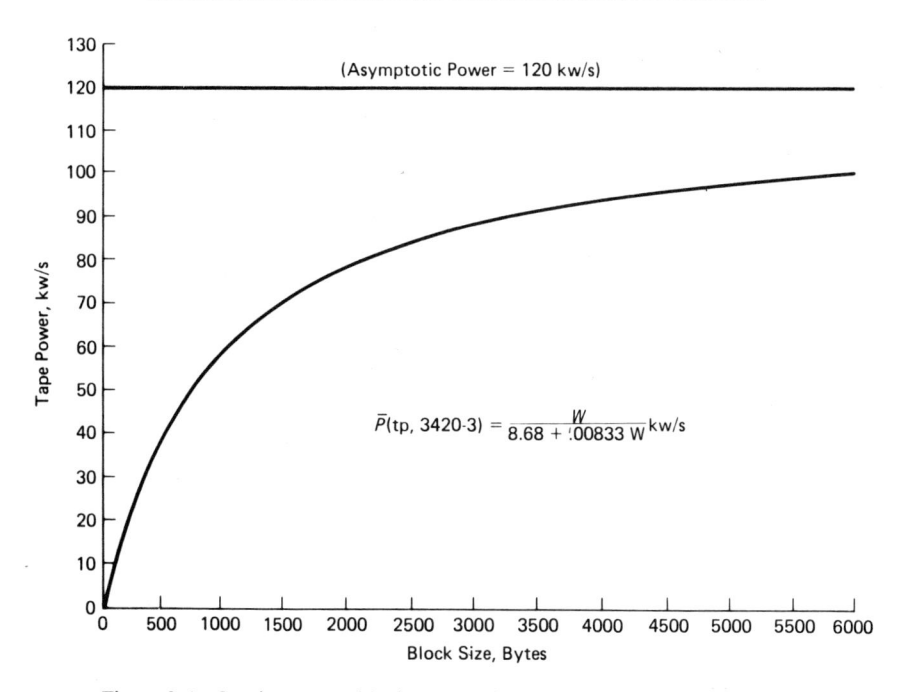

Figure 9-1. Continuous read/write power for IBM 3420 Model 3 tape drives.

198 COMPUTER PERFORMANCE EVALUATION

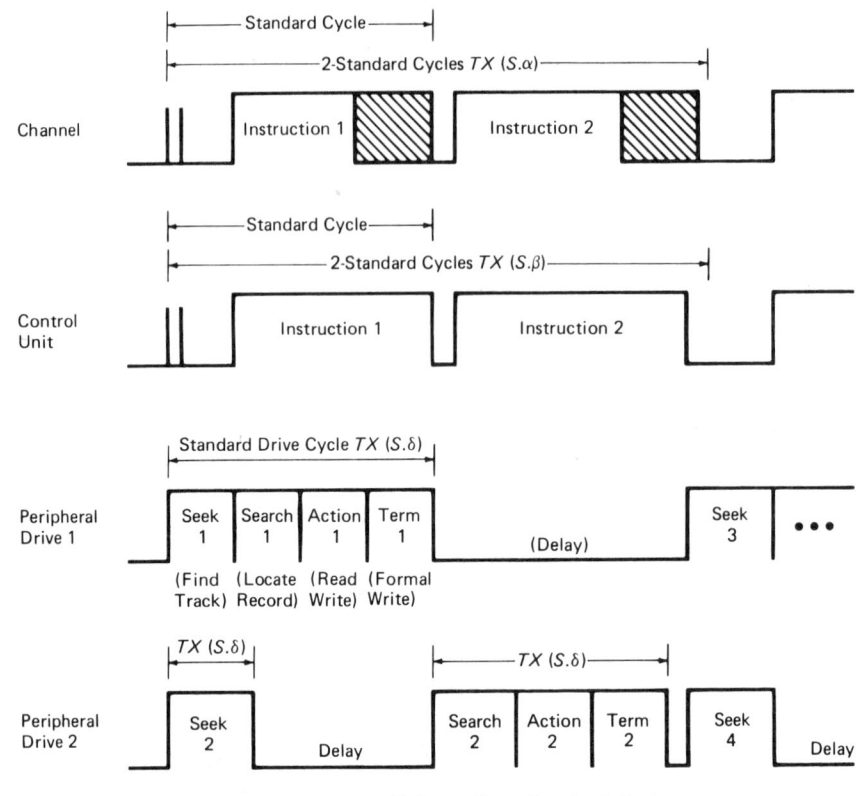

Figure 9-2. Type 2 I/O State Chart Standard Cycles.
(IBM 3330 disk Drives in Non-RPS Model)

I/O). Then the absolute power available from a disk drive control unit configuration is equal to:

$$\frac{N \times W}{\text{av. seek time} + N \times (\text{av. search time} + \text{av. data xmit time})}$$

For an IBM 3330, IBM's quoted values for average seek and search time are:

average seek time = 20 milliseconds
average search time = 8.3 milliseconds

SOFTWARE PHYSICS 199

The average data transmission time for a 4096-byte block is (1.24 microseconds/byte) × (4096 bytes) = 5.1 milliseconds. Therefore, the absolute software power for a 4096 byte average block size equals:

$$\text{power} = \frac{N \times (4.096) \times 10^6}{20 + N \times (8.3 + 5.1)} = \frac{N \times (4.096 \times 10^6)}{20 + N \times (13.4)}$$

This equation is solved and tabulated in Table 9-1 for one through eight spindles.

The capacity or software power of a *channel* subconfiguration with only one disk control unit subconfiguration attached is the same as shown in Table 9-1. Without demonstrating the calculations, the channel configuration disk power for this type of equipment is effectively unchanged when more disk control unit subconfigurations are added to the channel. Because of this, a practical starting assumption is that adding disk control units to a channel only increases online storage and not software power. This approximation also holds for adding disk spindles to a control unit.

Such calculations may be made for any type of peripheral drive and any combination of drives, control units, and channel architectures. After these calculations have been done for a given set of control unit subconfigurations and the subconfiguration with maximum theoretical I/O software power has been identified, this form of configuration is referred to as the *Ideal I/O configuration*. The ideal I/O configuration for disks like those of Example 5 occurs when there is one channel for each control unit.

Table 9-1. IBM 3330 disk drive with one control unit.

NO. OF SPINDLES N	POWER	POWER AS A MULTIPLE OF 1 SPINDLE POWER
1	122.6 kw/s	1.00
2	175.0	1.43
3	203.8	1.66
4	222.6	1.82
5	235.4	1.92
6	245.3	2.00
7	251.3	2.05
8	257.6	2.10

The absolute power of the central processor or processors in a configuration is most easily obtained by direct measurement with a hardware monitor. In software physics, processor power may be expressed in terms of an instruction mix. In practice, the instruction mix will vary with the workload so that the average power value is more useful and is generally all that is needed.

The maximum *theoretical throughput power* of a configuration is equal to the sum of the powers by equipment class (the sum of the CPU power and I/O power by channel subconfiguration). For an *ideal configuration,* the I/O power is the sum of the ideal I/O subconfigurations. The effective I/O power of the control unit subconfigurations is used.

Example 6

Consider a simple configuration with one IBM 3330 disk control unit subconfiguration, made up of 8 drives on channel 1, operating in a non-RPS mode with an average block size of 4096. By the previous calculations, the maximum I/O disk power is 258 kw/s (see Table 9-1). Also assume that the CPU is an IBM 370/158 with an average CPU power of 8000 kw/s. Ignoring the printers, card readers, and so forth, the configuration capacity or theoretical throughput power is the work that can be done in one second:

$$\begin{aligned} \text{CPU work/sec} &= 8000 \text{ kw/s} \\ \text{disk work/sec} &= 258 \text{ kw/s} \\ \text{tape work/sec} &= 102 \text{ kw/s} \\ \text{total capacity} &= 8360 \text{ kw/s} \end{aligned}$$

The ideal workload for this configuration would use all of this power. This workload would cause complete overlap of all equipment classes and operate all at 100% utilization of software power. Note however that the channel 1's percent of utilization would be less than 100% because the channel is not busy during disk seeks. The importance of this is that it is known that channel 1 in this configuration cannot be used 100% of the time.

The software work *unit vector* for the ideal workload is calculated by dividing total software work into the software work by equipment class. Since the total work possible in one second is 8360 kw, the ideal workload unit vector is:

$$\text{unit vector} = \begin{bmatrix} \text{CPU} : 8000 \div 8360 \\ \text{disk} : 258 \div 8360 \\ \text{tape} : 102 \div 8360 \end{bmatrix} = \begin{bmatrix} .957 \\ .031 \\ .012 \end{bmatrix}$$

This unit vector in conjunction with the total work per second characterizes the ideal workload for the equipment.

APPLICATIONS

Real workloads never correspond to ideal workloads and equipment is rarely in an ideal configuration. A method is needed to identify the extent to which real workloads are in balance with real configurations and to determine the most cost-effective methods for obtaining a desired configuration throughput power. The basic technique for doing this in software physics uses an *execution time profile*. An execution time profile is similar to a normal system profile except that any-device-busy times for subconfigurations are used rather than channel-busy times.

Example 7

An execution time profile may be developed as follows. (The configuration used in Example 6 is also used here.)

1. Measure the execution times by equipment class by using a software or hardware monitor.
2. Measure or calculate the work done concurrently (overlap) by equipment class. Plot this information as in Figure 9-3 to show the power usage levels of the equipment classes.

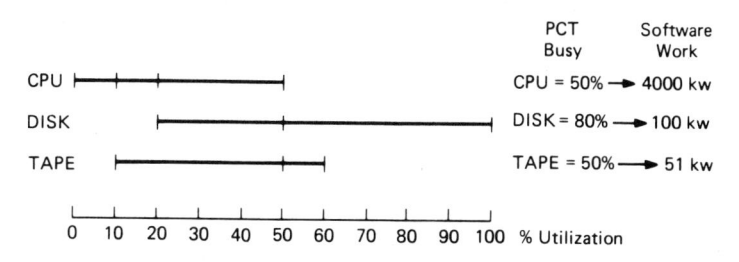

Figure 9-3. Sample execution time profile.

The tape work would be 51,000 units (or 51 kw) per second of elapsed time (the absolute tape power for Figure 9-1 was 102 kw/s based on a block size of 6000 bytes and the tapes were 50% busy). Assume that 100 kw of disk work per second of elapsed time was observed. Since the percent utilization was measured as 0.8, the absolute power would be 125 kw/s (100 ÷ 0.8) or slightly more than "one spindle power" with the assumed block size of 4096 (see Table 9-1). The CPU power was assumed to be 8000 kw/s, so the CPU work done in a second of elapsed time would be 4000 kw (50% × 8000). The total work done per elapsed second would be 4151 kw (4000 + 100 + 51) and the throughput power would be 4,151 kw/s. Comparing this actual throughput power (4151 kw/s) with the theoretical throughput power of Example 6 (8360 kw/s) indicates the maximum potential improvement possible with the current configuration.

The execution time profile (Figure 9-3) shows that the work by equipment class is not completely overlapped. A certain amount of CPU work must be done when no disk or tape work is in process. This work is called a *CPU-offset*. The CPU-*disk* offset, from the profile, is 1600 kw (0.2 × 8000), the CPU-*tape* offset is 800 kw (0.1 × 8000).

The CPU–disk concurrent work would be 2400 kw (0.3 × 8000) and the CPU-tape concurrent work would be 3200 kw (0.4 × 8000). This expresses the disk and tape work which is overlapped with CPU work in the same terms as CPU work. Similarly the CPU–disk slack work is 4000 kw (0.5 × 8000). The meanings of CPU-*offset, concurrent,* and *slack* work are that overall system performance improvement efforts directed at disk operation will have no positive effect on CPU–disk offset time, they may or may not affect the CPU–disk concurrent time, and they definitely will have positive effects on the CPU–disk slack time. The same may be said for CPU-tape offset, concurrent, and slack times.

Example 8

A work concurrency chart may now be developed for the configuration of Examples 6 and 7. The units of CPU work developed for disk and tape are an expression of the total workload reduced to a *standard second* of elapsed time. This standard second is used as the base line for plotting the various concurrencies and nonconcurrencies in the Sample Work Concurrency Chart of Figure 9-4. The value of using this standard second is that predicted performance changes may be converted directly into percentage projections. This is demonstrated in later examples.

This work concurrency chart can be used to evaluate the impact of either equipment changes or performance improvement activities. It could also be used to define a configuration which would operate at a desired level of throughput power.

Example 9

Suppose that a performance improvement project was undertaken to raise the disk multiprocessing level to two spindles from the level of one spindle as observed in Example 6. The new disk power for an average 4096-byte block size (See Table 9-1) would be 175 kw/s instead of 125 kw/s.

The disk performance improvement would not reduce the CPU-disk offset work, but it would reduce CPU-disk slack by a factor of 0.7143 (125 kw/s ÷ 175 kw/s or old disk power ÷ new disk power). The CPU-disk concurrent work would

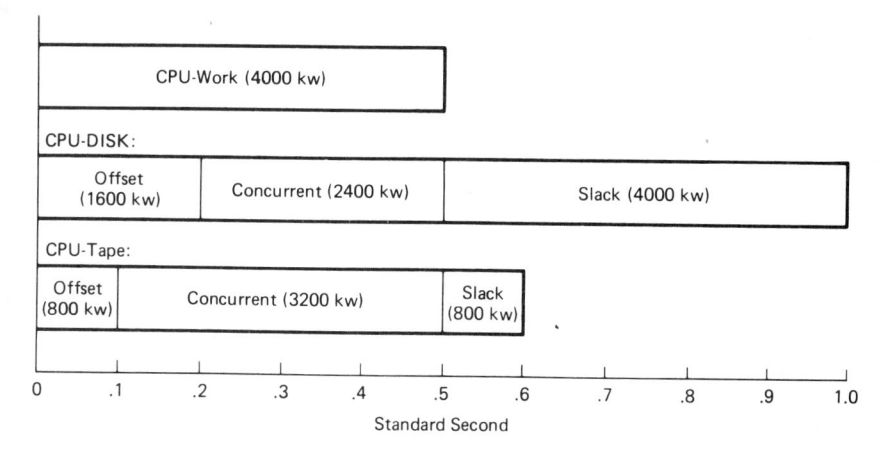

Figure 9-4. Sample work concurrency chart.

be reduced by an amount in a range determined by examining the CPU and disk dependencies of CPU-disk concurrent work. At worst, no CPU-disk concurrent work improvement would occur. At best, CPU-disk concurrent work could be reduced by 686 units of software work, but the uncertainty of the change would all show up in the prediction of the altered system's CPU-disk *slack* work. The predicted work concurrency chart information for this disk power improvement is given in Table 9-2.

The sample predicted work concurrency chart shown as Figure 9-5 is a plot of the new data in Table 9-2 along with the original CPU and CPU-tape data from Examples 7 and 8. At this point, a decision may be made on the merit of actually implementing the performance improvements which would cause the disks to operate at the higher software power level. Note that the software work of the disks remained unchanged throughout this discussion as did the CPU and tape work. This is generally the case in typical system "tuning" projects: the same workload gets handled more quickly. The purpose of this exercise is to demonstrate how approaches developed in software physics may be used to quantify the impact of changes in terms of the present system's overall performance before the changes are made.

Once the changes have been made to improve disk performance, new measurements should be made to determine the average disk power level. Suppose that the new run time was the best case of the range predicted (this would normally be the outcome in this type of project unless there were unusual interdependencies between disk

Table 9-2. Predicted performance improvements.

CPU-DISK:	PRESENT	PREDICTED WORST	PREDICTED BEST	
Concurrent	2400 kw	2400 kw	2400 kw	
Slack Work	4000 kw	2857 kw	2171 kw	(686 difference
Offset Work	1600 kw	1600 kw	1600 kw	shows in predicted
CPU-disk Total Work	8000 kw	6857 kw	6171 kw	slack)
Elapsed Time (standard sec.)	1.00 sec	0.86 sec	0.77 sec	
Predicted Improvement in Run Time	—	14%	23%	

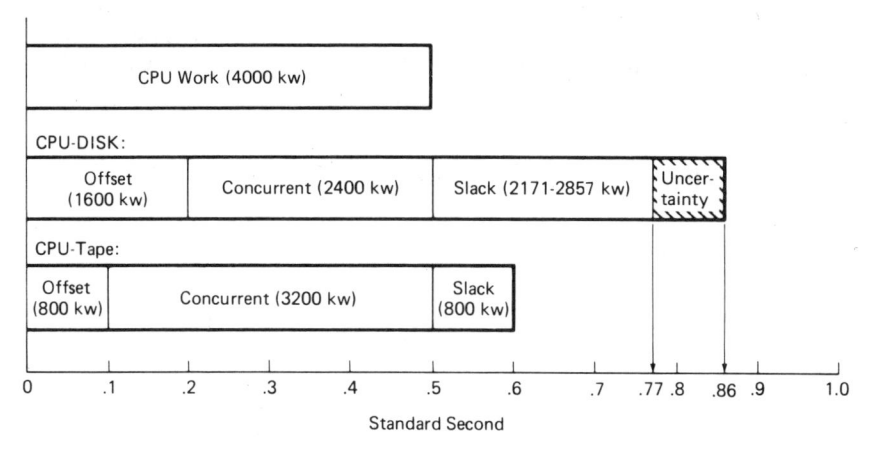

Figure 9-5. Sample predicted work concurrency chart.

and CPU processing); then the altered system would run in 23% less time and the disk power would be 175 kw/s instead of 125. Tape and CPU powers remain unchanged at 102 kw/s and 8000 kw/s, respectively.

Example 10

It is now possible to construct an execution time profile for the altered system. Since the work done in the original standard second now requires only .77 times as long, the new percent busy levels which should be observed may be calculated ahead of time. (Note that CPU-disk concurrent work plus CPU-disk slack work requires .57 standard seconds in Figure 9-5 while they required .80 standard seconds in Figure 9-4. This may be seen more clearly by observing that since *power = work/time*, then *time = work/power*; work remained constant at 100 kw while power changed from 125 kw/s to 175 kw/s, so time which was .80 seconds (100/125) must change to .57 seconds (100/175).) The percent busy levels of the altered system are determined by dividing busy time by elapsed time.

% CPU = (.50/.77) = 65% or .65 standard seconds
% disk = (.57/.77) = 74% or .74 standard seconds
% tape = (.50/.77) = 65% or .65 standard seconds

Now the amount of work which will be completed may be calculated. Again based on the definition of power = work/time, it should be clear that *work* = *time* × *power*.

CPU work = .65 sec × 8000 kw/s = 5200 kw
disk work = .64 sec × 175 kw/s = 130 kw
tape work = .65 sec × 102 kw/s =   66 kw

The overlaps of CPU, disk and tape usage will be in the same proportions as shown in Figure 9-5.

% CPU-disk offset   = .20/.77 = 26%
% CPU-disk concurrent = .30/.77 = 39%
% CPU-disk slack   = .27/.77 = 35%

% CPU-tape offset   = .10/.77 = 13%
% CPU-tape concurrent = .40/.77 = 52%
% CPU-tape slack   = .10/.77 = 13%

Plotting this information produces the altered systems execution time profile as seen in Figure 9-6.

Direct comparisons may also be made to see the overall improvement in this system's throughput power. Example 6 showed that the *theoretical* throughput power of this configuration was 8360 kw/s and Example 7 showed that the actual throughput power was 4151 kw/s before improvement. From Example 10 and the data in Figure 9-6, the new throughput power is 5396 kw/s (5200 + 130 + 66).

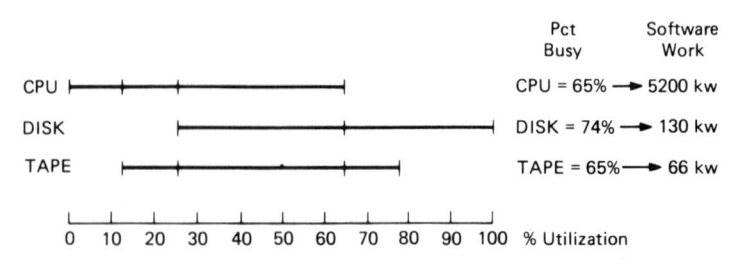

Figure 9-6. Altered system's execution time profile.

The throughput power increase is therefore 1245 kw/s (5396 − 4151):

% throughput power improvement = (1245/4151)
$$= 30\%$$

Summarizing the information in these examples and stating the work in unit vector notation allow comparisons to be made which indicate the stability of the unit vector as a way of stating the characteristic composition of an installation's work. (Differences may be seen if the calculations are carried out to four or five places; however, differences of these magnitudes are generally considered in the same way as measurement errors—they are too small to be significant.)

$$\begin{array}{cc} \textit{ideal workload} & \textit{initial workload} \end{array}$$

unit vectors:
$$\begin{bmatrix} 8000/8360 \\ 258/8360 \\ 102/8360 \end{bmatrix} = \begin{bmatrix} .957 \\ .031 \\ .012 \end{bmatrix} \quad \begin{bmatrix} 4000/4151 \\ 100/4151 \\ 51/4151 \end{bmatrix} = \begin{bmatrix} .964 \\ .024 \\ .012 \end{bmatrix}$$

$$\textit{improved workload}$$
$$\begin{bmatrix} 5200/5396 \\ 130/5396 \\ 66/5396 \end{bmatrix} = \begin{bmatrix} .964 \\ .024 \\ .012 \end{bmatrix}$$

The reader is strongly encouraged to assume other changes in the example configuration to try out these techniques. Suppose that the worst case in improvement had resulted and try using the data in Figure 9-5 to determine that the new throughput power would only be 4816 kw/s. If the disk power usage level can be increased beyond 175 kw/s, or if the CPU-disk offset can be reduced, the limiting factor on throughput power may become the tape power. The impact of changing to some other tape blocking factor may also be evaluated.

Given a workload forecast in the form of a software work vector, and an execution time profile, a work concurrency chart can always be constructed. Once the elapsed time to process the work has been decided (and this is a management decision), the overall throughput power required and the absolute power required within each equipment class are easily calculated. This specifies the required capacity for the installation. Comparing this capacity to observed power usage levels and to theoretical power levels of the existing capacity would permit development of a combined equipment and performance improvement plan to meet projected workload requirements.

10
Reporting Performance to Management

The understanding of how computer systems work and what they do usually decreases dramatically at each level of management above the computer center. This fact does not excuse the performance analyst from reporting information in terms that can be understood by higher-level managers. The final report that results from a CPE project is normally the only thing about the project that receives management attention. Chapter 2 gave a usable format for preparing written performance reports. Generally, the periodic written reports which cover individual CPE projects are not enough performance information for managers. A regular and continuing information flow about installation performance is also needed.

ELEMENTS OF A PERFORMANCE MANAGEMENT REPORTING SYSTEM

Managers at every level want to know trends. That is, are things better, worse, or the same as they usually have been in the past? Because of this, some facility for incorporating trend information should be a feature of any performance reporting system. Trends are most easily understood when they are depicted graphically or as a picture; however, managers at the working level may require trend information in more detail such as may be given in a computer-generated listing using exception flags to highlight unusual variances from past performance.

Terminology

On rare occasions, very high-level managers have specified the information that they wish to have reported to them about computer performance. In these cases the words used in the reports are familiar management terms like productivity, availability, capacity, service, satisfaction, control, waste, timeliness, and so forth. More commonly, first-level managers and technicians track and report computer performance in terms like CPU busy, megabytes of memory used or available, percent busy for channels and peripherals, EXCPs per CPU second, ABEND rates, and so forth. Very few higher-level managers have either the time or the interest to understand such working terminology. Wherever possible, commonly understood words should be used for reports that will circulate outside the computer center. The specialized vocabulary, or jargon, of computer technicians is extremely handy for discussing and solving problems but such language is a hindrance to communication outside the computer environment.

The term that is most readily understood by managers is *money*. Reports that stress such performance indicators as revenue per hour, cost per product, and variations from planned revenues or costs are usually welcomed at all management levels. There has been an understandable hesitancy to prepare and report such numbers in many computer installations. This has probably been due to the difficulty of making and meeting precise plans involving the full cost of computer services. The tools and techniques of CPE make more accurate planning and better cost and revenue projections possible. As the CPE capability at an installation matures, there is generally more willingness to report to higher management in terms of money.

Consistency

It should be recognized that—no matter how expensive they may seem—computer expenditures are a small part of the operating costs of most companies. Because of this, there is virtually no interest in the details of computer performance at the higher management levels unless the computer installation is thought to be poorly managed. One major cause of such suspicion is erratic or inconsistent reports on the computer center's activity. Short, periodic reports that always contain the same reporting parameters and that include historical trends for comparison with the latest figures can reduce this problem.

When consistent reports are furnished from one reporting period to the next, it should be expected that some periods will look bad and some will look good. There are usually explanations for such variations that are easily understood outside the computer room. The standard reports should never be altered or skipped to deemphasize or to hide some set of figures that show "bad" performance or to place unusual stress on figures indicating "good" performance. This type of reporting activity makes managers skeptical about the value of the regular reports. A better approach is to report as usual but to offer a very short, narrative explanation for those categories that look too "bad" or too "good."

Figure 10-1 shows one type of management report that has been effective at many installations and which is acceptable at the highest corporate levels. This report shows the latest month's revenue per hour along with the actual revenue figures for the past twelve months as contrasted with the expected values of past months and projections for the next six months. Limits on revenue per hour are also shown. The only narrative that would accompany this report would be to explain why either limit was violated as shown in notes *1. and *2. of the figure and to state why the "theoretical" limit will

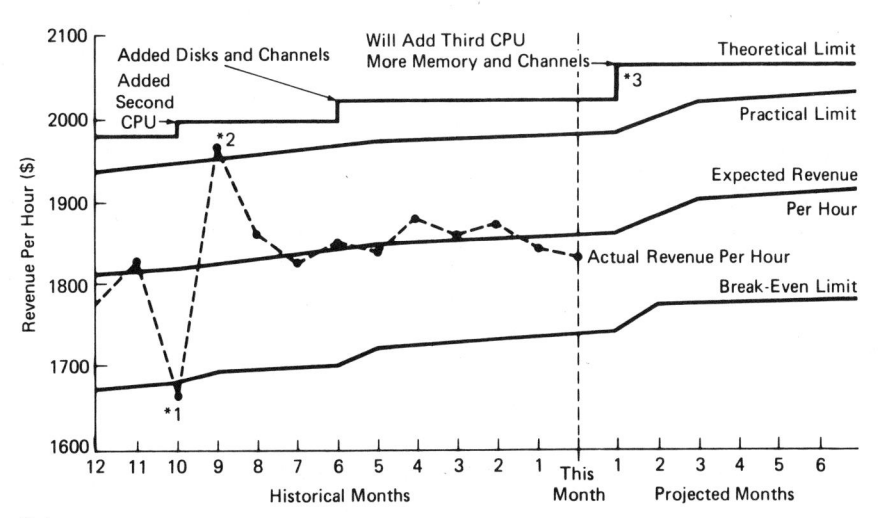

Notes:
*1. Lost four days of production: one due to equipment installation problems, three due to snow.
*2. Unusual effort expended to clean up backlog from preceding month.
*3. Planned capacity increase to support online order processing system for central region warehouses.

Figure 10-1. A management report.

be changed in the future (note *3.). Such a report shows management whether the computer is paying its own way or not, and alerts management at least six months ahead that some change in total capacity is planned.

There is always a temptation when reports like that of Figure 10-1 show a bad month (like the one that causes note *1.) to elaborate the reasons or to put the report into different terms. For instance, this report might have been recalculated to include a figure for "revenue per hour *in service.*" This would serve to factor out the four days that were lost and would probably make the "bad" month look closer to "normal." Such a report might be generated as an additional page to the regular report, but changing a standard or agreed-on format to focus on one month's problems should never be done. This should not be taken as a suggestion that reports which no longer serve a useful purpose be continued indefinitely, only that useful and accepted reports not be altered for short-term purposes.

Management Reporting Goals

There are only a few major goals that need to be considered when a reporting system or individual report is to be created. The primary goal is that the report serve to enhance the management process. This goal may be much broader than simply managing the computer installation. For instance, users may find their management task much easier if they are given reports that highlight their own activities which involve the system. Providing meaningful management information to users is another goal for performance reports.

Performance reports should be designed to depict performance achievements objectively. The reports should relate to understandable units that are important to the operation of the company or agency which the computer serves. The reports should be as simple and uncluttered as possible. Reports should encourage productive dialogues between the computer center and other departments. Finally, an important goal of performance reports is that they serve to strengthen management control of all automated systems.

It is not realistic to expect that every performance report would meet every reporting goal; however, the total system of performance management reports should be created with all goals in mind. These goals are given in summary form in Figure 10-2.

A Performance Reporting System Should:
- Enhance the Management Process.
- Provide Meaningful Management Information.
- Objectively Depict Performance Achievements.
- Be in Understandable Units.
- Relate to Corporate Goals.
- Have Simple, Uncluttered Reports.
- Encourage Productive Dialogue with Data Center Personnel.
- Strengthen Management Control of Automated Systems.

Figure 10-2. Performance management reporting system goals.

Performance Indicators

There is no general agreement about what computer activities are the best indicators of overall system performance, but there are a few guidelines that can help an individual installation decide what to create as indicators for their reporting systems. In industries with only one or very few end products, performance indicators may be based on the cost of computer service per product. For example, an insurance company might track performance in terms of computer cost per policy serviced or per policy in force. A bank might use checks processed or demand deposits as their distribution factor for computer costs. An aircraft company could report dollars of computer costs per airplane produced while an automobile manufacturer could use cost per car. Along with these single-number indicators, the reports should show previous highs, lows, and the average value of the reporting unit. The concept of "stock market" reports (high, low, and latest for the past year) is a good one to use to promote management understanding and acceptance. There are many ways to display these and other types of indicators which will be shown later in this chapter under "Reporting Formats." Numerous other indicators will also be suggested there that are useful in centers which can not relate costs to one or a few company products.

Information Sources

A comprehensive performance management reporting system should include more than just the output from the measurement tools that are covered in this book. These tools provide the largest share of reporting information which is automated and in machine-accessible form, but more information is usually needed to relate performance data to the goals of the various automated systems. Such information is normally in manual records covering such things as system development data, users' requirements, production control policies, and costs. Other information may be in either manual or automated records. This information includes historical records, performance goals, system models, and scheduling data. These sources should be considered as representative: not all sources are available at every installation and other sources of performance information may be available at other sites. Figure 10-3 shows the concept of a performance management reporting system based on these information sources.

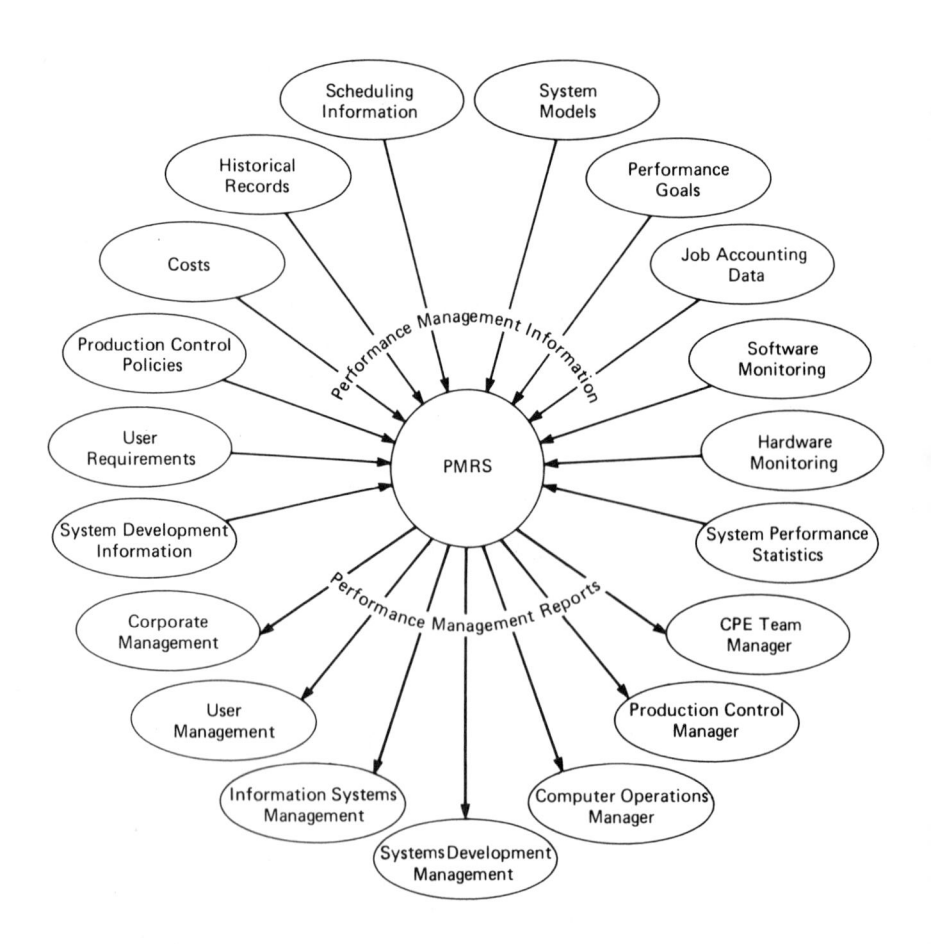

Figure 10-3. Performance management reporting system concept.

Performance Standards

An ideal time to develop standards of performance is during the design and development of a performance reporting system. The reporting system must necessarily provide reports that show when any performance standard is violated and, ideally, would provide periodic reports that show the level of compliance to standards even when there are no violations. The kinds of standards that can be included are: percent of the time that critical reports are delivered on time, percent of general products delivered on time, percent accomplishment of system development goals, and variations from norms of resource usage and service levels.

This last item regarding variations has come to be a very useful area for performance reporting and for setting standards where no standards have existed previously. It is both easy and realistic to state standards for both resource usage and service levels in terms of past performance. That is, the average or mean value of, say, CPU usage over the past six-or-so months is a fair estimate of the CPU usage for next month. Further, the observed high and low values, or more accurately, the statistical level of one standard deviation above and below the means, are reasonable limits to set on what should be expected in any particular performance category in the near future. An even simpler set of limits that is in use is percent variation. For example, if an indicator varies by more than plus or minus 10% from its previous average or its predicted value, the indicator may be flagged by underscoring or asterisks in a listing-type report or noted with a comment in a graphical report. In many cases, plus or minus 10% is considered a flag for management attention while plus or minus 15% would be a flag that might start a CPE project to address the problem described by that indicator's variance. Limits like these can serve as standards while experience is being gained that would allow more realistic standards to be set. This idea of setting limits of allowable variations is widely used in production applications outside the computer environment. These limits are called *control limits.* Variations within control limits are expected; variations outside these limits call for some reaction.

Figure 10-4 shows a performance report prepared for the production control manager which flags items that are outside the 10 to 15% control limits and lists individual applications with variances exceeding 15%.

216 COMPUTER PERFORMANCE EVALUATION

PRODUCTION CONTROL REPORT – MONTHLY

Operations Summary

Item	Norm	This Month	Variance Indicator
Resource Usage:			
CPU (Min)	51.8K	52.2K	
I/O (Min)	106.2K	105.4K	
Memory (KWH)	134K	153K	* +
Disk (MBytes)	3.2K	3.5K	
Online (Hours)	3.0K	3.2K	
Print Lines (1000s)	43.3K	45.0K	
Wait Time (Hours)	1.0K	1.1K	* +
Transactions/Day	3500	3300	
% Capacity Recovered (S)	82.2	80.8	
Service Level:			
Time Critical Reports on Time	1482	1604	
Time Critical Reports Late	14	8	** –
Response Time Avg (Sec)	13.8	12.0	* –
Avg Cost/Product (S)	47.11	43.91	
Avg Cost/Transaction (S)	3.48	3.15	
Avg Cost/Job (S)	6.50	6.67	
Batch Jobs Completed	27607	26311	
Production Jobs Aborted-Cost (S)	4950	5104	* +
Production Jobs Aborted-Number	550	538	
Number Production Reruns	326	361	
Development Tasks Completed	412	406	

Performance Exceptions

System	Performance Area	Percent Variance
EHF	CPU	+29.3
DCF	I/O	–28.4
BAE	Memory	+28.3
BBB	Disk	+22.2
ACD	Print Lines	+22.1
FBH	Disk	+21.4
AJB	Wait Time	+20.0
AEB	Number Batch Jobs	–19.4
BDB	Number Batch Jobs	–18.9
CHD	Time Critical Reports	+16.3
HCD	Transactions/Day	–16.1
IBE	Number Aborts	+15.8
EFJ	Number Reruns	+15.8
EAC	Response Time	–15.6
FAB	Hardware Cost	+15.2
EEE	Output Volume	+15.1
BGD	Avg Cost/Job	+15.0
BAH	Development Tasks Completed	+15.0

Note: Performance variances in excess of ±10% and ±15% are single and double asterisked respectively.

Figure 10–4. A production control report.

REPORTING FORMATS

There are many formats available for performance reports. The types of formats discussed here are those which have found acceptance in management reporting in many installations, not necessarily those which are used at a working level in the course of conducting CPE projects. (Examples of working level report formats are best obtained from vendors of CPE products.) Management-reporting formats are generally tailored to the individual computer center by members of the center or by management-consulting firms. The formats given here should be taken as starting points for developing meaningful management reports, not as fixed or unmodifiable formats. In all cases, the indicators that are plotted in the following examples are for illustration and to suggest indicators that might be useful. Each installation should determine which indicators are important enough to report to their own management.

The types of formats discussed here are mainly graphics that should be manually generated for maximum effect. The first type is the computer-generated listing which can be graphical but is, of course, automatically generated. Next, line graphs and bar charts are covered, and Gannt charts, a special version of bar charts, are also introduced. Then other formats that are newer and probably less familiar are explained. These formats have been called "Kiviat Graphs" and "Schumacher Charts." In all cases, explanatory text is omitted in the formats themselves because, once the report format is understood, the report should be self-explanatory. The exceptions to this rule are mainly to explain variances (as was done in Figure 10-1).

Computer Listings

This type of performance report is easily the most abused. Listings are often generated that are several pages long for presentation to management. Listings that require more than one page are almost never acceptable as management reports. Figure 10-4 is a listing that covers one month of performance, is related to past performance, and reports each system that has significant variation from that system's norm. This report may be considered graphical in that only those items which are noteworthy have attention called to them by the simple use of asterisks. If every performance item had significant variance so that all were asterisked, then the report would lose a great deal of its graphical attribute.

Any number of variables and any time period may be reported using even a one-page listing format if thought is given to what is important before creating the format. Figure 10-5 shows another listing report which was prepared for the manager of system development. It covers only one system to show how the first three months of production experience compare with the design specifications that were prepared before the system became operational. The purpose of such a report is to provide the development manager information for correcting the system to come closer to the design specifications, discussing the way the system is being used by the users, or revising the way that estimates are made in the design process. It is possible to look at this single page and see which measures are on target, which are off but getting better, and which indicators appear to need attention. The final column showing the average statistics for the first three months of operation could be incorporated as the "norm" for future months if it was decided that the system could not be made to fit all of the design specifications.

Line Graphs

Line graphs are most useful when only two variables are to be displayed over some fixed time. Figure 10-1 is a line graph showing "revenue per hour" versus "month". The fixed time is nineteen months. On occasion line graphs show several variables, perhaps with differently scaled vertical axes on the right and left. Unless the variables are very well behaved, this type of line graph is usually too confusing to use. A better approach is to make several single-line graphs with the horizontal axes all the same and aligned with each other as in Figure 10-6. The report recipient can visually connect the variables quite easily when they are portrayed in this fashion.

Line graphs shown in Figure 10-6 use indicators that might be useful for the information system's manager to see the overall trends of major categories of work. Any indicator with two or more data points could be displayed on a line graph.

REPORTING PERFORMANCE TO MANAGEMENT 219

SYSTEM DEVELOPMENT REPORT – PERFORMANCE ANALYSIS, HISTORICAL PERSPECTIVE

System: BGD (Inventory Update – Batch)

System Resource	Design Specifications (Monthly)	First Month Actual	First Month Variance Flag	Second Month Actual	Second Month Variance Flag	Third Month Actual	Third Month Variance Flag	Average Actual	Average Variance Flag
CPU Usage (Min)	102	136	** +	127	** +	122	** +	128	** +
I/O Usage (Min)	369	442	** +	381		384		402	
Memory Usage (KWH)	206	193		201		214		203	
Disk Storage (MBytes)	5.0	5.4		5.6	* +	5.4		5.5	
Number Jobs	160	149		152		154		152	
Job Hours	19.4	24.1	** +	21.2		20.9		22.1	* +
Online Hours	0	0		0		0		0	
Number Reruns	5	4	** –	5		4	** +	4.3	* –
Number Aborts	4	9	** +	7	** +	6	** +	7.3	** +
Number Support Manhours	20	22	* +	20		18	* –	20	
Input Transactions	5685	5840		5744		5782		5789	
Output Reports	67	72		71		70		71	
Total System Cost ($)	4560	6214	** +	6013	** +	5993	** +	6073	** +
Hardware Cost ($)	1961	2614	** +	3017	** +	2980	** +	2870	** +
Other Cost ($)	2599	3600	** +	2996	** +	3013	** +	3202	** +
Avg Job Cost ($)	4.67	6.10	** +	5.82	** +	5.64	** +	5.85	** +
Avg Input Cost ($)	.13	.17	** +	.16	** +	.16	* +	.16	** +
Avg Output Cost ($)	.92	1.32	** +	1.27	** +	1.07		1.22	** +

Note: Performance variances in excess of ± 10% and ± 15% are single and double asterisked respectively.

Figure 10-5. Listing format for system development management.

220 COMPUTER PERFORMANCE EVALUATION

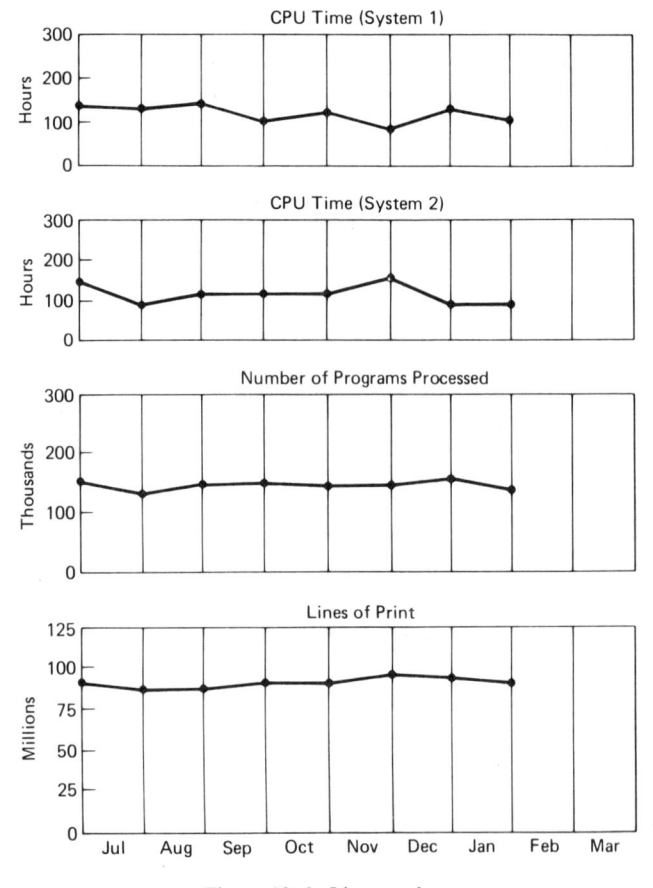

Figure 10-6. Line graphs.

Bar Charts

This type of format is used in two distinct ways: one to show several different variables over some fixed time, the other to contrast the changes in a few variables over a period of time. Figure 10-7 is a bar graph of the first type showing the use of various computer components. These kinds of indicators may be useful to an operation's manager for studying the relative use of the various computer resources at the installation.

The second type of bar chart is given in Figure 10-8. The variables plotted in this figure are the type that production control managers

REPORTING PERFORMANCE TO MANAGEMENT 221

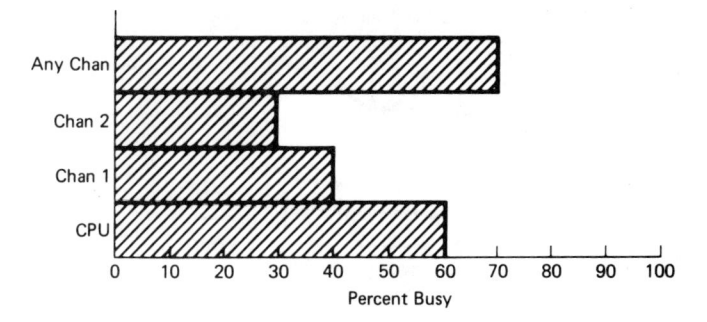

Figure 10-7. Bar chart—type 1.

often track to see how much time was spent in production versus other time that was used. A variation of this type of bar chart which spaces the bars and then connects the various elements that make up each bar is shown in Figure 10-9. This might be regarded as a cross between a line graph and a bar chart as the trends of each variable may be seen more easily than in charts like Figure 10-8. The data

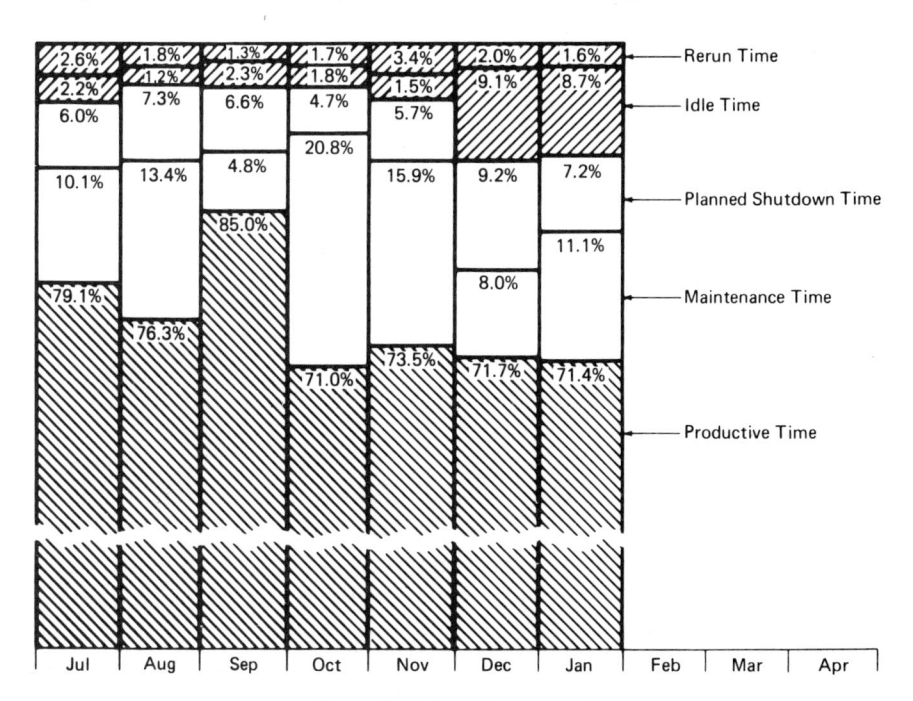

Figure 10-8. Bar chart—type 2.

222 COMPUTER PERFORMANCE EVALUATION

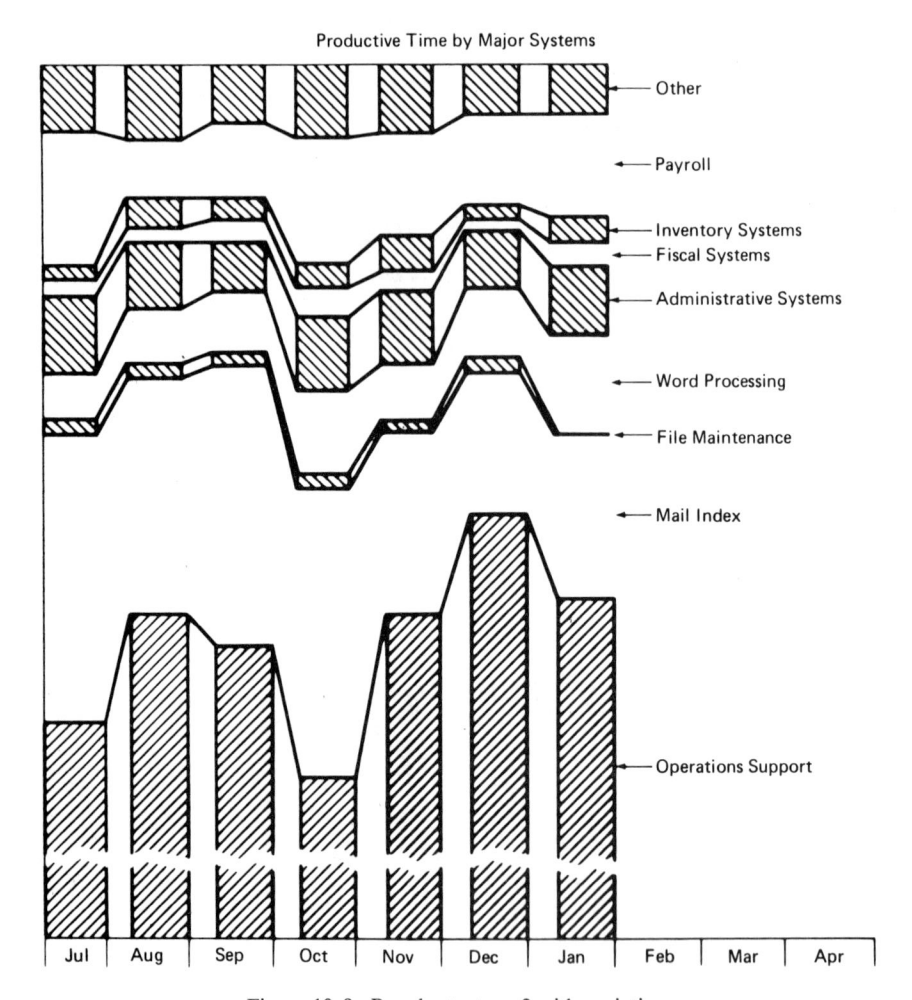

Figure 10-9. Bar chart—type 2 with variation.

plotted in Figure 10-9 are the types of overview information that are often useful to user management and to information system management to observe how the various elements of the production work vary from month to month. It is sometimes helpful to print the value of each bar right on the chart so that closer comparisons can be made. Note that this was done in Figure 10-8 for the production control manager who would normally be expected to want more detail than many of the other managers.

There is a type of bar chart that is often generated by computer which shows one variable horizontally across the page with each new line representing a step in time. Sometimes these are referred to as *histograms*. These are not normally suitable for management reports unless time is taken to go over the individual lines with a marking pen to make the trends of the variable easier to follow. This type of bar chart should be restricted to one-time or infrequent reports to management as they quickly become very easy to ignore in favor of more interesting presentations. Histograms are extremely helpful in the conduct of a CPE project at the working level but they should not be considered acceptable for continued management reporting.

Gantt Charts

This format might also be considered as a variation of the bar chart; however, Gantt Charts have a different property than bar charts. It is possible to see the simultaneous use, or overlaps, of resources when the same information that is plotted on bar charts is shown on Gantt Charts. The data plotted in Figure 10-7 are replotted as a Gantt Chart in Figure 10-10. Even though no new data are introduced, the Gantt Chart allows a better understanding of the relationships of the variables than does the bar chart of the same data. Note that it is easy to deduce that there must be more than the two channels shown which are part of the system plotted in Figure 10-10. (There are times when "any channel" activity is present but neither Channel 1 nor Channel 2 is active.) This can not be seen when the same information is shown as a bar graph as in Figure 10-7.

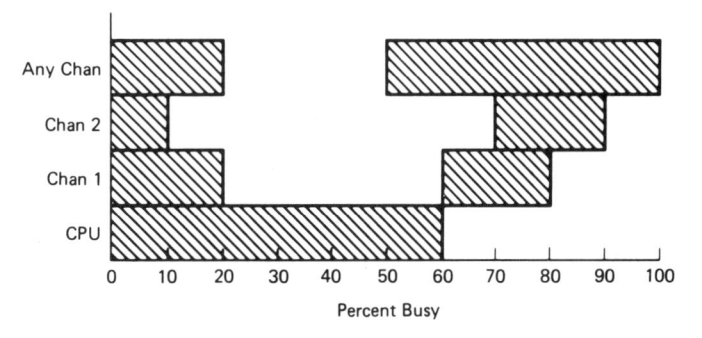

Figure 10-10. Gantt Chart.

Gantt Charts are often used by the manager of the CPE team to understand the balance and overlaps of the use of computer resources. Most often, Gantt Charts are produced automatically—typically by the data reduction programs that are obtained from or developed for using one of the measurement tools described in earlier chapters. This format is not only useful as a management reporting vehicle, it is also widely used as an analysis tool at the working level.

Kiviat Graphs

Kiviat Graphs have received considerable attention in the CPE community since their development in 1973. They are particularly useful for reporting "before" and "after" conditions of computer performance to higher management levels.

There are two forms of the Kiviat Graph in use. The first, much more widely used, requires that the user of the graph select an *even* number (usually eight, ten, or twelve) of performance indicators that are important at that user's installation. Half of these indicators are taken to be "good" when they increase in numerical value. The other half are considered "bad" when they increase in value. These indicators are numbered alternatively, beginning with a "good" indicator, then a "bad" indicator, and so forth until all "good" indicators have been assigned an *odd* number and all "bad" indicators an *even* number. These indicators are plotted on the radii of a circular diagram where each radius is evenly spaced around the circle with radius number "1" in the topmost, vertical position, and then numbered sequentially until all axes have been numbered. Then the indicators are plotted on the numbered axis corresponding to their number. Note that the outer ring of the circle represents the maximum value of each variable and the center is the minimum value. Because of this limit, it is easiest to plot percentages on this type of Kiviat Graph with 0 at the center and 100% at the outer ring of the circle.

Following these conventions, two eight-axis Kiviat Graphs are shown in Figure 10-11. The graph on the left represents an untuned IBM system while the graph on the right is of a tuned IBM system. As long as these conventions are followed, the more a system is improved, the more closely its Kiviat Graph will approach a "star

REPORTING PERFORMANCE TO MANAGEMENT 225

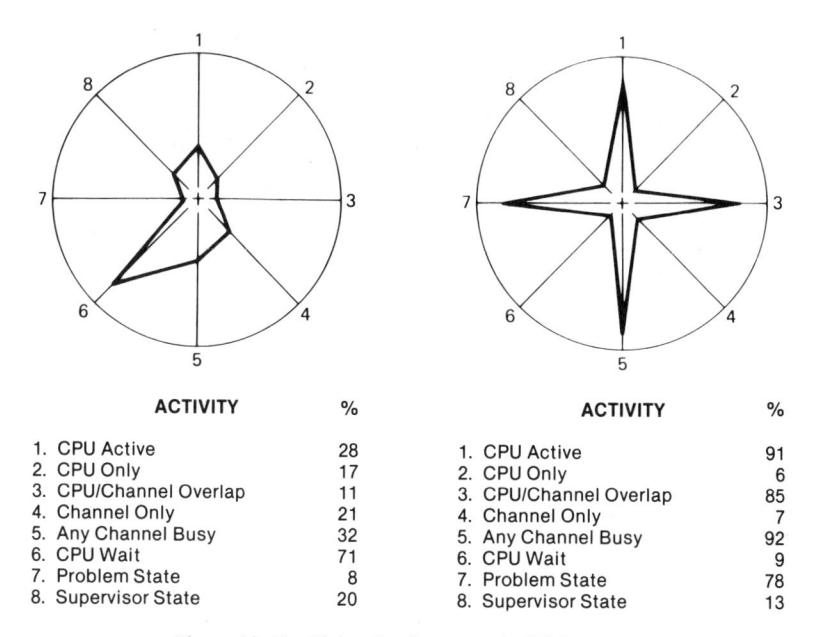

ACTIVITY	%
1. CPU Active	28
2. CPU Only	17
3. CPU/Channel Overlap	11
4. Channel Only	21
5. Any Channel Busy	32
6. CPU Wait	71
7. Problem State	8
8. Supervisor State	20

ACTIVITY	%
1. CPU Active	91
2. CPU Only	6
3. CPU/Channel Overlap	85
4. Channel Only	7
5. Any Channel Busy	92
6. CPU Wait	9
7. Problem State	78
8. Supervisor State	13

Figure 10–11. Kiviat Graphs—type 1: IBM system.

shape." Once it is explained that the star shape indicates performance which is close to the goals implied in the selected indicators, this format is easily and immediately understood by every level of management.

It is very important that the particular indicators plotted be chosen by the site which plans to use Kiviat Graphs in their reporting. The eight indicators shown in Figure 10–11 may be of no importance at most installations. In the installation where these two graphs were developed, the balance of resource usage of these particular eight indicators was considered important to the CPE project manager. These particular indicators have been used widely in articles describing the use of Kiviat Graphs and have gotten the aura of *the eight important* indicators. They are not generally important at all. They are simply a set of indicators that were chosen for use in one CPE project to portray the changes in the distribution of resource usage brought about by a tuning project.

Another CPE project involving a different architecture used a totally different set of indicators but, because the same rules described above were used, the "after" picture clearly approached the desired star shape. Figure 10-12 shows the Kiviat Graphs that applied to this project. The only change in the Control Data Corporation (CDC) system was the addition of "extended core storage" (ECS). Note that not all of the plotted indicators in this figure would normally range from 0 to 100%. In this case, reasonable maximums and minimums were selected for individual variables and the observed values were scaled between them so that they could be plotted as "percentages" in the Kiviat Graphs of the system. The tendency towards a star shape after the ECS addition should demonstrate to any level of management that the change allowed the workload and the equipment to attain a better match with regard to these indicators.

Trends may also be shown on this type of Kiviat Graph by plotting previous highs and lows for each variable. Another approach which indicates the stability of each indicator is to plot the statistical mean along with the one standard deviation (high and low) statistics as points on each axis. Unfortunately, either of these approaches tends to make the Kiviat Graph rather "busy" and harder to understand at a single glance.

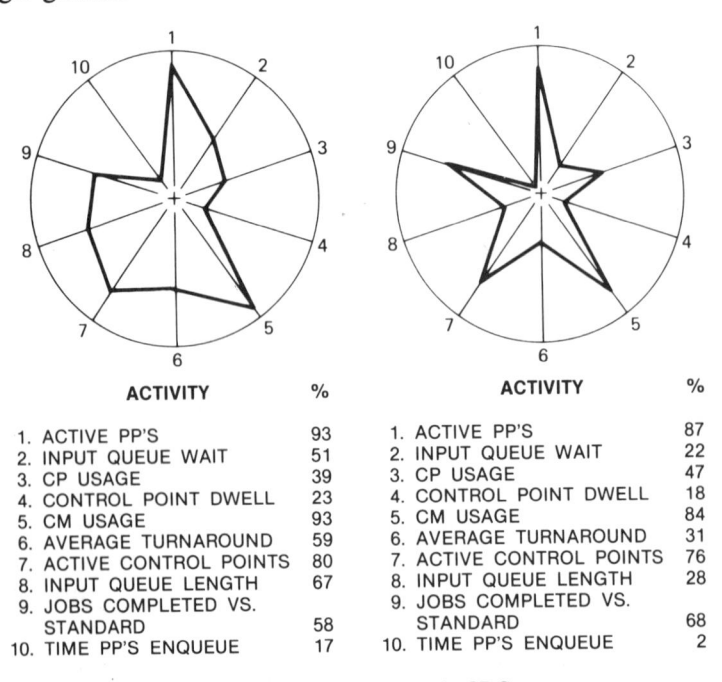

ACTIVITY	%	ACTIVITY	%
1. ACTIVE PP'S	93	1. ACTIVE PP'S	87
2. INPUT QUEUE WAIT	51	2. INPUT QUEUE WAIT	22
3. CP USAGE	39	3. CP USAGE	47
4. CONTROL POINT DWELL	23	4. CONTROL POINT DWELL	18
5. CM USAGE	93	5. CM USAGE	84
6. AVERAGE TURNAROUND	59	6. AVERAGE TURNAROUND	31
7. ACTIVE CONTROL POINTS	80	7. ACTIVE CONTROL POINTS	76
8. INPUT QUEUE LENGTH	67	8. INPUT QUEUE LENGTH	28
9. JOBS COMPLETED VS. STANDARD	58	9. JOBS COMPLETED VS. STANDARD	68
10. TIME PP'S ENQUEUE	17	10. TIME PP'S ENQUEUE	2

Figure 10-12. Kiviat Graphs—type 1: CDC system.

A second type of Kiviat Graph has evolved more recently and incorporates the statistical history of the indicator into the graph itself. Figure 10-13 shows a Kiviat Graph of the second type with 24 axes. The conventions outlined for type 1 Kiviat Graphs do not apply for type 2 graphs. Again, a circular display is used, but here each axis is divided into one-half standard deviation increments with the midpoint of each axis representing the statistical mean of the variable to be plotted on that axis. The concentric circles outward from the circle connecting the means are one-half standard deviation steps above the mean; inward from the mean the circles are deviations below the mean. For example, in the type 2 graph on the left of Figure 10-13, beginning at the center of the circle which represents all observations at or below 2½ standard deviations below the mean, the smallest concentric circle would be for minus 2 standard deviation plots, next for minus 1½, then minus 1, minus ½, 0 (or the mean value), plus ½, 1, 1½, and 2. The circumference of the circle, or the outer ring, represents all observations at or above 2½ standard deviations above the mean. As long as all previous observations over some past period (typically one year) are included in the statistical calculation of the

— Statistical mean

— "Normal" performance circle — includes all observations within one standard deviation from the mean.

All other concentric circles represent deviations above and below the mean in one-half standard deviation steps

All other concentrial circles represent deviations about +1 standard deviation or below −1 standard deviation in one-half standard deviation steps.

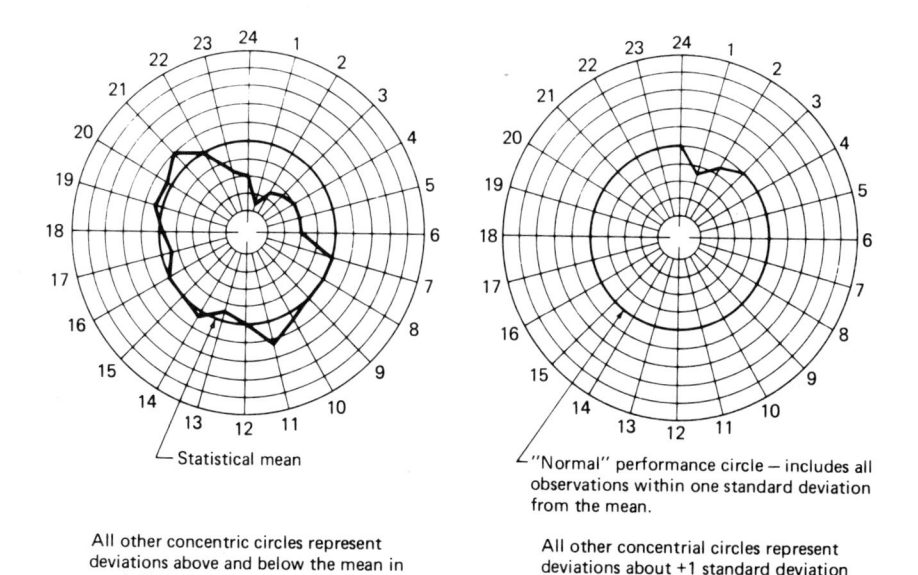

Figure 10-13. Kiviat Graphs—type 2.

latest observation, the behavior of the trend of the current figure is shown by its plotted value. (This type of Kiviat Graph is harder to explain than it is to understand.)

Kiviat Graphs of this second type are more useful if all observations between minus one and plus one standard deviation are regarded as "normal" and plotted on the same concentric circle. Statistically, this would mean that nearly 70% of all observations are taken to be normal or, perhaps, within "control limits." The graph on the right in Figure 10-13 is a replot of the same data as is in the left-hand graph but, on the right, the circle connecting the midpoints of each axis contains all observations from minus one to plus one standard deviations. By collapsing the plus and minus one standard deviation area, only those plots which are unusual would stand out. Note that axes 1, 2, and 3 show abnormal behavior of the plotted indicators; all other plots are on the "normal" ring. Some explanatory note should accompany this graph to state why performance was unusual on axes 1, 2, and 3.

The information plotted in Figure 10-13 was revenue per hour for a large center of a computer service company. Each axis represented one hour of one day. On the day used for these plots, the configuration was shut down for extensive maintenance from the day preceding these plots until about 0130 of this day. The system did not attain its full capability until after 0300 of the day plotted here.

This second kind of Kiviat Graph may have any number, odd or even, of axes. Different indicators may be plotted on each axis as was shown for type 1 Kiviat Graphs or several observations of only one indicator might be plotted as in Figure 10-13. There is no need to separate "good" and "bad" performance indicators, only to have a history of each indicator so that the deviation from the statistical mean may be calculated and plotted. There is no implication of "good" or "bad" in the shape of the plotted figure, rather the highlighted performance indicators are abnormal while those falling on the central ring are regarded as normal.

Schumacher Charts

When Kiviat Graphs are created by using the statistical conventions of type 2, many feel that there is no particular need to use a circular format. Another graphical management reporting format that can show the same kind of information as the type 2 Kiviat Graph is the Schumacher Chart. Figure 10-14 shows a portion of a Schumacher Chart.

The same plotting conventions are used here as for type 2 Kiviat Graphs but the way that Schumacher Charts are usually structured provides a facility for displaying both management and technical terminology in a way that promotes understanding of the relationships between the two types of terms. The idea is that, first, general management terms like those suggested earlier (see "Terminology") are chosen as major headings for individual reporting categories. These terms are usually either selected by, or at least coordinated with, higher management to be sure that each reporting area is one that management wants to know about. Then the technical indicators that translate into each management area are determined, usually by the CPE group. The major heading shown in Figure 10-14 is "Effectiveness." This is broken down into technical areas (Percent of General Products On Time, Percent of Critical Products On Time, and Percent of Cost Recovered) and the values of each

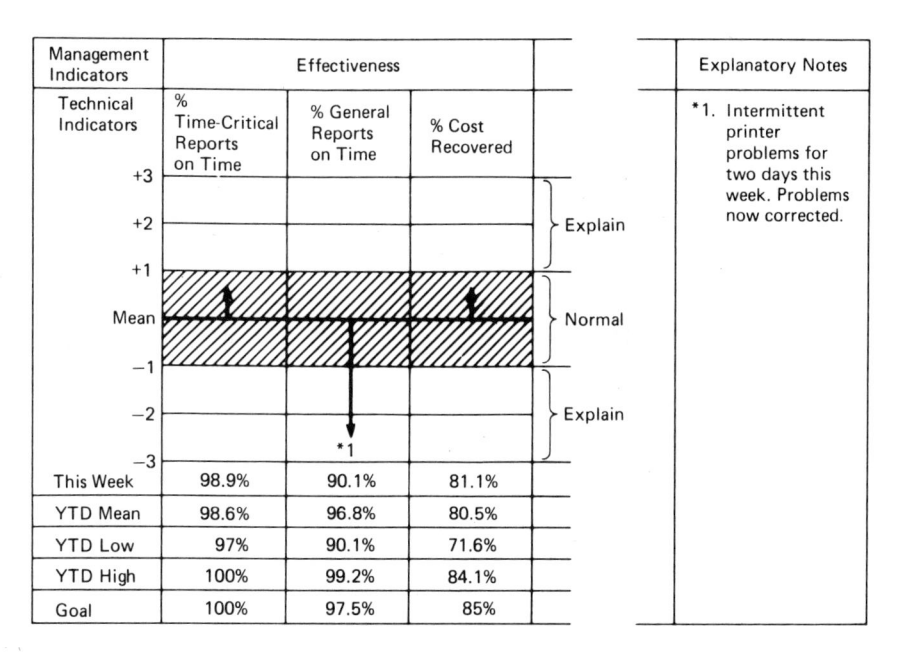

Management Indicators		Effectiveness			Explanatory Notes
Technical Indicators	% Time-Critical Reports on Time	% General Reports on Time	% Cost Recovered		*1. Intermittent printer problems for two days this week. Problems now corrected.
+3				} Explain	
+2					
+1				} Normal	
Mean					
−1					
−2			*1	} Explain	
−3					
This Week	98.9%	90.1%	81.1%		
YTD Mean	98.6%	96.8%	80.5%		
YTD Low	97%	90.1%	71.6%		
YTD High	100%	99.2%	84.1%		
Goal	100%	97.5%	85%		

Figure 10-14. Schumacher Chart—effectiveness.

230 COMPUTER PERFORMANCE EVALUATION

technical indicator are shown below the respective plot as "stock market" type, historical information. Only those indicators which plot outside the plus or minus one standard deviation band would be explained in notes to the graphic.

As an example of another set of management-technical indicators, consider the management interest in "Waste." Every industry has waste of some sort. Most industries set limits for the acceptable level of waste based on studies of the cost of producing 100% perfect products versus the cost of having to discard or redo some small percentage. The computer field seems unique in its aspiration for perfection but examination of the numbers of reruns and abnormal terminations of production programs at any installation quickly shows that this aspiration is never fulfilled. Higher management should be told how much is wasted in its computer facility just as in any other part of its production. Technical indicators for waste are readily available from the accounting data for most computers. These are called things like ABENDs, operator discontinued, reruns, and so forth. Figure 10-15 shows a Schumacher Chart for waste.

Management Indicators	Waste			Explanatory Notes
Technical Indicators	% Production Jobs Aborted	% Productions Jobs Rerun	$ Cost of Production Reruns	
+3				Explain
+2				
+1				Normal
Mean				
−1				
−2				Explain
−3				
This Week	9.7%	6.1%	$2407	
YTD Mean	12.6%	5.3%	$2110	
YTD Low	7.2%	1.2%	$1214	
YTD High	16%	8.7%	$3756	
Goal	4%	2%	$ 500	

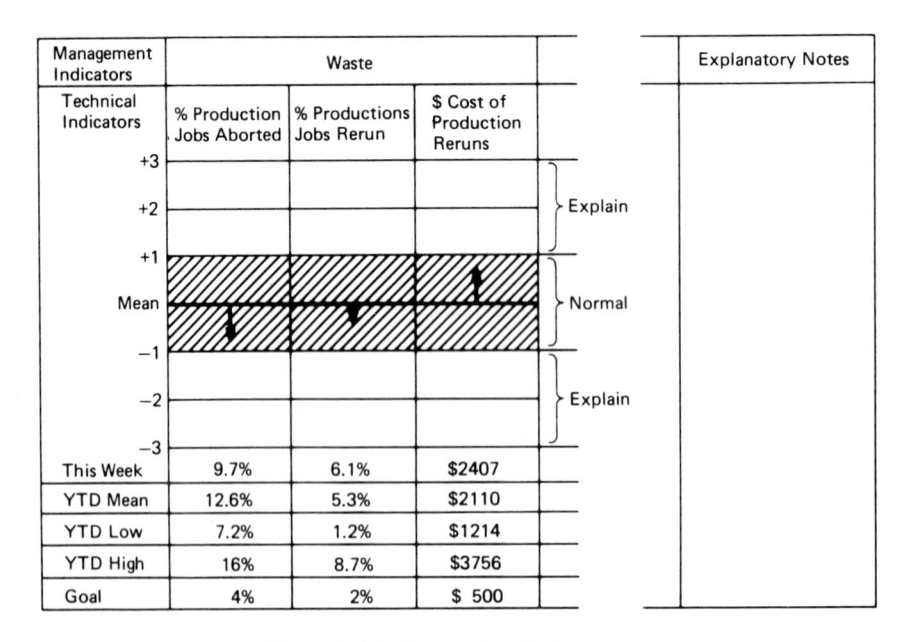

Figure 10-15. Schumacher Chart—waste.

When this kind of information is provided to the management of information systems or to corporate management, a regular project for waste management often results which enables controls to be developed over this important area.

Schumacher Charts may be prepared using one page for each management term when several technical terms are needed to support that area. When only two or three technical terms expand a management area, more areas can be displayed on a single page. It is best at first to keep the number of management areas down to six or so rather than trying to be too comprehensive. As experience grows and management becomes accustomed to seeing Schumacher Charts, new management areas may be added.

Schumacher Charts are sometimes quite useful at the technical level for such things as portraying general profiles of the total system and of large, individual programs. In such cases, all indicators would be technical, like: CPU busy, individual channel and device activity, memory usage, and so forth. Used this way, Schumacher Charts of benchmarks can be compared with the workload that they represent for a very quick proof of benchmark representativeness.

DEVELOPING A PERFORMANCE MANAGEMENT REPORTING SYSTEM

Comprehensive reporting systems that consider activities from the level of computer operations through corporate management and incorporate a full range of both automatically and manually generated information are necessarily unique to each company or agency. Because of this, there are no packaged products available that can be applied across the potential spectrum of users. There are reporting systems commercially available which collect data from several CPE tools and generate useful working level performance reports; however, management reporting as covered in this chapter requires either an in-house effort or use of a management consulting firm. Several of the larger consulting firms, particularly public accounting practices, have recently become very strong in developing computer performance reporting systems.

The effort needed to create a comprehensive reporting system is substantial. Four distinct phases must be accomplished to complete this effort. The phases may be called: survey, analysis, service-level review, and design.

The survey phase is usually the shortest and perhaps requires two to four staff weeks of effort. The major tasks of the survey are to develop an understanding of the needs and requirements of management and users and, if not already known, the general operational capability of the computer installation. Also during the survey, the programs which will be reported in detail need to be identified. Typically, those programs which constitute between 80 and 90% of the system's total resource usage would be selected for such reporting. The balance of the programs would be lumped together as "all others." As was pointed out at the beginning of this book, the number of programs which use this amount of resources is usually small—say 20 to 25% of the total number of programs. In larger installations, information about the range and availability of CPE tools would also be collected during this phase.

The analysis phase involves determination of baseline performance profiles for the individual programs selected earlier and for the overall system as usage varies during each day. The techniques for collecting and consolidating manual and automated information are also developed along with statistical routines to create historical trend information. It may also be necessary during the analysis phase to examine the function and organizational placement of the CPE effort in large data processing facilities. When this phase is handled by management consulting firms, recommendations are often made regarding the possible improvement of the organization's structure and reporting channels before the analysis is completed.

The service-level review phase is usually the longest of the four phases and requires the most effort. Here quantitative measures must be developed for the measures which management regards as important. Then these measures must be related to service levels and performance goals which are expected by the system's users. Initial performance standards are also developed and documented in this phase. By the end of the service-level review, a complete set of documentation should have been developed which defines all data elements to be included in the reporting system, all performance measures and how they are derived from the data elements, and detailed specifications for the initial reports which are to be produced by the system.

The final phase is quite straightforward in most computer installations. It is the design, programming and implementation of the programs which create the performance management reporting system. The system should be designed to have the greatest possible flexibility for producing special, one-time or continuing new reports. The extra time needed to provide this flexibility is usually repaid manyfold as managers begin to make special demands of the reporting system.

With exception of the first phase, it is not possible to estimate how long it would take to create a comprehensive management reporting system in general. There is some relationship between the size of the installation and the length of time required, but there is an even stronger relationship between the availability of information and the desire of management to have reports. It would not be unrealistic to spend between six months and one year in the total development effort. Consulting firms usually insist on completing the survey phase before they will give a binding estimate for the time and effort needed to finish the job.

11
A Structure for Continuing Computer Performance Evaluation Projects

This final chapter provides a practical structure for continuing, routine application of the CPE tools and techniques discussed throughout this book. The reader is encouraged to contrast the approach outlined here with the "Life Cycle" and management orientations of the first chapters and the tool-oriented approaches of subsequent chapters.

THE FLOW OF CPE PROJECTS

Figures 11-1, 11-2, and 11-3 show flow diagrams for applying CPE on a task-by-task basis. These tasks, which are also described below, are not meant to serve as a strict set of procedures that must always be followed. They are simply guidelines to help a manager or technician decide what task to try next when the priorities of the installation do not dictate some specific CPE project. It must be understood that activity conducted under these guidelines should be stopped or delayed whenever an installation-specific priority suggests a real need for some different type of CPE project than that which is underway.

One-time or even periodic application of the CPE flow diagrams of projects may be made even though a formal CPE group has not been established. In such cases, one or two analysts may be assigned tasks shown on a part-time basis. It is also possible and reasonable to spread the assignment of tasks to various sections of the computer department so that work on several tasks may be conducted simultaneously.

Very large installations or centralized groups that are responsible

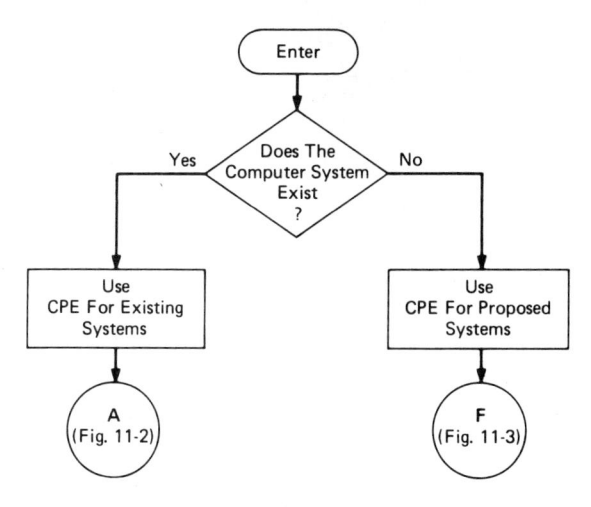

Figure 11-1. The first decision.

for management of multiple computer installations may be able to justify continuing full-time projects in any of the general task areas shown in these figures. For example, a large CPE team might be formed into specialty sections such as: control system tuning, applications program optimizing, equipment analysis, system modeling, scheduling, or into combinations of these specialties.

The flow diagrams should not be interpreted as oriented only towards computer equipment and its supporting operating system *or* sets of applications *or* the total set of equipment, operating system, and applications. The importance of this is seen in Figure 11-1. The only question is, "Does the computer system exist?" This consideration is seldom skipped when equipment is in mind, but it is too often overlooked when applications are to be examined. Whatever the "system" is comprised of, the first important question should be, "Does it exist?" If it does, it may be measured and examined using the full range of CPE tools and techniques; if it does not, modeling will be the only alternative.

CPE FOR EXISTING SYSTEMS

The first decision when examining an existing system is a value judgment that must be made by management. If management determines that the existing capacity is meeting requirements and that the ex-

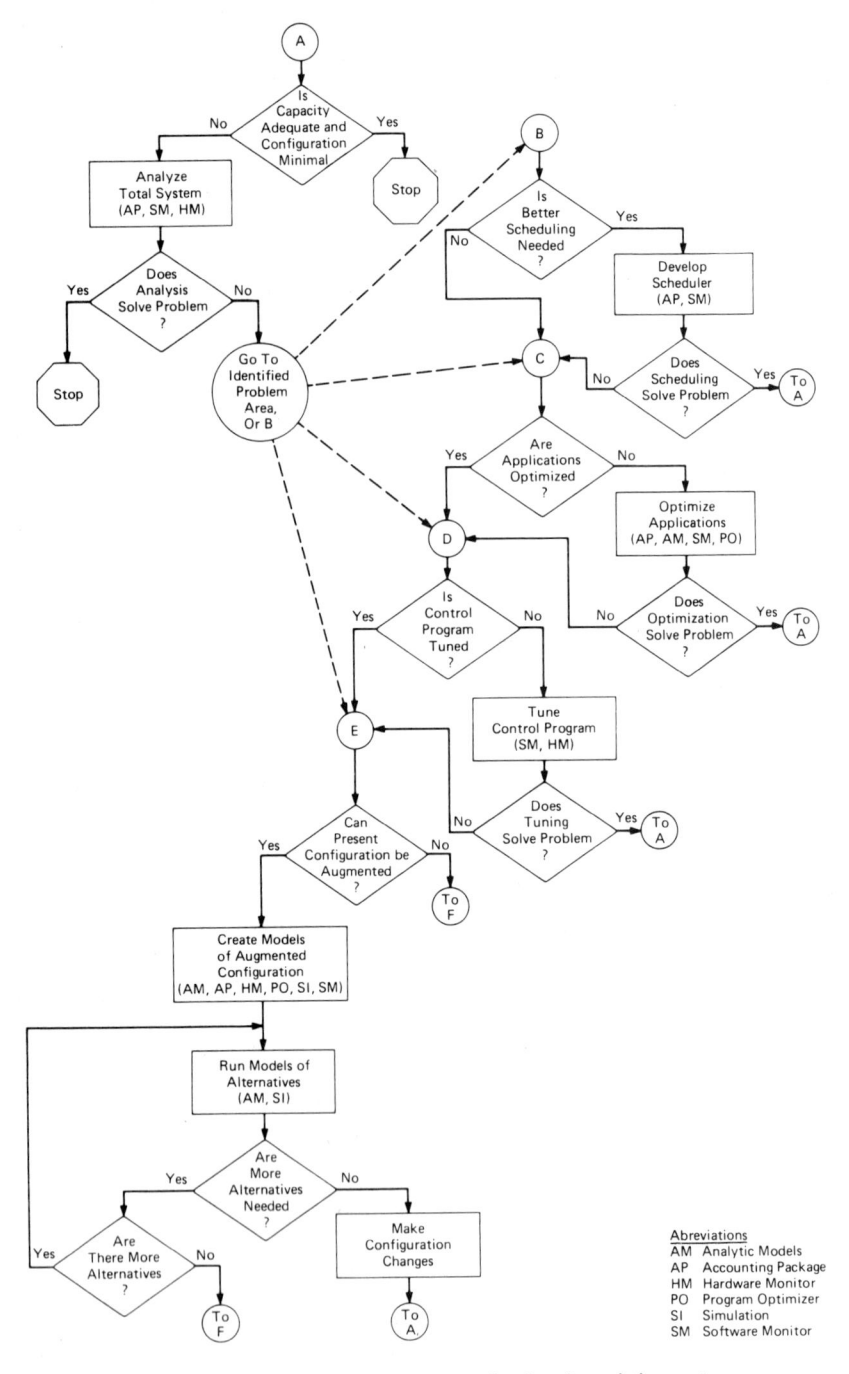

Figure 11-2. Computer performance evaluation for existing systems.

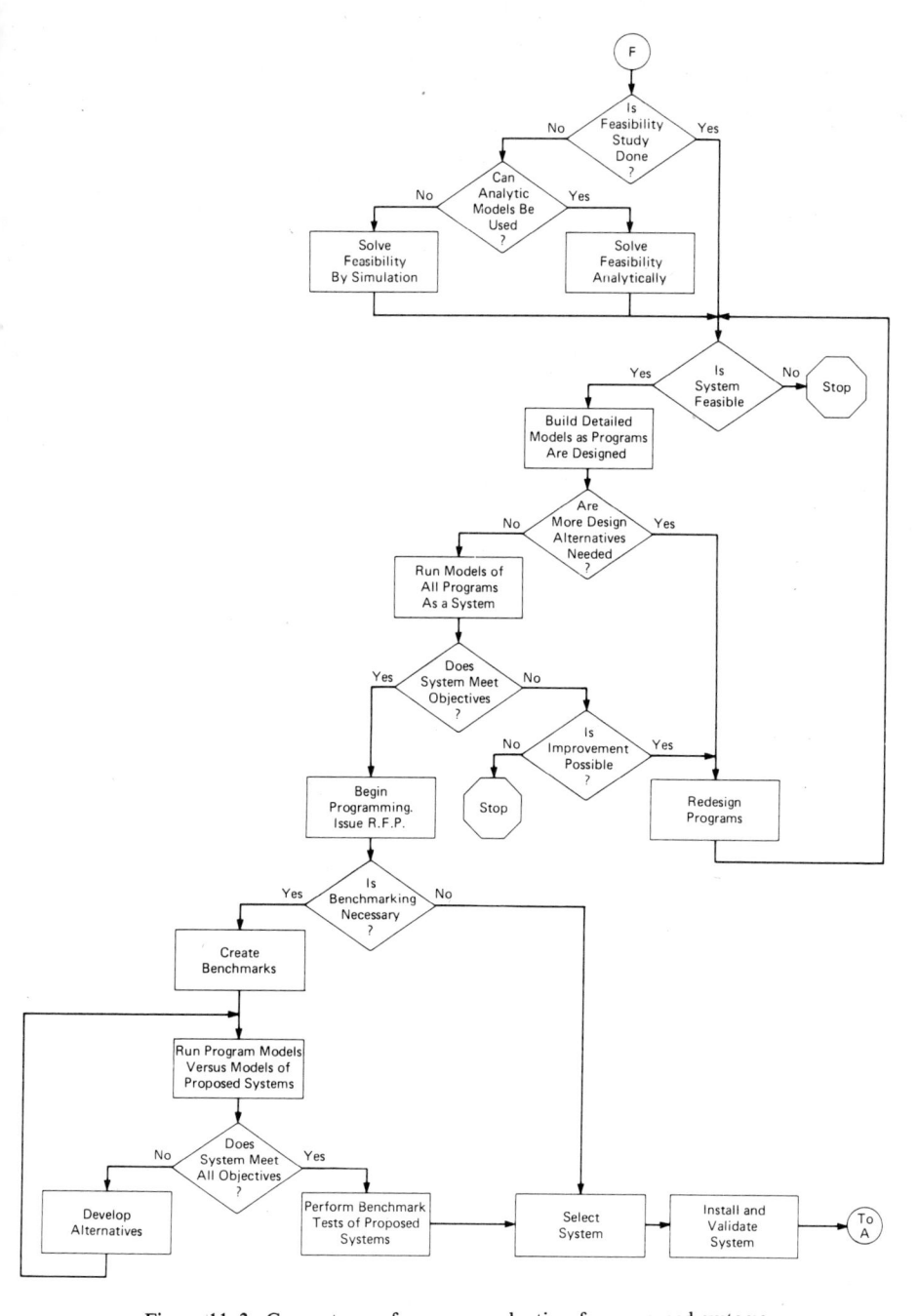

Figure 11-3. Computer performance evaluation for proposed systems.

isting configuration should not be reduced, then the ultimate goals of CPE are already met. No further effort should be expended on CPE until something occurs to change this management decision.

Analyze the Total System

When the determination has been made that there is either too much or too little capacity, analysis of the total system is in order. The purpose of this analysis is to determine the area within the system where there is the greatest potential for improvement.

The analysis needed might be compared to a "gross"-level audit of the installation. Examination of the workload's characteristics and of the way in which the workload and the equipment match, is the first step of such an analysis. Each program that uses a significant amount of the computing resources should be checked to ensure that the program is "legal" and that it is being used as intended. Potential "bottlenecks" in the equipment configuration should be noted. Kiviat Graphs on Schumacher Charts of system activity that are begun during this analysis may serve to point out workload/equipment imbalances.

During this analysis, visual observation or inspection plays a significant role in spotting problem areas that may need further examination. Although the outcome of visual observation is normally only that reasonably good intuition is developed for areas where problems exist, occasionally these inspections cause the problems to disappear without further work. This happens when unauthorized work or very poor operating procedures are discovered during the observation. In very rare instances, preliminary inspections may identify equipment components that are installed but that are not physically connected or usable to the system.

If the problem causing inadequate capacity or excessive equipment is resolved by analysis, then the CPE effort should be stopped until a problem is again perceived by management. If it is not resolved, the installation should be in a good position to determine whether a CPE team might be productive enough to justify its establishment. The installation personnel should also have a reasonable idea of where the initial, detailed studies should be undertaken.

The four basic areas where detailed CPE projects are productive on a continuing basis are described below. The areas are listed in the order in which they should be attacked *if* the analysis does not clearly indicate that one area (or, perhaps, some special project) deserves priority attention.* The four basic areas for CPE projects are:

1. Improved scheduling
2. Optimizing applications
3. Control program tuning
4. Configuration enhancement

Given that the computer system already exists, it is wise to cycle through these four areas periodically, whether a formal CPE team is available or not. Major effort should be directed at improving scheduling techniques and optimizing applications.

Only after examining the schedule and applications is it wise to spend time making changes to tailor the control program to the installation's unique workload and schedule. After these three areas are addressed, minor configuration changes may be assessed to tailor the equipment to the well understood demands at the installation. Adding hardware is usually the first proposal for improving system performance. In general, adding hardware should be the last alternative.

Improved Scheduling

Installations that have grown without particular attention to efficient operation are usually very well rewarded by any effort that is directed at improving the scheduling of jobs. There are commercial products that can provide quantum improvements in efficiency by the simple expedient of lining up applications to cause as little interference with each other as is reasonably possible.

In-house efforts using only accounting data and manual analysis can also produce quantum improvement. It is a simple (but time-consuming) task to prepare tables of the resources used by the major applications at an installation and then to arrange these table entries so that head-on conflicts between large users of the same resources are minimized. It may be worthwhile in a large installation to have

---

* In large IBM systems which use the "MVS" control program, "control program tuning" should be done before the other three areas.

one individual who is responsible for scheduling programs before they are introduced to the computer.

The best individual to involve in efforts to improve scheduling is the person that most operators seek out when they have questions about priorities or demands of specific programs. This is usually either one of the senior operators or a system programmer. This individual need not necessarily be the one to do the scheduling improvement, but he should at least be consulted regularly for ideas and opinions on proposed improvements.

When the scheduling methods have been improved to the point that further changes make little impact on system efficiency, the question should again be posed as to whether there still exists a problem with the computer system. If problems still are in evidence, or if scheduling is found to be so important that a person is assigned the task on a full-time basis, the CPE effort should be redirected towards the improvement of applications.

Optimizing Applications

This area has been addressed repeatedly throughout preceding chapters. It is the area that is most often thought of when CPE is considered. It is the domain of program optimizers and software monitors, with an initial role played by accounting packages. The technique for CPE projects in this area is to use accounting data to identify applications that are major system impactors and then to use software monitors and program optimizers to identify specific improvement areas within these applications.

When the major programs have been optimized and some method of continuing program surveillance is established, the CPE effort should be directed at control program tuning.

Control Program Tuning

Some software and hardware monitors make it possible to examine the internal workings of control programs at a sufficiently detailed level to make minor changes in the operating system. It is also possible through manual analysis to conclude that particular features of an operating system are either so little used that they should only be memory-resident when actually in use, or so often used that they should always be memory-resident.

Most control programs have options that are variable by externally set parameters. Some variables may be set, or reset, each time a program is initiated. Examples of such variables are Honeywell's and IBM's "Job Control Lanaguages" or JCL. Too often advantage is not taken of such control program features. The tuning effort should be aimed primarily at detailed examination of the small changes that will take advantage of the operating system's performance features. This is also an unusually productive area on a continuing basis. It is becoming common to find a specialist at many installations whose only job is to ensure that each application makes efficient use of operating system variables.

When full advantage is being made of the control program's performance options, the question is again asked as to whether problems still exist at the installation. If they do, it is time to examine possibilities of adding or changing equipment components within the existing system's options.

Configuration Enhancement

If it is suspected that only added equipment can solve a problem at an installation, the domain of modeling is entered. (Of course, it may be possible to make test runs on equipment that is under consideration at some other site; but, unless elaborate preparation can be made, the effect of the enhancement would not be measurable with the actual workload until after the enhancement is made.)

The construction of analytic or simulation models should depend on all available CPE tools and on data generated during earlier CPE projects. Proposed equipment alternatives may be modeled as long as there are feasible alternatives until some acceptable enhancement is identified. Once identified and selected, the new equipment will cause the characteristics of the installation to change in some way. This change makes it desirable to cycle through the previous three areas at least once to ensure that the enhanced system is reasonably well tuned. If no feasible alternative is found within the structure of the installed system, it may be necessary to consider replacing the entire configuration. This puts the problem into the context of CPE for proposed systems.

CPE FOR PROPOSED SYSTEMS

With the exceptions of benchmarking during the final phases of equipment acquisition and source program optimizers during the testing of new programs, CPE projects for proposed systems are exclusively within the domain of modeling. Whether the modeling is via specially written programs or through the use of one of the modeling packages will depend on the level of detail desired and the duration of the period considered by the analysts. In general, simulation packages get the larger amount of use in the type of work described here, but there is no reason to conclude that simulation packages are the only tool that should be used. As in nearly every other CPE project, the problem should determine the tool that is used. Many major procurement actions use several simulation tools and analytic models in combinations to take full advantage of the specific strengths of each approach.

CPE for proposed systems entails work in five areas:

1. Feasibility testing
2. Model building
3. Alternative testing
4. System creation
5. Validation

These areas should not be confused with the "steps" of conducting a simulation project as discussed in Chapter 7. (Define the Problem, Select a Solution Method, Develop Models, Validate Models, Simulate Alternative Solutions, Select and Implement "Best" Alternative, and Validate Simulation Predictions.) Each of the first three "areas" might entail all seven of the "steps". The System Creation area involves either program optimizers or benchmarks as the primary CPE tool, while Validation here is substantially the same as the final "step" in the modeling processes described earlier.

The CPE areas encountered when working with proposed systems are not nearly so distinctly separable as those for existing systems. For example, models developed during the feasibility testing may be used intact or refined for use later in testing the alternatives. System Creation, particularly when it is a system of applications programs, may begin during the feasibility tests and continue long after the system is operational. CPE projects in the Validation area actually cannot be completed until the system does exist, yet this is clearly a function of developing the proposed system and not of solving a problem with an existing system.

Feasibility Testing

The downfall of many data automation schemes may be traced to the failure to conduct a simple test of the feasibility of the scheme before a commitment was made to creation of the system. Even worse, a few of the more spectacular bad ideas that have failed in "computerization," were the subjects of rigorous feasibility studies that indicated they were bad ideas at the outset. But, in spite of better judgment, expediency demanded that the bad ideas be implemented. Whenever a new system is proposed, its feasibility should be examined.

The first level of feasibility testing is primarily a management task outside the view of CPE work. It requires that management ask and satisfactorily answer the "editorial" questions: "Who? What? Why? When? Where? How?" That is, management needs to know: *who* the system is for, *who* authorized it, and *who* will pay for it; *what* the reason is for it, *what* must be done to obtain it, and *what* the system is; *why* it is needed, *why* simpler alternatives are impossible, and *why* it wasn't needed before; *when* it is needed, *when* it can be obtained, and *when* it would be usable; *where* it would be obtained, *where* it would be installed, and *where* it would be controlled; and *how* much the system would cost, *how* it would be implemented, and *how* badly it is needed. Unless all of these questions can be answered, there should be doubt about the feasibility of the proposed system.

Given that management has determined system feasibility to their satisfaction, the CPE technician can begin the technical role. This requires that unbiased estimates be made of the quantity, space, and time needed to create the system. Analytic models should be used to make these estimates whenever possible. That is, when deterministic values are known for such things as the location and number of terminals in a proposed teleprocessing system, the volume and traffic characteristics of messages, and the total demands that would be made on the central computer facility; then a direct calculation of total system size may be possible. If there is a high level of uncertainty associated with such values, or when they are known to span ranges according to some rules of probability, then simulation would be needed to test the proposed system's feasibility.

Technical questions relating to the quantity, space, and time demands of the proposed system will have to be converted into cost and manpower by the CPE technician. This allows a management decision based on the real determinants of system feasibility. (It seems fair to say that virtually any system would be feasible if neither cost nor manpower were factors.) The specific questions that the CPE technician will have to resolve during the feasibility testing are highly problem-dependent. No general list comparable to the "editorial" questions given above for management can be enumerated. It can only be said that all of the foreseeable requirements should be examined at an acceptable level of detail. Then the likely cost in money and people should be put to management for their decision on "feasibility".

Feasibility testing should occur at the earliest part of the Procurement Phase of a computer system's life cycle. The CPE technician who becomes involved at this point has an unusual opportunity to establish good relations with the people who are setting system requirements (the people that must provide information for the feasibility study). The communication set up with these individuals should be carefully maintained as it will have great value much later during the Operational Phase of the life cycle when Validation of the models against the real system takes place.

Model Building

Once the proposed system is ruled feasible, construction of detailed models of the applications may begin. This task may continue far into the operational life of the implemented system so it is worthwhile to create detailed models that can be varied over any foreseeable workload range and that can be expanded to incorporate changes that may become needed.

The concepts and methodology of model building are covered in detail in Chapters 7 and 8 and will not be repeated here. Every alternative that is suggested may be modeled, but time and common sense will dictate that only those alternatives with good chance of implementation should be turned into workable models.

Alternative Testing

As soon as a few working models have been created, testing of the various design alternatives may begin. This entails the running of the models to estimate the resources that each design alternative would demand and to select the "best" of the available alternatives. "Best" must be recognized as a relative word in this area. Testing alternatives, like testing feasibility, often comes down to the question of manpower and cost. The "best" technical solution may have to be abandoned in favor of some cheaper alternative.

An example of this is often seen when new equipment is to be acquired for a large existing workload. It is so often cheaper and faster to convert the existing programs without modification that this will be done no matter how inefficient the programs may be. When this happens, only equipment alternatives need testing to ensure that the existing programs can be processed on the proposed configurations.

When enough of the proposed system has been through the alternative selection process to constitute a "representative" workload, simulation runs of the total applications set may begin. At this stage the total set is checked to ensure that all objectives of the system will be met by the selected designs. If necessary, more design alternatives may be generated to bring the system into line with requirements. This may entail modification or recreation of models of those applications that must be redesigned.

Programming typically begins as soon as the first few program designs have been completed. However, the System Creation area is not fully underway until the total system's design is judged to meet all of the system's objectives.

System Creation

When the proposed system is comprised of both applications and equipment, this is a very busy period for the CPE technicians and for the computer group. The programming must be accompanied by regular tests that use program optimizers on some available equipment while the iterative modeling and benchmarking tasks are underway to select equipment.

System Creation spans the Procurement and Installation phases of the system's life cycle. As the system begins to take on its final form, the applicability of the full range of CPE tools broadens to match that of "CPE for Existing Systems" as shown in Figure 11-2. Acceptance Testing may be thought of as both the last activity of "CPE for Proposed Systems" and the first activity of "CPE for Existing Systems."

Validation

After the new system is operational, one CPE task remains that is truly a function of "CPE for Proposed Systems." This is the task of ensuring that the detailed models of applications and equipment accurately represent the system that becomes operational. There is no specific time when this task is done but it is best to do it as soon as possible.

The value of model validation to the CPE group is very high. First, it provides a documented record that the system is as it was designed to be, or indicates where the variations from the design occur. And, second, the validated models created for the proposed system are extremely useful during the Operational Phase of the system's life cycle in support of continuing CPE projects.

When the Validation area is skipped or put off for too long, much of the detailed and difficult work of model building will be wasted. It is not a particularly difficult task to ensure that the models do match the implemented programs. Further, the validation activity fits quite nicely into the continuing duties of a CPE group and can serve as a focal point for selecting specific projects as the system ages and changes.

GENERAL

The flow diagrams of Figures 11-1, 11-2, and 11-3 are not all-inclusive. Many of the CPE projects mentioned throughout this book do not lie conveniently in any of the boxes of the diagrams. Beyond their use as decision-assistance tools, the flow diagrams may also be used for time and cost accounting purposes. As each block's activity is conducted, the manpower expended and the span time used may be recorded. Once the activity in a block has been conducted a few times, the observed resources used for past CPE projects can be used to make time and cost estimates for future CPE projects.

A further purpose that may be served by this structured approach is that of scheduling the use of CPE tools and technicians. As the value of CPE projects becomes established in an installation, requests for CPE projects tend to outpace the group's ability to perform projects. Categorizing nonpriority tasks into their places in the diagram should allow the CPE team to cover several related tasks in their logical order. When a history of CPE activity is available, it becomes easy to estimate the delay before each newly requested project will be initiated.

The earliest work that led to the development of these diagrams was undertaken to associate times and costs with each of the CPE activities at a major, centralized computer management organization.* The times and costs associated with each task did prove to be reasonably constant for any one group. However, each of the groups that have used this approach found such widely varied costs that it would be misleading to offer any numbers here as "representative." The costs for each category of CPE project, like the value of each project, are installation- or organization-dependent.

IN CLOSING

This book is intended to provide a reasonable basis for beginning and continuing CPE efforts. The stress is on practical applications that have worked in real computer installations. There are many ways of identifying and solving problems of inefficient computer usage. The variety of tactics and viewpoints discussed in this book should enable computer managers and technicians to look carefully at some of the many alternative ways of improving the efficiency of "their" computer.

It is feared that structuring this book by "tool and technique" may suggest that the first concern should be with what CPE tool to

* Bell Telephone Laboratories, Business Information Systems, Piscataway, New Jersey.

buy. Such a conclusion would be wrong. The first step should always be to identify and understand specific problems. The tools needed for this step are *common sense* and *visual observation*. If these two tools are not available in the beginning, additional CPE tools won't help at all.

The problems must dictate which tools should be used for their solutions. Dr. Thomas E. Bell, one of the pioneers of the CPE field, made this point very succinctly in his article, "Computer Measurement and Evaluation—Artistry or Science?"*

> ... If the designated people begin [a CPE project] by asking what sort of tools to acquire, the probability of an unsuccessful effort is high.

Buying tools before specific computer problems are identified just adds the problem of what to do with the tool. The goal of Computer Performance Evaluation is solutions, not more problems.

---

* *Performance Evaluation Review,* **1**, Number 2, ACM/SIGME, New York, June 1972, pp. 4–10.

Suggested Readings

Accounting Data

Coughlin, Donald T., "Introduction to Cost Accounting," *Computer Measurement Group Transactions,* Nos. 23-24, pp. 3-2 through 3-13, Mar./June 1979, The Computer Measurement Group, Inc. POB 26063, Phoenix, AZ 85068.

Read, Emma, "Time Sheet Accounting," *Journal of Systems Management* **30,** pp. 32-35, Jan. 1979, Association for Systems Management, 24587 Bagley Road, Cleveland, OH 44138.

A *Guide to Major Job Accounting Systems: The Logger System of the UNIVAC 1100 Series Operating System,* National Bureau of Standards Special Publication 500-43, Dec. 1978.

"Charging for DP Services: Two Methods Analyzed," Dan Bernard, *Government Data Systems,* pp. 23-24, Jan./Feb. 1978.

"Cost of Using Excess Capacity," Edwin L. Heard, *Journal of Systems Management,* pp. 24-27, Sept. 1976.

Guideline on Major Job Accounting Systems: The System Management Facilities (SMF) for IBM Systems Under OS/MVT, National Bureau of Standards Special Publication 500-40, Oct. 1978.

"Management Use of Job Accounting Data for Performance Evaluation," V. Banna, *Computer Measurement Group Transactions,* Mar. 1977.

"Managing Computer Performance With Control Limits," T. E. Bell, *Performance Evaluation Review,* pp. 21-28, Jan. 1975.

"The Computer Pricing Process," C. W. Axelrod, *Computer Measurement Group Transactions,* Dec. 1977.

Hardware/Software Monitors

Mead, C. W., "Hardware Monitors Help Services Firm . . . Forecast, Budget Growth For 11 Data Centers." *Computerworld,* **13,** pp. 54-55, Nov. 26, 1979, Computerworld, Inc. 375 Cochituate Road, Route 30, Framingham, MA 01701.

"A Guide to the Use of Hardware Monitors," Gary Carlson, *EDP Performance Review,* pp. 1-8, Sept. 1976, pp. 1-7, Oct. 1976.

"Effectively Using Your Hardware Monitor," Robert Bishop, *Computer Measurement Group Transactions,* Sept. 1976.

"Evaluation and Comparison of Software Monitors," *EDP Performance Review,* pp. 1-9, Feb. 1976.

"Fallacies of Intuition in Performance Tuning," Gary Carlson, *EDP Performance Review,* pp. 1-6, Apr. 1976.

"Making the Most of Performance Monitors," William B. Engle, *Computer Decisions*, p. 50, Nov. 1978.

"Software Monitoring: Principles of Design and Use," Duane Ray Ball, *Proceedings of the Computer Performance Evaluation Users Group 1976*, pp. 215-219, 1976.

"Techniques for Software Monitoring", T. B. Pinkerton, *System Tuning*, pp. 347-358, 1977.

"The Design of Software Monitors," I. L. Ramage, *System Tuning*, pp. 359-372, 1977.

"Tutorial: Computer System Monitors," Gary J. Nutt, *Performance Evaluation Review*, pp. 41-51, Jan. 1976.

Program Analysis/Optimization

Smith, Connie, "Methods For Improving the Performance of Application Programs," *Computer Measurement Group Transactions*, No. 22, pp. 4-2 through 4-35, Dec. 1978.

"COBOL Optimization and Flowcharting," M. M. Headrick, National Technical Information Service, Y/CSD/INF-77/1, 1977.

"Gaining An Awareness of the Performance of COBOL Programs," Paul J. Jalics, *Computer Measurement Group Proceedings*, pp. 61-65, 1978.

"Improving Performance the Easy Way," Paul J. Jalics, *Datamation*, pp. 135-137, Apr. 1977.

"Measuring Programming Quality and Productivity," T. C. Jones, *IBM Systems Journal*, **17**, No. 1, pp. 39-63, 1978.

"Performance Evaluation of Programs in a VS Environment," James R. Walker and Thomas E. McKittrick, *Computer Measurement Group Proceedings*, pp. 62-78, 1976.

Benchmarks

Oliver, Paul, "Software Conversion and Benchmarking," *Software World* **10**, No. 3, pp. 2-11, 1979, A. P. Publications Ltd., 322 St. John St., London EC1V 4QH, England.

"Benchmarking Distributed Systems: Objectives and Techniques," Thomas F. Wyrick, *Performance of Computer Installations*, pp. 83-101, D. Ferrari, Editor, North-Holland, 1978.

"Benchmarking in Selection of Timesharing Systems," D. J. M. Davies, *Computer Performance Evaluation Users Group Proceedings*, pp. 27-36, 1978.

Guidelines for Benchmarking ADP Systems in the Competitive Procurement Environment, National Technical Information Service, FIPS-PUB 42-1, 1977.

"Remote Terminal Emulation in the Procurement of Teleprocessing Systems," Shirley Ward Watkins and Marshall D. Abrams, *AFIPS Conference Proceedings—National Computer Conference*, pp. 723-727, 1977.

"Validation—All Important in Benchmarking," Arnold L. Johnson, *Computer Performance Evaluation Users Group*, pp. 75-83, 1977.

Simulation

"A Case Study of Simulation as a Computer System Design Tool," Gary J. Nutt, *Computer,* pp. 31-36, Oct. 1978.

"Computer Simulation: A Tutorial," Gerald Adkins and Udo W. Pooch, *Computer* (Magazine of the IEEE Computer Society), pp. 12-17, Apr. 1977.

"The Use of Simulation in the Evaluation of Software," N. F. Schneidewind, *Computer* (Magazine of the IEEE Computer Society), pp. 47-53, Apr. 1977.

Emshoff, J. R. and Sisson, R. L., *Design and Use of Computer Simulation Models,* Macmillan, New York, 1970.

Gordon, G., *System Simulation,* Second Edition, Prentice Hall, New Jersey, 1978.

Shannon, R. E., *Systems Simulation, The Art and Science,* Prentice Hall, New Jersey, 1975.

Roth, P. F., "Simulation" in *Encyclopedia of Computer Science,* A. Ralston and C. L. Meek, Editors, Petrocelli-Charter, New York, 1976, pp. 1259-1278.

Roth, P. F., "Simulation of Computers—An Introductory Tutorial" in the *Proceedings of the Symposium on Simulation of Computer Systems,* H. J. Highland, Editor, Boulder, CO, Aug. 12-14, 1975, pp. 1-5.

Roth, P. F. and Meyerhoff, A. J., "BOSS Simulation of a Time Sharing Message Processing System for Bank Applications" in the *Record of Proceedings, Third Annual Simulation Symposium,* Tampa, FL, Jan. 14-16, 1970, pp. K1-K13.

Proceedings of the Symposium on Simulation of Computer Systems:
Gaithersburg, MD, June 19-20, 1973
Gaithersburg, MD, June 4-6, 1974
Boulder, CO, Aug. 12-14, 1975
Boulder, CO, Aug. 10-12, 1976

Proceedings of the Conference on Simulation, Measurement, and Modeling of Computer Systems, Boulder, CO, Aug. 13-15, 1979.

Proceedings of the Winter Simulation Conference, H. Highland, T. Schriber, and R. Sargent, Editors, Gaithersburg, MD, Dec. 4-6, 1976.

Roth, P. F., "A Progress Report on the Use of BOSS for ADPE Performance Prediction," in *Proceedings of Computer Performance Evaluation Users Group,* Bedford, MA, Apr. 18-20, 1972.

Analytic Models

Lindzey, G. E. and Browne, J. C., "Response Analysis of a Multi-Function System." *Performance Evaluation Review,* **8,** pp. 19-25, Fall 1979, ACM Special Interest Group on Measurement and Evaluation, ACM, 1133 Ave of the Americas, New York, NY 10036.

"BEST/1—Design of a Tool for Computer System Capacity Planning," J. P. Buzen, et al., *Proceedings of AFIPS 1978 National Computer Conference,* pp. 447-455.

"A Queueing Network Model of MVS," J. P. Buzen, *ACM Computing Surveys,* **10,** 3 (September 1978), pp. 319-331.

"The Operational Analysis of Queueing Network Models," P. J. Denning and J. P. Buzen, *ACM Computing Surveys,* **10,** 3 (Sept. 1978), pp. 225-261.

Queueing Network Models of Multiprogramming, J. P. Buzen, Garland Publishing, New York, 1980.

General

Morris, Michael F., "What to Do About Those Expensive Computers," *Management Focus,* pp. 9-31 Jan./Feb. 1981.

"A Survey of EDP Performance Measures," Joseph R. Matthews, *Government Data Systems,* pp. 29-32, Jul./Aug. 1978.

"Computer Performance Analysis: Framework and Initial Phases for a Performance Improvement Effort," T. E. Bell, B. W. Boehm, and R. A. Watson, The Rand Corp., R-549-1-PR, Nov. 1972.

"EDP Effectiveness Evaluation," Corydon D. Hurtado, *Journal of Systems Management,* pp. 18-21, Jan. 1978.

EDP Performance Management Handbook, Applied Computer Research, 1978.

"Getting Started in Computer Performance Evaluation," Philip J. Kiviat and Michael F. Morris, *CMG Transactions,* Section 3, pp. 2-19, Dec. 1975.

"Guidance for Sizing ADP Systems," Dennis M. Gilbert, James O. Mulford and Mitchell G. Spiegel; *Computer Performance Evaluation Users Group,* pp. 305-330, 1978.

Guideline on Computer Performance Management: An Introduction, National Technical Information Service, FIPS-PUB-49, 1977.

"Kiviat Graphs and Single-Figure Measures Evolving," Michael F. Morris, *Computerworld,* pp. 17-18, Feb. 9, 1976, pp. 19-20, Feb. 16, 1976.

"The State of the Art In Analytical Modeling," Richard F. Dunlavey, *EDP Performance Review,* pp. 1-7, Nov. 1978.

The Value of Performance Measurement," Ivan Berti, *Computer Management,* pp. 57-58, Sept. 1978.

"What are We Measuring?" Robert B. Forest, *Infosystems,* pp. 92-94, May 1978.

Ferrari, Domenico, *Systems Performance Analysis,* Prentice-Hall (New Jersey), 1978.

Index

Index

absolute (software) power, 195–196, 198
accounting data, 10, 14, 47, 51–73, 81, 89, 99, 104, 114, 239–240
  acceptability of, 69
  applications of, 61–73
  as a startup tool, 69–70
  availability of, 3, 69
  computer resource, 51
  conditioning, 62
  cost of, 8, 58–59
  cross-validate, 70
  definition of, 51
  discrepancies in, 70
  evolution of, 3
  oldest form of, 52
  overhead, 8, 59, 70
  programmer information from, 66–69
  typical performance information from, 71
  suggested readings on, 249
  reduction packages, 3
  reduction programs, 2
accounting package(s), 5, 12
  common errors in, 62
  comprehensive, 57–58
  limitations of, 58
  standard reports of, 56
  system, 55–57
advantages (strengths) of,
  analytic models, 139, 182
  simulation, 162–163
  software monitors, 89–90
  software power, 190
analytic model(s) 7, 131–132, 164–183, 241, 243
  applying, 175–182
  data collection for, 171–172
  definition of, 165

equations, 168–169, 180
extensions, 180–182
  for batch programs, 182
  for time sharing applications, 182
  for transaction processing, 182
  limitations of, 182–183
  major advantage of, over simulation, 182
  parameters, 170–171
  suggested readings on, 251–252
  strengths of, 182
ALGOL, 81
alternative testing, 242, 245
application program, 4
  analyzers, 81–83
  optimizing, 239–240
arrival(s), 166
  rate, 170–171
asymptotic (software) power, 196–197
audit (or), 238
  internal, 9
  self (benchmark), 123, 127–128
  trail, 131

bar chart, 220–223
Bell, Dr. Thomas E., 248
Bell Telephone Laboratories, 247
benchmark(s) (-ing), 2, 9–10, 118–134, 246
  acceptable error, 129
  background, 119–120
  characteristics, 123–125
  cost of, 8, 132–133
  customer-supplied, 122
  definition of, 6, 118
  existing systems, 125–131
  existing workloads, 125
  frequent application of, 122
  how to, 124–125

253

254 INDEX

benchmark(s) (-ing) *(cont.)*
  instruction, 120
  instruction mix, 120
  job stream, 131
  kernal, 120, 127
  limitations of, 132-133
  objectives, 124-125
  overheads, 8
  parameters of a, 128-129
  programs, 6
  proposed systems, 131-132
  proposed workload, 125
  representative, 11, 133
  run time of a, 130
  self-auditing, 122
  suggested readings on, 250
  terminology, 120-121
  why, 121-123
billing, 51-52
  information, 53-55
  overhead, 55
block,
  count, 55
  size, 196-197
Boolean operations, 5, 96-98, 101
bottlenecks, 87, 178, 238
Burroughs, 91
  B3500, 116
Buzen, Dr. Jeffrey P., 164

cables, 99-101
  laying, 100
capacity, excess, 17
capacity management, 3, 43-45, 53
  definition of, 45
check flags, 3
code, extraneous, 86
common sense, 2, 248
  rules for connection and use of
    hardware monitors, 107-110
comparators, 100-102
comparisons (of computer systems), 119
computer listings, 217-219
computer manufacturers as largest
    simulation users, 162
computer performance evaluation (CPE),
  charter for, 28
  continuing, activities, 43-49
  cost of, tools *(See also* costs) 8
  data base, 43, 45-46

  decision to get started in, 19-21
  definition of, 2
  for existing systems, 235-241, 246
  for proposed systems, 237, 242-246
  goal of, 248
  introduction to, 1-18
  manager's responsibilities, 32-33
  managing, efforts, 19-50
  principle concern of, 9
  project administration, 30
  project goals, 17
  project management, 32
  project reports, 31
  rule of thumb, 21
  scheduling the use of, 247
  technicians and internal auditors, 9
  threshold for using, 16, 49-50
  tools, 8-10
  when to stop using, 16, 238
computer performance evaluation (CPE)
    project(s)
  a structure for continuing, 234-248
  adminsitration, 30
  analytic models in, 180
  costs of, 37, 247
  experiments, 39
  final report, 209
  flag to start a, 215
  goal setting for a, 21-23
  goals, 17
  level of detail, 36
  logical starting point for, 52
  management, 32
  managing the scope of, 36
  objectives, 35
  report production, 38
  reports, 31
  scheduling, 35
  the flow of, 234-237
  using accounting data for, 69-73
  validation in, 37-38
computer performance evaluation (CPE)
    team, 13, 23-26, 235
  attitude, 26
  basic skill areas, 30
  controls over, 29
  job descriptions, 29-30
  leader's responsibilities, 34-43
  maintaining skill levels of, 41
  members' background, 24

INDEX 255

minimum investment for a, 26
organizational placement of a, 26-30
organizing a, 35-36
potential members of a, 25-26
specialties, 235
types of people for a, 24-25
computer system(s)
  examples of, variables, 153
  problems with, applicable to simulation, 141
  queuing and probabilistic behavior in, 152
  sizing, using simulation, 160
computer resource accounting data. *See* accounting data
COMTEN, 111
concentrators, 99
confidence
  curves, 76-77
  interval, 76-77
configuration enhancement, 239, 241
console logs 47
consultant(s), 50, 117, 233
Control Data Corporation (CDC)
  Cyber 74, 112-113
  system, 226
  6600, 82
control limit(s) 46, 215
control progam, 12, 75, 84
  activity, 58
  analyzers, 81, 84-87
  optimization projects, 100
  third party, 86
  tuning, 239-241
  variables, 241
cost(s)
  accounting, 247
  allocation, 52
  benefit studies, 122
  estimates, 247
  hardware monitor project, 116-117
  of a CPE technician, 49-50
  of accounting data, 8, 58-59
  of benchmarks, 8, 132-133
  of CPE tools, 8
  of CPE projects, 37, 247
  of hardware monitors, 8, 116-117
  of modeling, 8
  of program optimizers, 8
  of simulation, 162

of software monitors, 75, 92
subject to reduction, 19
threshold level of, for CPE, 19

definition of
accounting data, 51
analytic models, 165
benchmarks, 6, 118
computer performance evaluation, 2
hardware monitors, 4, 93
modeling, 7
simulation, 132
software monitors, 3, 25-81
software power, 185-186
software work, 185
departures, 166
diagnostics, performance, 70-71
diagnostic routines, 13
discrete event simulation,
  example of, 152
  major elements of, 155
  output of, 158
  of resource contention, 152
documentation of simulation, 151-152
driver programs, 127, 129
DYNAPAR, 111-113

editorial questions, 243
EDP Performance Review, 134
effectiveness, 9, 17
efficiency, 9, 16, 47, 53, 240
  program, 81-82
elements of discrete event simulation, 155-156
emulation, 120
engineering test point. *See* probe point
equipment
  class, 186
  planning, 190
  selection, 11
  specification, 11
  usage analysis, 81, 87-89
establishing outside relationships, 43, 48-49
execution time profile, 201, 206-207
expense. *See* cost

feasibility testing, 242-244
flow diagrams of CPE activity, 235-237
flow of events, simulated, 157
forecast, 11

FORTRAN, 4, 75
free resource, 3

Gantt chart, 223-224
Gibson mix, 119
goal(s), 17, 248, 212-213
goal-oriented approach, 23
goal-setting for CPE, 21-23
guidelines for a CPE project, 234-248

hardward monitor(s) (-ing), 2, 4, 5-6, 10,
    14, 47, 61, 92, 93-117, 185-186, 240
  basic, 5, 8, 102-103
  bias, 93-94
  categories of, 102-104
  common injuries when using, 107
  common sense rules for connection and
    use of, 107-110
  complexity of, 93
  connection of, 93, 107
  cost of, 8, 116-117
  count mode, 95
  data reduction, 110
  definition of, 4, 93
  engineering test point. *See* probe point
  event mode, 95
  installation of, 115
  intelligent, 5, 8, 102-104
  internal clocks, 99
  limitations of, 114-116
  logic boards, 96-99
  logic pins. *See* probe points
  mapping, 5, 8, 102-103
  onsite assistance for, 107
  overhead, 8, 110, 114
  output, 110-114
  permission to connect, 115
  physical description of, 93-102
  probe, 94
  probe point, 48, 93-94, 105-107, 117
  raw, data, 111
  signals monitored by, 94-99
  suggested readings on, 249-250
  system independence of, 104-105
  time mode, 95
  using, 102-117
  when to use, 104-105
  work sheets, 99
histograms, 223
Honeywell JCL, 241

hypothesis, 63-65

IBM
  JCL, 241
  MVS, 239
  system, 110, 225
  360s, 114
  360/65, 82
  370s, 114
  370/158, 200
  3330, 196, 198
  3420, 197
ideal configuration, 195, 200
ideal I/O configuration, 199
identity data, 55
importance of environment, 59-61
independent variables, 165-166, 169
  determining the, 172-174
indicators, performance, 70-71
instruction level, 124, 131
integrating operations and measurement
  activity, 43, 46-47
internal audit, 9
internal report, 111

jargon, 210
job billing, 3
job catalog, 72
job scheduling, 3

Kiviat graphs, 224-228, 238
  conventions 224-225
  type 1, 224-225
  type 2, 227-229
Kolence, Kenneth W., 184

library control, 3
life cycle applications of simulation,
  160-161
life cycle of a computer system, 9, 11-15,
  234
  installation phase of, 10, 12, 161
  operation phase of, 10, 13-15, 161, 244,
    246
  procurement phase of, 10-11, 160, 244
  relative to CPE tools, 10
  simulation in the, 160
  transition phase of, 10, 15, 161
limitations of
  accounting packages, 58

analytic models, 182–183
benchmarks, 132–133
hardware monitors, 114–116
simulation, 162
software monitors, 89–92
line graphs, 218, 220
logic boards (logic panels), 96–99
  Boolean operators, 96
  counters, 98–99
  decoders, 96
  fan-outs, 96
  hubs, 96
  inverters, 96
logic pins. *See* probe points
logical record, 55

management, 8, 46
  decisions, 8, 46
  reporting, 62
  terms, 210, 230–231
mathematic(s) (-al)
  algorithmic timers, 146
  closed solutions, 169
  conventions of, 169
  impossibility of solutions, 146
measurement(s), 6
  frequency, 43–44
  of performance, 53
  prediction versus, 135
  simulation for reasonable estimates of, 149
  tools, 120–121
model(s) (-ing), 2, 6, 10–11, 45–46
  analytic, compared to simulation, 164
  analytic, in preference to simulation, 139
  applications in system life cycle, 159
  building, 242, 244–245
  characteristics of, 7
  characterized, 7
  computer systems, 136
  computerized, 137
  cost of, 8
  development of, 142
  definition of, 7
  discrete event, application, 146
  disk rotational latency, 154
  domain of, 241
  elements of discrete event, 155
  examples of discrete event, 152
  extensions, 180–182

  implementation of, 143
  inputs, 46
  languages, 7
  of a computer system, 167–175
  output, 46, 158
  overhead, 8
  packages, 7
  scope of, 137
  skills, 180
  supermarket shoppers, analogy, 137
  use in life cycle, 9
  testing validity of, 147
  validity compared to accuracy, 147
  verification and validation of, 146
monitor interval, 111
multiprocessing, 194
multiprogramming, 1, 43, 47, 51, 59, 194

natural forecast unit (NFU), 189

observational error, 189
operating system. *See* control program
operations logs, 52–53
operations phase, 92, 161
operational environment, 12
operator performance, 47
output of discrete event models, 159
organization's requirements, 11
overhead of
  accounting data, 8, 59, 70
  benchmarks, 8
  hardware monitors, 8, 104, 114
  program optimizers, 8
  software monitors, 79, 81, 90

performance characteristics, 13
performance evaluation uses of simulation, 138
Performance Evaluation Review, 248
performance management reporting systems (PMRS)
  concept of a, 214
  consistency in, 210–212
  developing a, 231–233
  elements of a 209–215
  information sources, 213
  performance indicators, 213
  performance standards, 215
  phases, 232–233
  reporting goals, 212–213
  terminology, 209–210

258 INDEX

performance standards, establishment of, 44
post-CPE project reviews, 42
PL1, 91
power usage
  absolute, 193
  relative, 193
predict(ing) (-ive), 6
  changes, 15
  tools, 121
price/performance ratio, 122
probes, 101, 103, 106
  connecting, 115–116
  disconnecting, 115–116
probe point(s), 48, 93–94, 105–107
  adapters, 94
  identification of, 106, 117
  locations, 106
  verification of, 117
problem program, 55
Problem Program Evaluator (PPE), 82
process of simulation, 140–150
procurement
  documentation, 11
  evaluation, 126
  phase, 160
  rules, 121
production environment, 12
productivity, 12
program
  analysis suggested readings, 250
  monitor, 75
  optimizations suggested readings, 250
  reviews, 14
program optimizer, 2, 5, 10, 74–92, 240
  cost of, 8
  definition of, 4, 75
  event-driven, 76
  overhead of, 8
pseudocounter, 103

quality control, 83
quantity data, 55
queues, 165–167
queuing in computer system exhibit, 152
queuing theory, 165–167, 180
  assumptions, 174–175
  prohibitive for solving models, 135
  simulation instead of, 139

random number, 130–131
real-time system testing, 139
records, 55
  card image, 72
  per block, 55
remote terminal emulator (RTE), 120, 133–134
report(s) (-ing)
  a management, 211
  a production control, 216
  bar chart, 220–223
  computer listing, 217–219
  consistent, 210–212
  erratic, 210
  for system development management, 219
  formats, 216–231
  Gantt chart, 223–224
  graphical, 217–218
  inconsistent, 210
  Kiviat graph, 224–228
  line graph, 218
  stock market, 213, 230
reporting performance to management, 209–233
  as revenue per hour, 210–211, 218, 228
  formats for, 217–231
  goals of, 212
  in money terms, 210
  performance standards in, 215
  variations in, 210–211
representative(ness), 123, 130, 133
  sample, 121, 122
  workload, 245
requests for proposals, 11
resources
  fixed, 156
  interconnectivity of, 156
  movable, 156
response time, 166–167
  overall system, 172
reuse analysis, 15

scheduling, 47, 88
  improved, 239–240
Schumacher chart(s), 228–231, 238
script, 121
self-auditing (benchmark), 123, 127–128

service time, 170-171
SIGMETRICS, 92
simulation(s), 135-163
   applications of, in life cycle, 159
   compared to analytic models, 164
   comparison of, implementation tools, 144
   decision to use, 142
   definition of, 136
   elements of discrete event, 155
   expense of, 162
   gives reasonable estimates of system, 149
   implementation tools, 144
   inaccuracies inherent in, 136
   limitations of, 162
   management decisions with, 163
   Monte Carlo, 154
   output data, 150, 159
   output of discrete event, models, 155
   predictive, not measurement, technique, 135
   primary use of, 138
   problem definition task of, 141
   process of, 140
   reasons for using, 140
   running, 149
   suggested readings on, 251
   strenghts of, 162
   trace-driven, 139
   use of, by manufacturers, 162
   used with other CPE tools, 139
   users characterized, 163
   validation of, 146
   verification of, 146
   when to use, 138
simulation language(s)
   algorithmic timer 146
   block-diagram-oriented 144-145
   comparison of 144
   computer-oriented 143, 145
   discrete event 146
   general-purpose 143-144
   packages 143, 145
simulation tools, 7, 142-146
smaller systems, considerations for, 49-50
software hook, 78
software monitor(s), 2-4, 10, 14, 61, 74-92, 99, 104, 114, 127, 186, 240
   categories of, 81-89

combination, 76, 80
commercially available, 79, 90
definition of, 3, 75-81
distinctions, 74-75
event-driven, 76, 78, 91
limitations of, 89-92
locally coded, 79
overhead of, 79, 81, 90
sampling, 76-78, 91
self-adjusting, 89-92
strengths of, 89-90
suggested readings on, 249-250
time-driven, 76, 79, 91
software physics, 73, 106, 184-208
   acceptance of, 184
   application of, 201-208
   examples, 187-189, 195-206
   theory of, 185
   three basic properties of, 185
software power, 73
   advantage of, 190
   definition of, 185-186
   for capacity calculations, 194-201
   theoretical, as capacity, 196
   software unit vector, 187-188, 200-201, 207
   stability of the, 207
software work, 73
   average, per job, 191
   definition of, 185
   repeatability of, 190
   unit of, 185
   vector, 186, 201
standard(s)
   enforcement, 3
   error, 129
   job, 192
   performance, 215
   second, 203
   setting, 44
storage occupancy, 185
strengths. *See* advantages
subconfiguration, 186, 199, 201
switches, option, 58
synthetic programs, 127-130
system(s),
   analogous, 136
   considerations for smaller, 49-50
   complex, 139

system(s) (*cont.*)
  cumbersome, 139
  creation, 242, 245-246
  described by discrete event models, 152
  dynamic, 136
  exhibit queuing and probabilistic behavior, 152
  expensive, 139
  history, 159
  incident reports, 47
  model output describes performance, 158
  non-available, 139
  random processes in, 154
  sizing, 160
  selection, 160
  target, 138
  variables, 153-154
  visibility, 15

task level, 124, 131
teleprocessing system, 59-60
test environment, 4
thinker, 24-25
throughput power, 192-194, 202
  theoretical, 200, 206
time data, 56
total error, 129, 132
trace routines, 3, 60
transition phase, simulation, 161
trend(s), 45, 209
  forecasting technique, 188
  long term, 46
  predicting growth, 14
tuning, 44, 85, 204
  configuration, 87-89

turnaround time, 53

UNIVAC, 91
users group(s), 84-85
utilization, 166-167

validate, 6, 8
validating results, 162
validation, 242, 246
  accuracy of, 147
  heuristic, 147
  of models, 147
  relative, 147
  testing, 141
value
  added, 53
  installation, 53
vector notation, 187
verify, 6
visits, 170
visual observation (inspection), 2, 238, 248

work concurrency chart, 202-205, 207
worker, 25
workload
  balancing, 88, 190
  conceptual design of, 9-10
  detailed specification of, 10
  forecast, 14, 187
  ideal, 194
  implementation, 13
  planned, 11
  requirements of proposed, 11
  tailoring the, 12
80/20 rule, 21